"Dan Berbecel's book is an excellent contribution to the literatures on presidentialism, how to limit the likelihood of executive takeovers of democracy, and Latin American politics. It shows that presidents' de facto powers diverge markedly from their constitutional powers. The book is well researched and written."

— **Scott Mainwaring**, *Eugene and Helen Conley Professor of Political Science, Notre Dame*

Presidential Power in Latin America

What explains variance in presidential power between countries? In *Presidential Power in Latin America*, Dan Berbecel provides a general, systematic theory for explaining presidential power in practice as opposed to presidential power in theory.

Using expert survey data from Varieties of Democracy (V-Dem) alongside interviews with high-level figures in politics, the judiciary, the public administration, NGOs, and academia in Argentina and Chile, Berbecel argues that constitutional presidential power (formal power) is a very poor predictor of presidential power in practice (informal power). Given the poor predictive value of formal rules, he provides an explanation for why hyperpresidentialism emerges in some countries but not in others. Berbecel attributes the root causes of hyperpresidentialism to three independent variables (the strength of state institutions, the size of the president's party in congress, and whether or not the country has a history of economic crises) which together determine how likely it is that a president will be able to concentrate power.

Presidential Power in Latin America will be of key interest to scholars and students of executive politics, Latin American politics, and more broadly, comparative politics.

Dan Berbecel is an assistant professor in the Department of Political Science at York University (the Glendon Campus) in Toronto, Canada. His main area of research interest is Comparative Politics, with a focus on Latin American Politics.

Routledge Studies in Latin American Politics

https://www.routledge.com/Routledge-Studies-in-Latin-American-Politics/book-series/RSLAP

Presidential Power in Latin America

Examining the Cases of Argentina and Chile

Dan Berbecel

NEW YORK AND LONDON

First published 2022
by Routledge
605 Third Avenue, New York, NY 10158

and by Routledge
2 Park Square, Milton Park, Abingdon, Oxon, OX14 4RN

Routledge is an imprint of the Taylor & Francis Group, an informa business

Library of Congress Cataloging-in-Publication Data
A catalog record for this title has been requested

ISBN: 978-0-367-69055-7 (hbk)
ISBN: 978-0-367-69691-7 (pbk)
ISBN: 978-1-003-14290-4 (ebk)

DOI: 10.4324/9781003142904

Typeset in Times New Roman
by codeMantra

I would like to dedicate this book to my parents, Cristina and Gheorghe Berbecel. Throughout my entire life, they loved and supported me, and I would never have gotten to where I am today without them.

Contents

Figures

Tables

Note about the Chilean Constitution

At the time of writing of this book, Chile was in the process of modifying its constitution, with the ultimate outcome still unknown. Every mention of the Chilean constitution in this book refers to the constitution in place as of 2021.

Acknowledgments

This book emerged out of my doctoral dissertation that I defended at Princeton University in June 2019. I would first of all like to thank the members of my dissertation committee, Deborah Yashar, Grigore Pop-Eleches, and Jennifer Widner, for their support. I had the pleasure of getting to know all three of them since the beginning of my graduate school journey. In the first two years of the PhD program, I took various courses with them, and they helped shape my understanding of the field of political science. In the dissertation-writing process, Deborah, Grigo, and Jennifer all spent long hours reading what were often very long drafts, and then provided valuable feedback and guidance which was critical to the success of this project. They also provided me encouragement during the more difficult phases of the dissertation-writing process, especially toward the end.

I would also like to thank Steven Levitsky, who provided me feedback during various stages of this project. More fundamentally, during my time at Harvard College, he was the person who inspired me to study political science.

I am also extremely grateful to all of the individuals in Argentina and Chile who sat down with me and allowed me to interview them. These interviews were a critical component of my book and provided me unique insight on the political systems in both countries. I am also grateful to VOICES! Research & Consultancy in Argentina for allowing me to add on several questions to their omnibus survey. I also wanted to thank Alicia and Gerardo Delle Donne. I first visited Argentina during my freshman college summer in 2009, and Alicia and Gerardo were my host family. They were very warm and kind to me, and one of the reasons that I fell in love with Argentina and its people (and chose to subsequently continue studying Argentina) was because of them.

I would also like to thank the following organizations at Princeton for their significant financial support to conduct fieldwork in Argentina and Chile: the Program in Latin American Studies (PLAS), the Princeton Institute for International and Regional Studies (PIIRS), and the Mamdouha S. Bobst Center for Peace and Justice.

I am also grateful to all of my former colleagues at Princeton University who provided me feedback in various settings, including the weekly department-wide Comparative Politics Seminar. I am also grateful to the Department of Politics at Princeton University for giving me such an outstanding platform from which I could pursue my PhD in political science.

I also wanted to recognize all of the undergraduate students that I have taught over the past several years. Although they did not play a direct role in helping me write this book, they helped me discover and pursue my passion for teaching, which helped give me motivation during the more challenging phases of the writing process.

Finally, last but not least, I would like to thank my current employer, York University (the Glendon Campus), for giving me my dream job of Assistant Professor of Political Science. This position has brought immense joy and meaning to my life, and I expect that this is the first of many books that I will publish as a professor at this institution. I would specifically like to thank my senior colleague, Willem Maas, for encouraging me to write this book as well as for all of his guidance and mentorship. I really enjoyed all of the discussions we had during our frequent walks, and I am very grateful to have him as a colleague.

Glossary of Some Key Terms for Argentina and Chile Most Relevant to This Book

Parties in Argentina

Cambiemos: This is the coalition that supported Macri, composed of the PRO, the Radical Party, and the Civic Coalition

Front for Victory (also known as the *Frente para la Victoria*, or FPV): This is the front of the Peronist party that supported Cristina Kirchner

Peronist party (also known as the *Partido Justicialista*, PJ, or Justicialist party): This party was born with Juan Perón, and while it provides rhetorical support for the working classes, it lacks a clear ideology (there have been both right-wing Peronists such as Carlos Menem and left-wing Peronists such as Néstor and Cristina Kirchner). Peronist presidents have often been hyperpresidential since democratization

PRO (*Propuesta Republicana*): This is the right-wing party to which President Macri belonged

Radical Party (also known as the *Unión Cívica Radical*, UCR, or Radical Civic Union): This is the second major party in modern Argentine political history and has opposed Peronism

Parties in Chile

Chile Vamos (formerly called the *Alianza*): This is the rightist coalition in Chile made up primarily of the UDI (furthest to the right) and the RN (center-right)

Christian Democrats: This is a party that was part of the left-wing *Nueva Mayoría* (Christian Democrats were the most centrist members of the coalition)

Nueva Mayoría (formerly called the *Concertación*): This was the leftist coalition in Chile made up of several parties including the Socialist Party, the Party for Democracy, the Christian Democrats, the Social Democratic Radical Party, etc. The coalition suffered a rupture in the 2017 elections, with the Christian Democrats running their own candidate for president

Key Political Leaders in the History of Argentina (Chronological Order)

Juan Perón (president between 1946–1955 and 1973–1974): He is the founder of the Peronist movement, and he and his wife **Eva Perón** gained immense popularity among the poor and working classes of Argentina

Military dictatorship (1976–1983): The military in this period is infamous for the "Dirty War" and the failed invasion of the Falkland Islands

Raúl Alfonsín (president from 1983 to 1989, non-Peronist, UCR): He became president after the country democratized in 1983

Carlos Menem (president from 1989 to 1999, Peronist, PJ): He was a right-wing Peronist and implemented a radical neoliberal economic program

Fernando De La Rúa (president from 1999 to 2001, non-Peronist, UCR): His term ended with the disastrous 2001–2002 economic crisis

Eduardo Duhalde (president from 2002 to 2003, Peronist)

Néstor Kirchner (president from 2003 to 2007, Peronist, FPV): He and his wife were leftist Peronists

Cristina Kirchner (president from 2007 to 2015, Peronist, FPV)

Mauricio Macri (president from 2015 until 2019, non-Peronist, PRO)

Key Political Leaders in the History of Chile (Chronological Order)

Salvador Allende (1970–1973): He was a Marxist president who was democratically elected

Augusto Pinochet (1973–1990): He governed Chile as a military dictator after the coup against Allende, and is known for making Chile one of the most free-market states in Latin America

Patricio Aylwin (1990–1994, left-wing *Concertación*, Christian Democratic): He was the first democratically elected president after Pinochet's military dictatorship

Eduardo Frei (1994–2000, left-wing *Concertación*, Christian Democratic)

Ricardo Lagos (2000–2006, left-wing *Concertación*, Party for Democracy)

Michelle Bachelet (2006–2010, left-wing *Concertación*, Socialist Party)

Sebastián Piñera (2010–2014, right-wing *Alianza*): This was the first time since the democratic transition that a right-wing president came to power

Michelle Bachelet (2014–2018, left-wing *Concertación*, Socialist Party)

Sebastián Piñera (2018 onward, right-wing *Alianza*)

Key Historical Moments in Argentina (Most Relevant to This Book)

1930 coup: Democratically elected president Hipólito Yrigoyen was overthrown. Several institutions notably declined in stature after this coup, including the Supreme Court

1943 coup: General Juan Perón comes to power, first as Secretary of Labor, and later as president

1976 coup: A bureaucratic-authoritarian military regime takes power

Democratic transition in 1983: The military had lost legitimacy amidst the economic crisis in the early 1980s and the failed invasion of the Falkland Islands

Economic crisis between 1988 and 1990: Argentina experienced a sharp economic decline in the late 1980s that involved hyperinflation. President Alfonsín resigned early so that President-elect Menem could tackle the crisis

Economic crisis of 2001–2002: In the late 1990s, the Argentine economy went into recession, which culminated in the 2001–2002 crisis. This was the most severe crisis in modern Argentine history, and unemployment reached almost 25%

Election of Macri in 2015: The election of Mauricio Macri in 2015 caused Argentina to move toward the political right

Heavy neoliberalism in the 1990s: Carlos Menem, a Peronist, with the support of the IMF implemented drastic market reforms that made Argentina one of the most neoliberal economies in Latin America

Political crisis of 2001: In 2001, the economic crisis morphed into a political crisis. President De La Rúa submitted his resignation on December 20, 2001 (he had to be airlifted from the presidential building, the *Casa Rosada*, because of heavy protests outside). Between December 21, 2001 and January 2, 2002, Argentina alternated between four presidents (Puerta, Saá, Camaño, and finally settling on Duhalde)

Sharp left turn in the 2000s: Between 2003 and 2015, Argentina was governed by Néstor Kirchner and then Cristina Kirchner, who were both populist left-wing Peronists. They nationalized many of the industries that had been privatized by Menem, and in order to raise money for public spending, they pursued an expansionary monetary policy that resulted in significant inflation

Key Historical Moments in Chile (Most Relevant to This Book)

1973 coup: In 1973, the military launched a coup that toppled the democratically elected government of Salvador Allende (Allende was a

Marxist, and the military was significantly more conservative). Pinochet would emerge as the predominant leader after the 1973 coup

1988 plebiscite (and the democratic transition that followed in 1990):   In 1988, a plebiscite was held where the population voted to determine whether Pinochet would stay in power. The population voted against Pinochet, elections were called, and the country democratized. Patricio Aylwin became the first democratically elected president since Allende

Other Key Terms for Argentina

Court-packing under Menem: After Menem came to power, he packed the Supreme Court with political allies. The Court was largely subordinate to the executive branch under Menem

NUD   (Necessity and Urgency Decree, also known as a *Decreto de Necesidad y Urgencia*, DNU): This is a type of decree that was abused by President Carlos Menem in the 1990s. Although this decree was meant only for matters of "necessity" and "urgency," Menem in practice regularly used this instrument to bypass congress

Other Key Terms for Chile

Constitutional Tribunal and Supreme Court: In Chile, the high-level judiciary is split between two courts. The Constitutional Tribunal is responsible for judicial review; the Supreme Court does not perform judicial review, and acts a final court of appeals for civil and criminal cases

Contraloría: This is an institution in Chile that among various functions, reviews presidential decrees

Exclusive initiative: Only the president can initiate laws in certain areas including the budget, any laws that involve spending, etc. (although congress may reject these initiatives, it cannot propose any new ones itself in these areas)

Urgencies: Urgencies are a tool through which Chilean presidents can ask congress to vote on a particular piece of legislation within a set number of days (there are three levels of urgencies with timeframes of 30, 10, and 3 days)

1 Introduction

In a comparison of presidential systems throughout the world, there is a fundamental paradox: although in theory many presidential regimes have systems of checks and balances in their constitutions, there is significant variation in the degree to which these checks and balances function in practice. In some countries, although there may be powerful constitutional constraints on the president, in practice, he/she may still be able to rule almost unilaterally under a type of system that I will refer to as "hyperpresidentialism." On the other hand, in other countries, although constitutional constraints may not be as strong on the president, in practice, he/she may rule in a highly consensual manner in which congress, the judiciary, and other institutions of horizontal accountability play a significant role.

The central question that this book will seek to answer is *what factors determine the degree to which a president will be able to concentrate power?* What is it about the structural conditions in some countries that allow presidents to become hyperpresidential and usurp power from institutions such as congress and the judiciary? At the same time, what is it about the structural conditions in other countries that prevent presidents from being able to concentrate power to an excessive degree? In short, the main variable that this book seeks to explain is presidential power in practice, and specifically, I will try to provide an explanation for when hypepresidentialism will emerge.

This book will examine two cases in particular, namely Argentina and Chile. Whereas Argentina has exhibited strong signs of hyperpresidentialism throughout the past three decades, in Chile, the president has been significantly constrained by institutions of horizontal accountability. This situation is paradoxical, since constitutionally the Chilean president is considerably more powerful than the Argentine counterpart. Although I will perform a comprehensive analysis of Argentina and Chile, this book will not be limited to these two countries. I also include a large-N analysis of presidential systems throughout the world (with a particular focus on presidential democracies in the Western Hemisphere).

This book is critically important in the context of the rising populism and democratic backsliding in many parts of the world. A trend

DOI: 10.4324/9781003142904-1

has emerged where more and more presidents are trying to concentrate power and where institutions that serve as checks and balances are being eroded. Through my book, I seek to provide a comprehensive theory that predicts when a country is likely to move toward a hyperpresidential system. In addition to its predictive value, my book also proposes an electoral design which would minimize the likelihood that a president will be able to concentrate power.

In this introductory chapter, I will begin in Part I with a conceptual analysis of my dependent variable, the degree of presidential power, and provide a comprehensive definition of hyperpresidentialism. In Part II, I will address the common belief throughout the literature that presidential power and hyperpresidentialism are directly correlated with how much constitutional power presidents are given; as my data will show, constitutional presidential powers have a very weak relation to presidential powers in practice. I will then discuss in Part III the theory that forms the basis of this book, and introduce my three independent variables. In Part IV, I will provide a literature review where I show how my book fits into the broader discussions within political science. In Part V, I present how this book is structured and give a brief roadmap of what will be discussed in each chapter. Finally, in Part VI, I provide a brief summary of modern politics in Argentina and Chile.

Part I: Defining Hyperpresidentialism and Presenting My Question

Conceptualizing Hyperpresidentialism

Before conceptualizing hyperpresidentialism, it is essential for me to go into detail about what I mean by a presidential system. By a presidential system, I refer to a system of government where the executive branch is separate from the legislative branch, and the survival in office of the president does not depend on the confidence of congress. In presidential systems, the president is also directly accountable to the electorate as a whole. I constructed a dataset of presidential systems throughout the world, and in this dataset, I will include semi-presidential systems, given that although there may be a prime minister in such systems, there is still a president with substantial powers who does not depend on the approval of congress to keep his job (although in many presidential systems the congress can impeach the president, given the high voting threshold that must be achieved, it is extremely difficult and completely different from the no-confidence vote in parliamentary systems). I would like to note that to qualify as a presidential system, the president must have substantial power at least on paper and cannot merely play a ceremonial role (e.g., Italy would not count as a presidential system; despite the existence of a president, in practice he possesses little meaningful power compared to the prime minister). Although the theory I will present is also applicable in determining the concentration of power by executives in parliamentary regimes (prime ministers), I will focus solely on presidential systems in this book.

For the purposes of this book, the term "hyperpresidential" will be used to describe a president who concentrates significant power at the expense of institutions of horizontal accountability such as congress and the judiciary. Rather than being serious institutions which can credibly threaten to derail a president's initiatives, congress and the judiciary are viewed as mere nuisances and fail to constrain a super-president. In a hyperpresidential country, presidents are able to enact sweeping projects with little congressional or judicial oversight. The concept of hyperpresidentialism is rooted in Guillermo O'Donnell's description of a "delegative democracy" which he defines as follows:

> Delegative democracies rest on the premise that whoever wins election to the presidency is thereby entitled to govern as he or she sees fit, constrained only by the hard facts of existing power relations and by a constitutionally limited term of office. The president is taken to be the embodiment of the nation and the main custodian and definer of its interests.[1]

Note that under my definition of hyperpresidentialism, I do not claim that congress and the judiciary have *no* power. In many hyperpresidential countries, these institutions can be strong enough to inconvenience the president. For example, congress may be able to extract concessions from the executive branch in the passage process for bills; the judiciary may also occasionally rule against the president. However, in a hyperpresidential system, these institutions will rarely be seen as an existential threat by the executive branch. While congress may have some ability to influence the content of a law that the president wishes to pass, any changes legislators enact will usually be on the margins (rather than on the centerpiece of the law). Similarly, while judges may occasionally issue rulings that the president does not like, the judiciary will generally not go against the president in areas most important to the executive branch.

To clarify, I am using an absolute scale to measure the degree to which power is concentrated in a president (as opposed to the use of powers relative to their constitutional authority).

There are two situations that characterize hyperpresidentialism, and these two situations are based on the fact that laws can be created either by the president through a decree or by the legislature through a statute. In the first situation, the president governs largely through the use of decrees and completely bypasses a congress that is either unwilling or unable to challenge the president. Similarly, the Supreme Court would not effectively take any action against these excessive presidential decrees.

This Supreme Court will often have undergone several court-packing attempts, and the members who form the majority are usually allies of the president. An example of hyperpresidentialism where excessive decrees were used is the case of Argentina under Carlos Menem, who abused decree power to push through his neoliberal agenda in the 1990s.

The second situation in which hyperpresidentialism occurs is when even though the use of decrees is limited (and most lawmaking is done through the legislature via statute), in reality, the president is still the dominant actor in the process, often by exercising strong control over one or more of the leading parties. This is especially the case in the context of unified government, where the president is able to exercise significant discipline over his party. Oftentimes, what may characterize this second scenario of hyperpresidentialism is that a piece of legislation proposed by a president receives little to no meaningful debate and passes with relatively few changes. A case of this second situation of hyperpresidentialism is Argentina under the presidency of Cristina Kirchner, who despite using relatively few decrees, exercised extremely tight control over congress (where her party for several years held a majority in both chambers).

Hyperpresidentialism will be contrasted in this book with regime types that I refer to as "representative systems" or "representative democracies." Unlike delegative democracies where vertical accountability exists but with little horizontal accountability, representative systems have both strong vertical and horizontal accountability. In this regime type, institutions such as congress and the judiciary fully perform their constitutional role of checking executive power. In countries with representative systems, the president is neither able to rule by decree nor able to persuade congress to simply rubber-stamp his/her proposals. My definition of "representative" systems is based off of Guillermo O'Donnell's concept of representative democracy, which he describes as follows:

> Vertical accountability, along with the freedom to form parties and to try to influence public opinion, exists in both representative and delegative democracies. But the horizontal accountability characteristic of representative democracy is extremely weak or nonexistent in delegative democracies...Because policies are carried out by a series of relatively autonomous powers, decision making in representative democracies tends to be slow and incremental and sometimes prone to gridlock."[2]

In terms of the informal interaction between the three branches, I conceive a representative system to involve a widespread consensus where all major political actors, including the president, perceive that laws should only be passed when there is agreement between congress and the executive; in other words, "going at it alone" by the president on major issues would be seen as taboo. There is also a widespread mentality in a representative system that laws declared unconstitutional by the courts should not pass. In short, respect for the constitutional role of each branch of government is the "only game in town." In a hyperpresidential system, this informal consensus does not exist among political actors; presidents view congress as merely an annoyance, and the judiciary as a hindrance which they should try to weaken at every opportunity.

Differentiating Between a Congress That Is a Rubber Stamp and a Congress That Approves a President's Project Because of a Similar Ideology

Some may take issue with my argument that a hyperpresidential regime can be characterized by the president using a majority in congress to pass laws through legislative statutes. Indeed, they may ask, *is it not natural that if a president has a majority in congress, that congress should approve all legislative projects proposed by the president?* The answer to this question is that while it is reasonable that in a unified government the executive and legislative branches will cooperate to a greater degree than in a divided government, in a representative system the legislature never falls to the level that it becomes a rubber stamp. Informal norms in a representative system ensure that a president would still have to involve congress in the process of drafting laws and would still have to make compromises over the concerns of individual legislators; overall, the executive would be expected to face some pushback. In other words, although the majority of legislators may be from the president's party, congress as an institution of horizontal accountability still has some degree of autonomy to check presidential power and will not automatically approve whatever legislative project the president decides to send. For example, at the beginning of President Barack Obama's first term in office when the Democrats held vast majorities in the House and Senate, Congress did not cease in its role as an effective institution of oversight, and Obama was aware and accepted that he had to work actively with the legislature to pass his proposals. This is in contrast to cases such as Mexico where for a large part of the second half of the 20th century, congress did indeed function like a rubber stamp during periods of unified government and fundamentally ceased in its role as a veto player. Congresses such as that of Mexico in the 20th century as well as that of Argentina during the Menem period would fall into the category of "subservient" legislatures. According to Cox and Morgenstern, "subservient majorities (very high percentages of members thoroughly beholden to the president) will accept essentially any proposal the president makes."[3]

Part II: The Weak Explanatory Powers of Constitutional Presidential Powers for Determining Presidential Powers in Practice

It is logical to assume that countries in which the president has more constitutional powers will be more hyperpresidential, whereas countries in which the president has fewer constitutional powers will be more representative, with a greater role for institutions of horizontal accountability like congress and the judiciary.

Nevertheless, as the cases of Argentina and Chile demonstrate, presidential powers in theory do not necessarily correspond to presidential powers in practice. The distinction between presidential powers in theory and presidential powers in practice is one of the most critical distinctions made in this book. Presidential power in theory (also referred to as "formal presidential power," "constitutional power," or "de jure power") refers specifically to power that the constitution grants the president. Presidential power in practice (also referred to as "informal power" or "de facto power") refers to how much power presidents wield in reality. A president may be constitutionally very weak, yet still hold significant power in practice. For example, Mexican presidents are among the weakest presidents constitutionally in the Americas, yet until the 1990s, they governed with few restraints. Argentine presidents also face strong constraints, yet since democratization, many Peronist presidents have governed almost unilaterally. In contrast, there are countries such as Chile where despite the fact that presidents are powerful constitutionally, in practice they have been significantly constrained by institutions such as congress and the judiciary.

Data confirms that *formal constitutional powers are an extremely weak predictor of presidential power in practice.* To demonstrate the weak predictive power of formal powers, I use the dataset I constructed of all presidential countries throughout the world (as I mentioned earlier, note that this dataset also includes semi-presidential systems).[4] For every country, I compare the constitutional powers given to the president with presidential powers *in practice*, but as the following results indicate, the correlation between these values is very weak.

To measure formal presidential power, I use data from the Comparative Constitutions Project,[5] which draws from the work of Zachary Elkins, Tom Ginsburg, and James Melton. For all the countries in my sample, I used the indicator "Executive Power" (based off of the constitution of that country). To measure presidential power in practice (informal power), I use expert surveys from the Varieties of Democracy Project, V-Dem (specifically, "Legislative Constraints on the Executive" and "Judicial Constraints on the Executive"). These expert surveys will assess the extent to which presidents were constrained by congress and the judiciary, and *fewer constraints on the president signal more presidential power* (and vice versa). This book is one of the first pieces in the literature to attempt to directly measure presidential power *in practice* as a dependent variable. Expert surveys such as the ones by Varieties of Democracy provide an innovative way to measure this dependent variable.

Both the "Legislative Constraints on the Executive" index and the "Judicial Constraints on the Executive" index are composite indices, which aggregate several indicators together (these indicators are established based on expert surveys with multiple country experts). After being asked questions, experts are asked to code their responses using various numerical options given to them.

Specifically, the "Legislative Constraints on the Executive" index aggregates together the following four indices: "Legislature questions officials in practice," "Executive oversight," "Legislature investigates in practice," and "Legislature opposition parties." Regarding "Legislature questions officials in practice," the question asked of experts is "In practice, does the legislature routinely question executive branch officials?" Regarding "Executive oversight," experts are asked:

> If executive branch officials were engaged in unconstitutional, illegal, or unethical activity, how likely is it that a body other than the legislature, such as a comptroller general, general prosecutor, or ombudsman, would question or investigate them and issue an unfavorable decision or report?

Regarding "Legislature investigates in practice," experts are asked:

> If the executive were engaged in unconstitutional, illegal, or unethical activity, how likely is it that a legislative body (perhaps a whole chamber, perhaps a committee, whether aligned with government or opposition) would conduct an investigation that would result in a decision or report that is unfavorable to the executive?

Finally, regarding "Legislature opposition parties," the question asked of the experts was "Are opposition parties (those not in the ruling party or coalition) able to exercise oversight and investigatory functions against the wishes of the governing party or coalition?"

The "Judicial Constraints on the Executive" index aggregates together the following five indices: "Executive respects constitution," "Compliance with judiciary," "Compliance with high court," "High court independence," and "Lower court independence." For "Executive respects constitution," experts were asked, "Do members of the executive (the head of state, the head of government, and cabinet ministers) respect the constitution?" For "Compliance with judiciary," experts were asked, "How often would you say the government complies with important decisions by other courts with which it disagrees?" For "Compliance with high court," experts were asked, "How often would you say the government complies with important decisions of the high court with which it disagrees?" For "High court independence," respondents were asked:

> When the high court in the judicial system is ruling in cases that are salient to the government, how often would you say that it makes decisions that merely reflect government wishes regardless of its sincere view of the legal record?

Finally, regarding "Lower court independence," experts were asked, "When judges not on the high court are ruling in cases that are salient to the government, how often would you say that their decisions merely reflect government wishes regardless of their sincere view of the legal record?"[6]

Regarding the experts asked to answer the above surveys, according to Varieties of Democracy:

> These experts are generally academics (about 80%) or professionals working media, or public affairs (e.g., senior analysts, editors, judges); about 2/3 are also nationals of and/or residents in a country and have documented knowledge of both that country and a specific substantive area. Generally, each Country Experts code [sic] only a selection of indicators following their particular background and expertise (e.g. the legislature).

There is an aim to have a "minimum of five Country Experts to code each country-year for every indicator," and several criteria are used to ensure that these experts are of high quality. For example, 60% of country experts should be "nationals or permanent residents of that country"; also efforts are made to ensure that the experts are impartial, and that people are not selected "who might be beholden to powerful actors... close association (current or past) with political parties, senior government officials, politically affiliated think-tanks or institutes is grounds for disqualification"; another important criterion includes

> obtaining diversity in professional background among the coders chosen for a particular country. For certain areas (e.g., the media, judiciary, and civil society surveys) such diversity entails a mixture of academics and professionals who study these topics. It also means finding experts who are located at a variety of institutions, universities and research institutes.[7]

In the scatterplot in Figure 1.1, on the x-axis, I illustrate the formal presidential powers for my sample using the "Executive Power" variable where higher scores indicate more constitutional powers given to presidents. On

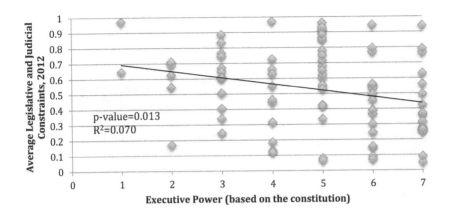

Figure 1.1 Scatterplot comparing Constitutional Executive Power with the average of Varieties of Democracy's 2012 Indicators, "Judicial Constraints on the Executive" and "Legislative Constraints on the Executive" for a sample of all presidential systems in the world (87 countries).

the y-axis, I computed the score received by that country in 2012 when averaging Legislative Constraints on the Executive and Judicial Constraints on the Executive (a higher average of these two values indicates more constraints *in practice*, and therefore *less* presidential power). Note that for each scatterplot in this book, I provide two values drawn from Stata: (1) the p-value and (2) the R-squared value.

As this scatterplot shows, as constitutional executive power goes up, legislative and judicial constraints on the executive do indeed fall as would be intuitively expected. Nevertheless, although this correlation is statistically significant at the 5% level, the relationship is small and overall has very weak explanatory power (in the scatterplot, the trend line is nearly flat). The small R-squared value of 0.070 further illustrates that constitutional powers explain informal presidential powers in only a very small percentage of cases (visually, in the scatterplot, this can be seen by the fact that few of the points are actually close to the regression line). Therefore, although constitutional powers do matter, their effect on presidential powers in practice is very small, and they overall have little predictive power.

The predictive capability of constitutional executive powers is even weaker in my second dataset based on a sample of 20 presidential democracies in the Western Hemisphere.[8] Figure 1.2 contains a scatterplot comparing the same variables as in Figure 1.1 (average Legislative and Judicial Constraints for 2012 vs. formal Executive Power).

Within this sample of 20 presidential democracies in the Western Hemisphere, the relationship between formal executive power and presidential

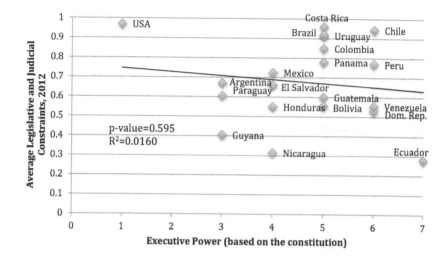

Figure 1.2 Scatterplot comparing Constitutional Executive Power with the average of Varieties of Democracy's 2012 Indicators, "Judicial Constraints on the Executive" and "Legislative Constraints on the Executive" for a sample of all presidential democracies in the Western Hemisphere (20 countries).

powers in practice was statistically insignificant, and the R-squared value was near-zero at only 0.0160.

We can observe a similarly weak correlation when instead of using the indicators from Varieties of Democracy to measure presidential power in practice, we use Polity IV's indicator, "Executive Constraints" (xconst). It is important to note that this indicator is not as effective as the expert surveys from V-Dem in assessing presidential power in practice. Specifically, the methodology by which Polity IV's value is calculated includes some measures that can be considered formal constraints. Examples of formal constraints coded by this index include "if there is a legislature it cannot initiate legislation" and "the legislature initiates some categories of legislation."[9] Nevertheless, Polity IV's index is still useful as a robustness test for the purposes of this book since the indicators it codes for also include measures of presidential power in practice that do not stem directly from the constitution (e.g., "the legislature delays implementation of executive acts and decrees" and "a council or legislature sometimes refuses funds to the executive"). The data in Figure 1.3 shows the weak relationship between formal constraints as measured by the Comparative Constitutions Project and presidential powers in practice as measured by xconst.

As the statistical output in the scatterplot in Figure 1.3 shows, the relationship between formal constitutional powers and the "Executive Constraints" indicator is very weak.

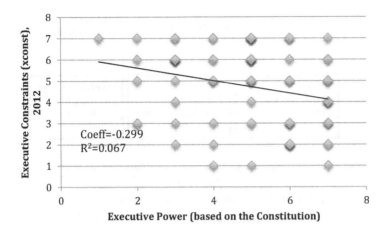

Figure 1.3 Scatterplot comparing Constitutional Executive Power with Polity IV's "Executive Constraints" for a sample of all presidential systems in the world.

Given that constitutional presidential power is such a poor predictor of presidential power in practice, the purpose of my book will be to establish a significantly more reliable prediction mechanism using my three independent variables.

Part III: Introducing the Theoretical Argument Behind the Emergence of Hyperpresidentialism

In this part, I will introduce the three independent variables which I have determined affect presidential power in practice and create fertile conditions that lead to hyperpresidentialism. The first critical factor in the development of hyperpresidentialism is the strength of state institutions in a country, with institutional weakness making hyperpresidentialism more likely. *Throughout this book, the terms "institutional strength" and "rule of law" will be used interchangeably* (since having strong rule of law implies having strong state institutions and vice versa). The second factor affecting the degree of presidential power is the size of a president's party in congress (a stronger working majority will result in more presidential power). The third factor that affects informal presidential power is the presence of recent economic crises in a country (with a greater number of recent crises making hyperpresidentialism more likely). The argument this book makes is illustrated in Figure 1.4.

Below, I will define these three independent variables and provide the theoretical foundation for why together they make it likely that hyperpresidentialism will emerge.

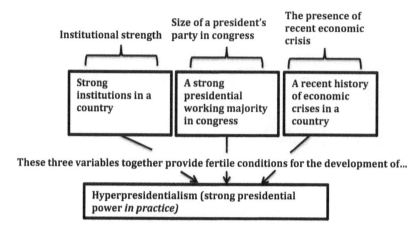

Figure 1.4 Central argument of the book.

Logic Behind These Independent Variables

First Independent Variable: The Strength of State Institutions in a Country

The first independent variable that contributes to the emergence of hyperpresidentialism is the strength of state institutions. On the surface, there is no obvious link between hyperpresidentialism and rule of law, and it is not apparent why a society that is lawless would necessarily gravitate toward a concentration of power in the executive (in fact, one would expect the opposite, that when a society has features of anarchy, there would be *less* concentration of power). The main reason, however, why weak institutions provide an extremely fertile ground for hyperpresidentialism to emerge is because when institutions charged with enforcing laws limiting a president's power are too weak or riddled with corruption to effectively perform their duties, they often do not rein in the abuses of populist/personalist leaders who desire to abuse power. For example, courts may often fail to enforce rules limiting the scope of presidential decrees and may fail to punish executive abuses in general.

Presidents will generally attempt to maximize their power relative to other institutions of horizontal accountability such as congress and the judiciary. In this sense, in any democratic system, policymaking can be seen as a direct struggle between the executive branch and other institutions of horizontal accountability that seek to constrain the president. Seen through this prism, it is logical that whenever these institutions of horizontal accountability are weak, the president encounters less resistance and is thus likely to be able to govern in a more unilateral manner.

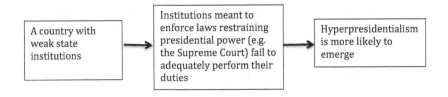

Figure 1.5 Illustration of the connection between institutional strength and hyperpresidentialism.

On the other hand, when these institutions are strong, presidents encounter significantly more resistance and are likely to have fewer of their proposals approved.

As I will describe in Chapter 3, institutional strength/weakness will be understood through the lens of four criteria: institutional prestige, technical capacity, independence from the executive branch, and respect for established rules/norms.

Second Independent Variable: The Size of a President's Party in Congress

The second main independent variable that determines whether it is probable that a president will be able to concentrate power is whether or not he/she has a working majority in congress, where by "working majority," I refer to a group of legislators who are likely to vote for whatever project the president proposes. Presidents are especially powerful in party systems where they wield significant control over a disciplined party. This method is akin to Shugart and Mainwaring's concept of "partisan powers" which Mainwaring describes as "the degree to which presidents can rely on disciplined majorities in congress."[10] A classical example of presidents being able to use partisan power to essentially render congress a rubber stamp is the aforementioned case of Mexico in the second half of the 20th century under the PRI.[11]

There are two theoretical reasons why I argue that having a working majority creates fertile conditions for hyperpresidentialism to emerge. First, congressional majorities increase the likelihood that the president's proposals will pass through the legislature. Notably, majorities would allow presidents to obtain greater control of key institutions, including the Supreme Court. Presidents often have powers of appointment in many of these institutions (with congressional authorization often required), and congressional majorities will allow presidents to more easily "stack" them with loyal appointees. These institutions in the long term will be less likely to challenge the president. Similarly, a president is more likely to have laws passed in the context of unified government, including possibly having them "rubber-stamped." Second, congressional majorities will be more likely to ignore presidential abuses of power (for example, if a president issues a controversial decree, the legislature is less likely to take action). In contrast, a congress controlled by a true opposition is more likely to confront the president.

Third Independent Variable: The Presence of Recent Economic Crises

The third independent variable that I will argue makes it more likely for a president to be able to concentrate power is the existence of recent economic crises. An economic crisis increases the likelihood of hyperpresidentialism because it generates *demand among members of congress* for strong, decisive leadership. An economic crisis also increases the likelihood of hyperpresidentialism because the emergency powers given to the president by congress to tackle the crisis can be either too broad or may lack adequate provisions to ensure that they will end once the crisis is over. Rather than limiting the president's authority to issue decrees to the narrow areas necessary for dealing with an economic crisis, congress perhaps out of fear or out of a lack of technical capacity to understand the measures needed to be taken to combat the crisis may "overshoot" and provide the president powers he/she does not need. Congress may also fail to include adequate provisions that would ensure that the decree powers end when the crisis is resolved. The result often can be that rather than simply giving the president the ability to act decisively in a moment of national emergency, congress will have in fact granted the president permanent decision-making powers that extend beyond the current downturn. In addition, the judiciary is less likely to challenge the president during a time of economic crisis.

Throughout this book, I will also discuss a specific kind of economic crisis that strengthens presidential power even further which I term a "bust-boom cycle." Although economic crises promote hyperpresidentialism through the mechanisms I mentioned above, presidents who come to power inheriting an economic crisis from their predecessor *and are able to restore growth* will be in an especially strong position to concentrate power. Presidents who take power during an economic crisis yet are able to promote a recovery will have benefitted from (a) the aforementioned demand by members of congress for strong leadership, which in many cases caused the legislature to confer the executive substantially greater authority, (b) a strong sense of legitimacy stemming from the fact that his/her government is associated with a return to economic growth, and (c) the greater resources available to the president during the boom period that they can use as patronage to coopt different groups in society.[12] The synergistic effects of this particular combination of a president taking power in a crisis and restoring rapid growth will become evident in my analysis of Argentina in Chapter 5.

In short, I have identified that economic crises are likely to promote the concentration of power in a president. I have also identified that a situation that is particularly likely to lead to hyperpresidentialism is when a president begins his term during an economic crisis yet is able to turn the economy around and claim credit for his economic management. This legitimacy arising from having successfully restored growth will give the president the political capital necessary to concentrate power.

Although I will discuss how my three independent variables worked in the Argentine and Chilean cases in Chapters 2–5, Table 1.1 summarizes how they apply in the two countries.

In Table 1.1, and throughout this book, I refer to Argentina as "hyperpresidential." However, as I elaborate in Chapter 2, Argentina has displayed some variation over time in the degree of hyperpresidentialism depending on whether there was unified or divided government. For example, as I will show, presidential power was higher under president Carlos Menem, who possessed working majorities in congress, than under Fernando De La Rúa, who did not have a majority in both houses of congress. However, despite the variations, Argentina can fairly be classified

Table 1.1 Summary of how my three independent variables worked in the cases of both Argentina and Chile

	Strength of state institutions	The size of a president's party in congress	The existence of recent economic crises
Argentina (hyperpresidential)	Argentina has weak institutions	Peronist presidents often had party majorities or near-majorities in congress (even when Peronists were technically slightly short of 50% of seats in the Chamber of Deputies, they still had de facto control)	From the late 1980s until 2019, there were two major economic crises, one at the end of the 1980s, and the other in the early 2000s. These two crises followed the pattern of a bust-boom cycle
Chile (president constrained in practice)	Chile has strong institutions	Presidents have never possessed *party* majorities since democratization	From the late 1980s until 2019, there were no serious economic crises

overall as being hyperpresidential, since even under the "weaker" presidents, presidential power was still extremely high. For example, with regard to the Chilean comparison, during all years since 1990, presidential power has been higher in Argentina than in Chile, regardless of the presidents in power.

Case Selection and Time Period Examined

In terms of case selection, Argentina and Chile provide a powerful most similar system design. These two countries are similar on many factors, most notably that since democratization, they have both been vibrant democracies. Other similarities include geography, economic development, and a history of bureaucratic-authoritarian military regimes; however, they critically differ on the extent to which the president was able to concentrate power. I will trace this difference to my three independent variables. Table 1.2 illustrates several of the similarities between Argentina and Chile.

In this book, I will mainly explore the time period in Argentina and Chile from democratization in the 1980s/1990 through 2019. My analysis will involve the presidencies up to and including Michelle Bachelet in Chile and Mauricio Macri in Argentina. I will not be examining Sebastián Piñera's second term in office or Alberto Fernández's presidency.

Part IV: How My Book Fits into the Literature

I will begin this part by describing how my book fits into several literatures across political science, namely the literature on measuring

Table 1.2 Similarities between Argentina and Chile

Geography	Economy	Armed conflict	Similar historical regime types
These countries are neighbors at the southern tip of Latin America. Argentina has a direct land border with Chile (among the longest borders in the world).	Similar GDP per capita levels and high scores on indices like health, education, etc. (among the highest in Latin America).	These countries have been free of the internal armed/civil conflict seen in other nations like Mexico, Colombia, and Peru.	Both countries experienced bureaucratic-authoritarian dictatorships and democratized in the 1980–1990 period. Today, both countries are vibrant democracies.

presidential power, the literature on the relationship between presidents and party systems, and the literature on democratization and democratic backsliding.

Literature on Measuring Presidential Power

Many authors in the literature, such as Metcalf 2000, Tsebelis 2002, Shugart and Carey 1992, Negretto 2013, and Frye 1997, have an underlying assumption in their research that to measure the strength of a president, one should look at what the constitution says. Various indices of presidential power have been created, but as I showed earlier in this chapter, these indices have the limitation that there is a large discrepancy between parchment rules and presidential power in practice.

Shugart and Carey 1992 divide presidential power into two categories: legislative and nonlegislative powers. Legislative powers include the veto, the decree, the ability to propose referenda, and the exclusive ability to introduce certain pieces of legislation. Nonlegislative powers include authority over cabinet appointees and cabinet dismissals. Each of these powers is measured on a 1–4 scale, and total legislative and nonlegislative power is calculated based on adding the points that presidents receive in each of these categories.[13] In a later piece, Carey further emphasizes the importance of formal rules in his discussion of "parchment institutions."[14]

In Figure 1.6, on the x-axis, I plotted the sum of Shugart and Carey's legislative and nonlegislative powers in 1992 for all presidential countries in their sample which coincided with my dataset from Figure 1.1 (all presidential and semi-presidential systems throughout the world).

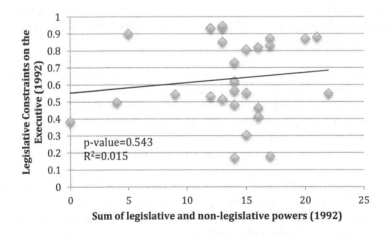

Figure 1.6 Scatterplot comparing the sum of Shugart and Carey's legislative and nonlegislative powers with Legislative Constraints on the Executive (the data is from 1992).

On the y-axis, I plotted the value received by those countries on the 1992 Legislative Constraints on the Executive index.

The results in this scatterplot not only fail to show a statistically significant relationship between constitutional presidential powers and presidential powers in practice, but the insignificant relationship that does exist is in the *wrong direction*. As the legislative and nonlegislative constitutional powers of presidents increase, this scatterplot indicates that constraints on the president *also increase* (when logically they should decrease).

Metcalf in his piece proposes several revisions to Shugart and Carey's model, but the revised model for measuring presidential power is still based on the same exact formal powers proposed by Shugart and Carey (although his methodology for calculating scores differs). Once again, this model relies on formal powers, and the problems inherent with this method of measuring presidential power are acknowledged by Metcalf when he writes that

> it is true that presidents may also have powers that are not defined in the formal written document. Although I do not discount the importance of this issue, I would argue that it is first necessary to measure the formal powers because these are a resource that will either be augmented or diminished by the informal powers.[15]

Frye 1997 proposes a mechanism of measuring presidential power using a similar method of looking at constitutional provisions and assigning a score to them. For example, whereas Shugart and Carey use a list of ten formal presidential powers, Frye expands this list to 27.[16] Frye in his piece, however, takes the step of acknowledging the potential significance of informal powers, which he describes as being possibly "strong and not encoded in formal rules."[17,18] He refers to these as "residual powers" and describes them as follows:

> As no specification of presidential power can account for all contingencies, residual power to make decisions "outside of the contract" must be assigned to either the parliament or the president...The power to make decisions in circumstances not specified in the constitution, such as a crisis, or to make binding decisions independent of the parliament gives the president a significant resource.[19]

Nevertheless, he ultimately views formal powers (or "specific" powers as he calls them) as more important, and argues that in a variety of countries he studies throughout the world (specifically post-communist societies), formal powers actually reflect informal powers very well. He claims that "if formal rules do not matter, then why did political actors expend vast resources to alter them in many cases?"[20]

Negretto in a 2013 book on constitutional design largely concurs with the methodology in Shugart and Carey's model (he describes that this index is "probably the best to date"[21] in measuring presidential power). The flaw he mentions in Shugart and Carey's piece is that their index is additive. He proposes an alternative model that takes into account how these presidential powers interact with each other in order to assess "their joint contribution to the overall power of the president."[22] Rather than adding these powers together in order to assess overall presidential power, Negretto proposes multiplying them and writes that a president who has moderate powers on two dimensions will have overall greater powers than a president who is very strong on one dimension but weak on the other.[23] Despite his proposal to change the methodology in Shugart and Carey's piece, Negretto's alternative mechanism for measuring presidential power still relies on formal, constitutional powers.

Similarly, in his work on veto players, Tsebelis gives the constitution a lot of weight in his assignation of the checks and balances that can exist in a political system. He argues that "the constitution of a country can assign the status of veto player to different individual or collective actors"[24] and calls these veto players generated by the constitution "institutional" veto players.

Helmke 2017 discusses inter-branch crises in Latin America, where she focuses on conflicts between the executive, legislative, and judicial branches. Although my book and Helmke's work intersect in certain areas, Helmke assigns significant weight to constitutional presidential powers. In a similar flavor to Shugart and Mainwaring 1997, she views presidential power in terms of both partisan power and constitutional power. Regarding the constitutional power component, she writes that:

> Obviously, there is still some slippage between the president's formal constitutional powers and his actual legislative powers, but this hardly invalidates the supposition that the president's formal legislative powers should provide a good indicator of his abilities to shape policy outcomes.[25]

Carlos Nino is another influential scholar who looked at presidential power, especially hyperpresidentialism. However, in his writings, he assigns constitutional provisions significant weight in determining presidential power in practice. For example, he describes that presidential power in Argentina, "both de jure and de facto, lie[s] in the 1853 Constitution."[26]

In his recent work, Corrales 2018 contradicts several explanations in the literature for the causes behind strong/weak presidential powers *in constitutions*, including the overall macroeconomic situation of a country and the ideological extremism of the president in power at the time the constitution is written. Rather, he claims that the fundamental factor influencing whether or not a country's constitution will grant the president significant power is what he calls "power asymmetries" between the incumbent president and the opposition.

My main critique of this overall literature is that it places too much emphasis on constitutional power and fails to take into account that presidential power in practice is often significantly different from presidential power in theory (as I showed in Part II of this chapter). There are endless cases of countries throughout the world where constitutions grant presidents relatively little power, yet they wind up governing in a very hyperpresidential manner. Similarly, there are many other countries where despite constitutions that grant significant power to presidents, executives often work in a cooperative and productive way with institutions of horizontal accountability such as congress and the judiciary. Recently, several scholars have begun to question whether formal rules actually constrain presidential power. For example, Palanza 2009 argues that the ability of Argentine presidents to govern unilaterally was not because the Argentine congress lacked the formal power to check the executive, but rather because it exhibited a lack of "institutional commitment."[27] Similarly, in her piece comparing hyperpresidentialism in Argentina and The Philippines, Susan Rose-Ackerman claims that "our study of the interactions between institutional structure and political power illustrates how often nominal legal constraints are undermined by determined Presidents."[28] Siavelis 2000 and Siavelis 2002 also describe how Chilean presidents, despite their strong formal powers, have in practice been relatively restrained. Helmke and Levitsky 2004 in their piece on informal institutions also discuss how rules on paper may not always apply in practice; they describe the concept of "competing" institutions, which occurs when informal practices explicitly contradict written rules. See also Morgenstern et al. 2013 for their discussion of "formal" and "reinforced powers."

My book is thus part of an emerging body of scholarship that questions the effectiveness of constitutional provisions in limiting presidential power, while much of the literature assumes that these constitutional "parchment" rules are the main determinant for presidential power in practice. So far, no systematic indicator has been created which measures presidential power without considering constitutional provisions, and it is for this reason that I use expert surveys as the main tool in numerically measuring presidential power in practice in this book.

Literature on Presidents and Party Systems

The analysis that I perform in this book about the effects of a legislative majority on presidential power also fits into the wider literature on presidents and party systems. In particular, my book both builds on the concept of "partisan power" described by Shugart and Mainwaring, and contradicts a lot of the discussion in the literature which views with pessimism the combination of presidentialism and a fragmented, undisciplined party system.

Shugart and Mainwaring 1997 introduce the concept of "partisan powers" of presidents. Whereas Shugart and Carey 1992 viewed formal constitutional powers as the only relevant factor in assessing the strength of presidents, Shugart and Mainwaring 1997 introduce this other dimension, partisan power, to assess presidential power. They write that:

> When observers classify presidents in terms of being "strong" or "weak," they tend to mean presidents' ability to put their own stamp on policy—to get an agenda enacted. We mean essentially the same thing. There are two principal ways that presidents can have such influence. One is to have constitutional powers inherent in the office of the presidency...Another is to have control over their own party and for that party to be in control of a majority of seats. Presumably, these two factors—which might be termed their *constitutional* and *partisan* powers over legislation—interact to determine the degree of influence presidents have over policy—and hence their strength.[29]

In my discussion of the second independent variable, I will build on Shugart and Mainwaring's concept of partisan powers by showing how in the case of Argentina, when the size of a president's party in congress increases, informal presidential power will tend to increase.

One of the dominant views in the literature on presidents and party systems that this book will contradict is the view that presidential systems produce optimal outcomes in the context of a small number of disciplined parties (where the president is likely to benefit from unified government). Mainwaring and Shugart argue that "other things being equal, presidentialism tends to function better where...parties are at least moderately disciplined, and party systems are not highly fragmented."[30] Similarly, Shugart and Mainwaring state that "undisciplined parties create problems in presidential democracies."[31] Mainwaring 1993 and Ames 2001 also viewed with pessimism presidential systems which were dominated by a high number of parties and where it was difficult for presidents to form majorities in congress. Mainwaring, for example, feared the immobilism and gridlock resulting from multiparty presidentialism, and feared that there would be "potentially deleterious consequences for democratic stability and/or effective governance."[32] Similarly, Ames 2001 in his piece on democracy in Brazil also views presidentialism in the context of a fragmented, undisciplined party system as a flawed combination (he specifically decries the open-list PR system). He writes that the electoral system in Brazil leads to "policy immobility."[33]

In my book, I will fundamentally contradict the assertion that presidentialism works poorly in the context of fragmented, undisciplined parties. Rather, I will claim that a fragmented, undisciplined party system ensures that presidents are not able to abuse their power and eliminates the possibility that hyperpresidentialism will occur through an excess of partisan power.

My book also fits well in the context of the recent edited book by Alemán and Tsebelis 2016. Their work, *Legislative Institutions and Lawmaking in Latin America*, discusses the legislative process across several countries and emphasizes the interaction between presidents and congress when passing laws. This work also directly relates to one of the independent variables in my book, since my book emphasizes the role of presidential majorities in the lawmaking process.

More generally, my work expands on the debate about the strengths and potential risks associated with presidential systems (see Shugart and Mainwaring 1997 and Linz 1990).

Literature on Democratization and Democratic Backsliding

This piece also fits well with the literature on democratization and democratic backsliding.

Beginning in the 1960s through the early 2000s, the political science literature was preoccupied with determining the causes of democratization (see, for example, Lipset 1959, Moore 1966, Przeworski and Limongi 1997, Rueschemeyer et al. 1992, Huntington 1991, Rustow 1970, Boix 2003). This book adds to the literature given its thorough analysis of two fledgling democracies which transitioned as part of Huntington's "Third Wave."

During the late 1990s and 2000s, when democratization seemed irreversible, several pieces focused on why certain countries did not participate in this democratic trend. For example, Ross 2001 famously tried to explain why certain oil-rich countries were resistant to democracy, and similarly, Bellin 2004 attempted to explain why authoritarianism has persisted in the Middle East. As well, Diamond 2004 tried to analyze why the United States failed to establish a thriving democracy in Iraq.

Levitsky and Way (2002, 2010) discuss "competitive authoritarianism," which often involves the concentration of power in a president (see also Levitsky and Loxton 2013 for a discussion of competitive authoritarianism in the Andes region of Latin America specifically[34]). Similarly, Zakaria 1997 describes his category of "illiberal democracies."[35] For a conceptual discussion of "democracy with adjectives" and "diminished subtypes" such as illiberal democracies, see Collier and Levitsky 1997. In terms of the Latin American literature specifically, several authors have written about the recent erosion of democracy, including Weyland 2013 (who claims that "for the first time in decades, democracy in Latin America is facing a sustained, coordinated threat"[36]) and Pérez-Liñan and Mainwaring 2015. Mazzuca 2014 talks about authoritarian backsliding in the context of what he calls "rentier populism."[37] There is also a recent literature on the populist, authoritarian left in Latin America, including Weyland et al. 2010 and Levitsky and Roberts 2011 (especially their concept of a "populist left" and "populist machine").

This book also adds to the extensive literature that analyzes countries with excessively powerful presidents, including the case of Argentina. Notably, Palanza in her recently published book provides a very insightful discussion of the conditions under which presidents will decide to use either decrees or statutes to enact their projects.[38] In other words, under what conditions will presidents choose to go through congress rather than simply use decrees to pass their proposals? In a similar vein, Remington 2014 discusses the use of decrees in modern Russia. Rose-Ackerman in her article also provides an analysis of hyperpresidentialism in Argentina and talks about the "weakness of institutional checks on the presidency."[39]

In the context of my third independent variable, my argument that economic crises promote a greater concentration of power in an executive is consistent with the various theories in the literature linking wealth with democracy, and economic crises with democratic reversals (see Lipset 1959, Huntington 1991, Przeworski and Limongi 1997, Diamond and Linz 1989). My theory also builds on the arguments in Przeworski 1991 about the feasibility of market reforms in the context of democratic versus authoritarian regimes.

A new trend has recently emerged, with several authors and political commentators discussing the *reversion toward authoritarianism* among not only fledgling democracies (which had not experienced Linz and Stepan's "democratic consolidation"[40] where democracy became the "only game in town") but also established democracies. Such works dovetail well with the themes in this book. In their recent book *How Democracies Die*, Levitsky and Ziblatt highlight how formal constitutional checks and balances will not serve as a barrier to leaders with authoritarian tendencies. Rather, this barrier comes in the form of "unwritten rules" that govern the behavior of political actors. In their discussion of American democracy, they make a similar argument to the one I make in this book, namely that formal rules are not a strong predictor of how a regime will function *in practice*. They write that "historically, our [American] system of checks and balances *has* worked pretty well—but not, or not entirely, because of the constitutional design by the founders. Democracies work best—and survive longer—where constitutions are reinforced by unwritten democratic norms."[41] Similarly, in his recent book *The People vs. Democracy: Why Our Freedom Is in Danger & How to Save It*, Yasha Mounk discusses the backsliding of democracy throughout the West in general. Like in the Levitsky and Ziblatt piece, Mounk's work also emphasizes the importance of informal norms for the proper functioning of democratic institutions.

This book also fits well with the work of Kim Scheppele on constitutions and the separation of powers in the context of stress. For example, my discussion of economic crises fits well with Scheppele 2004, where she examines abuses of power that may occur during crisis situations. This book also ties in with her recent work on democratic backsliding in Hungary and the attack on rule of law (see, for example, Bánkuti et al. 2012, "Hungary's Illiberal Turn: Disabling the Constitution").

Most fundamentally, this piece adds to the literature on democracy by shedding light on how democratic countries transition toward authoritarianism. Although the concept of hyperpresidentialism that I address in this book is not synonymous with authoritarian governments (since it is possible to have hyperpresidentialism in the context of democracy as under Menem in Argentina), usually a strengthening of presidential power is done in the context of a general backsliding of democracy. For many democratic countries, the increasing concentration of power in presidents represents a series of important steps in the erosion of democracy. By challenging the widely-held belief that a concentration of power in the presidency is the result of constitutional design and by proposing an original three-part theory to explain hyperpresidentialism, this book makes a strong contribution to the literature on democratization and democratic backsliding.

Part V: Structure of the Book and Roadmap of the Argument

Summarizing the Book Chapters

In Chapters 2–5, I will discuss my case analysis of Argentina and Chile in detail. In Chapter 2, I will explain how my dependent variable, presidential power, differed across the two cases. I will show how, in practice, whereas Argentine presidents for most of the period since democratization have been able to concentrate significant power, Chilean presidents were more restrained by institutions of horizontal accountability. I will also discuss formal (constitutional) presidential powers in these two cases and explain how on paper, it is in fact the Chilean president who is stronger than his Argentine counterpart. This case analysis will serve as an illustration for how presidential power in theory may not correspond to presidential power in practice. In Chapter 2, I also notably expand on the variation in presidential power *within* the Argentine case. Whereas Argentina for the vast majority of the post-democratization period has been a case of hyperpresidentialism, there have been periods when presidents were more restrained.

In Chapter 3, I discuss how my first independent variable, differences in the strength of state institutions, applies in the cases of Argentina and Chile. I will show how Argentina by all measures has significantly weaker institutions than Chile, and explain how this difference in institutional strength helped create the divergence that exists in presidential power between these two countries. In this analysis, I go across various institutions in both Argentina and Chile. In Argentina, I discuss the weakness of congress, the judiciary, the *Auditoria General de la Nación*, the *Defensor del Pueblo*, and the Central Bank. I will contrast the weakness of these institutions to the strength shown by the following Chilean institutions: congress, the judiciary (the Supreme Court and the Constitutional Tribunal), the *Contraloría*, the *Consejo para la Transparencia*, the Central Bank, and the *Ministerio Público*. In this chapter, I will also include a large-N analysis across (a) a dataset of all presidential systems throughout the world and (b) a dataset of all presidential democracies in the Western Hemisphere.

In Chapter 4, I discuss my second independent variable, the size of a president's party in congress. I will show how presidents in Argentina, specifically Peronist presidents, have enjoyed strong working majorities in congress, and how they were able to use these majorities to minimize congress's role as a veto player. I will then contrast the majorities enjoyed by Argentine presidents with the significantly smaller party shares of Chilean presidents. I will explain how Chilean presidents have never held party majorities in congress since democratization, and that even though presidents from the *Concertación* (later called the *Nueva Mayoría*) possessed coalitional majorities, these coalitional majorities were considerably more heterogenous and a far cry from the cohesion of the Peronist party in Argentina. I will show how this difference in the size of the president's party in congress led to the differing levels of presidential power in Argentina versus Chile.

In Chapter 5, I will go into detail about my third independent variable, namely whether or not a country has experienced recent economic crises. I will discuss how since democratization, Argentina has experienced many years of economic crisis, whereas Chile through 2019 experienced no economic crises. I will then show how presidents in Argentina were able to use these economic crises to concentrate power, unlike Chilean presidents who did not have this opportunity. I will also discuss the two bust-boom cycles in Argentina, and how certain Argentine presidents were able to benefit from these cycles of economic crisis followed by strong growth. In this chapter, I will also include the results of the survey I performed, which indicates whether or not presidents concentrate power because the electorate desires a stronger president.

Part VI: Modern Political History of Argentina and Chile

Origins of the Two Traditional Parties in Argentina

In Argentina, the two traditional political parties have been the Radical party and the Peronist party. In this section, I will briefly describe the history behind both political movements.

The history of Peronism begins with Juan Perón's rise to power in 1943 as Secretary of Labor following a coup d'état. Perón would become the president of Argentina starting in 1946 and was in office until 1955. Perón had deep ties to organized labor, and during his time in office, workers gained important rights including a minimum wage. Juan Perón and his wife Eva Perón became immensely popular among the poor and working classes in Argentina, and the movement that emerged from Juan Perón and his wife came to be known as Peronism. Even after Juan Perón was exiled in 1955, Peronism remained one of the dominant political forces in the country and would be a source for the instability that would eventually lead to a coup in 1962, a coup in 1966, and the coup in 1976.[42] After the 1976 military coup, during the "Dirty War" throughout the military dictatorship between 1976 and 1983, Peronism suffered severe repression, and many Peronist figures were imprisoned or tortured. What is remarkable is that the Peronist movement has been extremely resilient, and immediately reemerged as a political force once the military left (although it did not win the presidential elections in 1983). The tension between Peronist and anti-Peronist factions in society was one of the defining features of post-WWII Argentina and has continued to this day.

It is difficult to precisely define Peronism. An Argentine would have the same difficulty in defining Peronism as an American would in defining Trumpism, since neither political ideology fits clearly across the left–right spectrum. Indeed, there have been both right-wing Peronist presidents such as Carlos Menem and left-wing Peronist presidents such as Cristina Kirchner. This lack of a programmatic policy is described by Seawright, who claims that "over time, the Peronist party occupied virtually every imaginable position between the center left and the center right on the Argentine ideological spectrum."[43] Levitsky echoes this sentiment, and in addition to describing the Peronist party as "fluid," writes that:

> Peronism has long been characterized by its heterogeneity, ideological eclecticism, and malleability. Its electoral coalition was always more heterogeneous than those of most European working-class parties. In urban areas, Peronism originally drew from both the established industrial working class and an expanding pool of poor migrants from the interior, while in the less developed provinces of the interior, it was supported by a heterogeneous mix of rural workers and lower-to-middle-income townspeople. This heterogeneity and ideological eclecticism has made Peronism very difficult to label in left–right terms, and as a result, many scholars have simply characterized the movement as "pragmatic."[44]

Despite the difficulty in defining Peronism, it is possible to identify four elements of the political movement that have remained relatively consistent across time: (1) a strong base of support among organized labor, (2) a rhetorical commitment to improving the lives of the working classes, (3) an affinity for strong leaders, where internal debate among party officials is discouraged in favor of top-down control, and (4) an emphasis on the use of clientelism to obtain votes.

Peronism would eventually morph into the Peronist party, which is also known as the Justicialist party (*Partido Justicialista*) or PJ.

The other major political movement that emerged in Argentina during the 20th century is the Radical party, also known as the Radical Civic Union (*Unión Cívica Radical*), UCR, or simply "Radicals." The Radical party was founded in 1891, and the first Radical president was Hipólito Yrigoyen, who served from 1916 until 1922 and then from 1928 until 1930. Unlike Peronism whose base of support lies with the poor and working classes, Radicalism has its roots in the urban middle classes. Also, whereas Peronism has a focus on strong leaders and a top-down culture that discourages dissent within the party ranks, Radicalism has a strong emphasis on respect for institutions and democratic deliberation.

Brief Summary of the Modern Political History of Argentina

The military government that ruled Argentina between 1976 and 1983 lost power amid humiliation, since it was blamed for two dual catastrophes. First, Argentina suffered a severe economic downturn in the 1981–1982 period. Second, Argentina suffered an embarrassing defeat in the Falkland Islands War. In this context, the country democratized, and Radical president Raúl Alfonsín came to power. He served as president until 1989, and his term was characterized by economic stagnation (including inflation) and labor unrest (there were 13 general strikes in Argentina during Alfonsín's term). He resigned amidst a sharp economic downturn at the end of the 1980s which involved hyperinflation.

Alfonsín's successor, Carlos Menem, was a right-wing Peronist. After coming to power in the context of the economic crisis that emerged during the last part of Alfonsín's term in office, Menem adopted a radical set of neoliberal reforms that included privatizations and the pegging of the Argentine *peso* to the US dollar. Although these reforms initially produced an economic recovery in the early to mid-1990s, the economy slowed down during the late 1990s just as Menem's successor, Fernando De La Rúa, was taking office. De La Rúa was a Radical, and unlike Menem, he did not enjoy the support of either congress or organized labor. Argentina became difficult to govern under De La Rúa, especially since Menem had delivered him an economy that was slipping into recession. The recession accelerated during De La Rúa's term and peaked in the 2001–2002 period. Ultimately, the economic crisis reached a boiling point in December of 2001, when De La Rúa resigned and was forced to flee the *Casa Rosada* (the presidential palace) in a helicopter due to protests outside.

After a succession of three presidents whose terms in office collectively lasted less than two weeks, Peronist leader Eduardo Duhalde eventually emerged as the president. Duhalde's rise to power represented the return of Peronism to Argentine politics. Nearly a year and a half later in April of 2003, presidential elections were held where Néstor Kirchner, also a Peronist, won. In the following election in 2007, Néstor Kirchner's wife Cristina Kirchner was elected president (she had previously been a senator). Cristina Kirchner would go on to obtain reelection in 2011.

Collectively, Néstor Kirchner and his wife Cristina Kirchner governed Argentina for approximately 12 and a half years. During their time in office, the Argentine economy rebounded and grew sharply due to the commodity boom that increased demand for many Argentine agricultural exports (including soybeans). Unlike Menem, Néstor and Cristina Kirchner were leftist Peronists, and they were part of the Latin American "left turn."

Collectively, Duhalde and the Kirchners ensured that Argentina would be under Peronist control for nearly 14 years between January 2002 and December 2015. During the presidential election in 2015, Mauricio Macri defeated Peronist candidate Daniel Scioli (who had been vice president between 2003 and 2007 under Néstor Kirchner). After well more than a decade of leftist Peronist presidents, Macri's victory represented a turn back to the right. Macri took office under difficult conditions, since the economy was slowing, and he did not possess a majority in congress.

Brief Description of Modern Politics in Chile

The most critical starting point in an analysis of Chilean political history for the purposes of this book is the Allende presidency. In 1970, Allende took office pledging to promote Marxism in a democratic context. By 1973, the economy had plunged into a sharp recession, and inflation soared. It was in this context that on September 11, 1973, the military launched a coup against Allende and took power. Under the leadership of Augusto Pinochet, the military would remain in power until 1990. In 1988, a referendum was held where Chileans were asked whether they would like for Pinochet to remain in power for another eight years, and by a 56–44% margin, the population voted "no." Overall, the Pinochet period can be characterized as one of strong economic growth (with the notable exceptions of 1975 and 1982–1983) and neoliberal economic policies.

Following the return of democracy in 1990, the Chilean party system can be understood as being composed of two blocs: the right-wing bloc and the left-wing bloc.

The beginnings of the leftist coalition in Chile can be traced to the final years of the Pinochet regime, as the population was getting ready for the plebiscite to determine if Pinochet would stay in power and new elections would be called. During this period, several leftist parties decided to campaign together to encourage Chileans to vote "no" in the referendum. The "Concertación de Partidos por el NO" (*The Coalition of Parties for NO*) would later band together to form an alliance, *Concertación de Partidos por la Democracia*. After the plebiscite, one of the first acts of the parties of the *Concertación* was to name as their presidential candidate Patricio Aylwin, who would go on to win the 1989 presidential election. Initially, the Communist Party had been excluded from the *Concertación* coalition, but this would later change in 2013 when the *Concertación* was dissolved. After the dissolution of the *Concertación*, it was replaced with the *Nueva Mayoría*, which contained the Communist Party. The *Nueva Mayoría* presented a leftward shift from the *Concertación*, which had been criticized as sticking too closely to the neoliberal model left by Pinochet and not doing enough for the poor and working classes. The main parties in the leftist bloc have been the Socialist Party (PS), the Party for Democracy (PPD), the Christian Democrats (DC), and the Social Democratic Radical party. Note that in 2017, the *Nueva Mayoría* coalition suffered a major rupture, since the Christian Democrats decided to go against the coalition and field their own candidate, Carolina Goic, for the presidential election.

On the opposite end, there has been an alliance of right-wing parties in Chile, known historically by various names, notably the *Alianza*, and now called *Chile Vamos*. The two primary parties in the right-wing coalition are the UDI (*Unión Demócrata Independiente*) and the RN (*Renovación Nacional*). The UDI is a deeply conservative party whose ideology in many respects mirrors that of Pinochet. The RN is a more centrist right-wing party.

The return of democracy in Chile has largely been dominated by presidents from the leftist *Concertación*. Between 1990 and the time of writing of this book, of the seven presidential administrations, only two were from the right-wing coalition. In fact, between 1990 and 2010, all Chilean presidents were from the leftist coalition (Aylwin 1990–1994, Frei 1994–2000, Lagos 2000–2006, Bachelet 2006–2010). From 2010 to 2014, rightist president Sebastián Piñera came to power and was succeeded by Bachelet who governed for a second term from 2014 to 2018. Whereas the left in Argentina under Néstor and Cristina Kirchner took on a populist form, the left in Chile since the return to democracy has been far more moderate and pragmatic. In the most recent presidential election in 2018, Piñera won and as a result is once again president in what marks a turn to the right for Chile.

Notes

1 O'Donnell 1994; pp.59–60.
2 O'Donnell 1994; pp.61–62.
3 Cox and Morgenstern 2001; p.173.
4 The specific countries in this dataset are: Afghanistan, Algeria, Angola, Argentina, Armenia, Belarus, Benin, Bolivia, Brazil, Burkina Faso, Burundi,

Cameroon, Cape Verde, Central African Republic, Chad, Chile, China, Colombia, Comoros, Congo, DR, Congo, Rep, Costa Rica, Cyprus, Djibouti, Dominican Republic, East Timor, Ecuador, El Salvador, Equatorial Guinea, France, Gabon, Gambia, Georgia, Ghana, Guatemala, Guinea, Guinea-Bissau, Guyana, Haiti, Honduras, Indonesia, Ivory Coast, Kazakhstan, Kenya, Liberia, Lithuania, Madagascar, Malawi, Maldives, Mali, Mauritania, Mexico, Mongolia, Mozambique, Namibia, Nicaragua, Niger, Nigeria, Panama, Paraguay, Peru, Portugal, Philippines, Romania, Russia, Rwanda, Sao Tome and Principe, Senegal, Seychelles, Sierra Leone, South Korea, Sri Lanka, Sudan, Syria, Taiwan, Tajikistan, Tanzania, Togo, Tunisia, Turkmenistan, Uganda, Ukraine, USA, Uruguay, Uzbekistan, Venezuela, Zambia, Zimbabwe, and Yemen.

5 Comparative Constitutions Project 2016.
6 Varieties of Democracy Codebook.
7 Varieties of Democracy Methodology book.
8 The specific countries in this dataset are Argentina, Bolivia, Brazil, Chile, Colombia, Costa Rica, Dominican Republic, Ecuador, El Salvador, Guatemala, Guyana, Honduras, Mexico, Nicaragua, Panama, Paraguay, Peru, Uruguay, USA, and Venezuela.
9 Polity IV Project; pp.62–63.
10 Mainwaring 1997; p.56.
11 For further information, see Levy and Bruhn 2006; p.103, and Domínguez 2015; p.256.
12 For more information about how resources from an economic boom can increase presidential power, see Mazzuca 2014.
13 See Shugart and Carey 1992; p.155.
14 Carey 2000.
15 Metcalf 2000; p.663.
16 See Frye 1997; p.548.
17 Frye 1997; p.526.
18 Relatedly, see also Neustadt 1990 for a discussion of informal presidential powers in the context of US presidents.
19 Frye 1997; p.526.
20 Frye 1997; p.527.
21 Negretto 2013; p.82.
22 Negretto 2013; p.82.
23 Negretto 2013; p.83.
24 Tsebelis 2002; p.19.
25 Helmke 2017; p.80.
26 Nino 1996; p.167.
27 Palanza 2009.
28 Rose-Ackerman 2011; p.333.
29 Shugart and Mainwaring 1997; pp.40–41.
30 Mainwaring and Shugart 1997; p.449.
31 Shugart and Mainwaring 1997; p.53.
32 Mainwaring 1993; p.215.
33 Ames 2001; p.51.
34 Levitsky and Loxton 2013.
35 Zakaria 1997; p.23.
36 Weyland 2013; p.19.
37 Mazzuca 2014.
38 Palanza 2019.

39 Rose-Ackerman 2011; p.329.
40 Linz and Stepan 1996.
41 Levitsky and Ziblatt 2018; p.8.
42 For more information about this instability, see O'Donnell 1973 where he discusses the "impossible game".
43 Seawright 2012; p.117.
44 Levitsky 2003; p.27.

Bibliography

Alemán, Eduardo, and George Tsebelis. *Legislative Institutions and Lawmaking in Latin America*. Oxford: Oxford University Press, 2016.

Ames, Barry. *The Deadlock of Democracy in Brazil*. Ann Arbor: University of Michigan Press, 2001.

Bánkuti, Miklós, Gábor Halmai, and Kim Scheppele. "Hungary's Illiberal Turn: Disabling the Constitution." *Journal of Democracy*. Vol 23, Iss 3 (July 2012), pp. 138–146.

Bellin, Eva, "The Robustness of Authoritarianism in the Middle East: Exceptionalism in Comparative Perspective." *Comparative Politics*. Vol 36, Iss 2 (January 2004), pp. 139–157.

Boix, Carles. *Democracy and Redistribution*. Cambridge: Cambridge University Press, 2003.

Carey, John. "Parchment, Equilibria, and Institutions." *Comparative Political Studies*. Vol 33, Iss 6/7 (August/September 2000), pp. 735–761.

Collier, David, and Steven Levitsky. "Democracy with Adjectives: Conceptual Innovation in Comparative Research." *World Politics*. Vol 49, Iss 3 (April 1997), pp. 430–451.

Corrales, Javier. *Fixing Democracy: Why Constitutional Change Often Fails to Enhance Democracy in Latin America*. Oxford: Oxford University Press, 2018.

Cox, Gary, and Scott Morgenstern. "Latin America's Reactive Assemblies and Proactive Presidents." *Comparative Politics*. Vol 33, Iss 2 (January 2001), pp. 171–189.

Diamond, Larry. "What Went Wrong in Iraq?" *Foreign Affairs* Vol. 83, Iss 5 (September–October 2004), pp. 34–56.

Diamond, Larry, and Juan Linz. "Introduction: Politics, Society, and Democracy in Latin America." *Democracy in Developing Countries: Latin America*. Eds. Larry Diamond, Juan Linz, and Seymour Martin Lipset. Boulder: Lynne Rienner, 1989, pp. 1–58.

Domínguez, Jorge. "Mexico's 2012 Presidential Election: Conclusions." *Mexico's Evolving Democracy: A Comparative Study of the 2012 Elections*. Eds. Jorge Domínguez, Kenneth Greene, Chappell Lawson, and Alejandro Moreno. Baltimore: Johns Hopkins University Press, 2015, pp. 252–270.

Frye, Timothy. "A Politics of Institutional Choice: Post-Communist Presidencies." *Comparative Political Studies*. Vol 30, Iss 5 (October 1997), pp. 523–552.

Helmke, Gretchen. *Institutions on the Edge: The Origins and Consequences of Inter-Branch Crises in Latin America*. Cambridge: Cambridge University Press, 2017.

Helmke, Gretchen, and Steven Levitsky. "Informal Institutions and Comparative Politics: A research Agenda." *Perspectives on Politics*. Vol 2, Iss 4 (December 2004), pp. 725–740.

Huntington, Samuel. "Democracy's Third Wave." *Journal of Democracy*. Vol 2, Iss 2 (1991), pp, 12–34.

Levitsky, Steven. *Transforming Labor-Based Parties in Latin America*. Cambridge: Cambridge University Press, 2003.

Levitsky, Steven, and James Loxton. "Populism and Competitive Authoritarianism in the Andes." *Democratization*. Vol 20, Iss 1 (2013), pp. 107–136.

Levitsky, Steven, and Kenneth Roberts. *The Resurgence of the Latin American Left*. Baltimore: The Johns Hopkins University Press, 2011.

Levitsky, Steven, and Lucan A. Way. "The Rise of Competitive Authoritarianism." *Journal of Democracy*. Vol 13, Iss 2 (April 2002), pp. 51–65.

Levitsky, Steven, and Lucan Way. *Competitive Authoritarianism: Hybrid Regimes After the Cold War*. Cambridge: Cambridge University Press, 2010.

Levitsky, Steven, and Daniel Ziblatt. *How Democracies Die*. New York: Crown Publishing Group, 2018.

Levy, Daniel, and Kathleen Bruhn. *Mexico: The Struggle for Democratic Development*. Berkeley: University of California Press, 2006.

Linz, Juan. "The Perils of Presidentialism." *Journal of Democracy* Vol 1, Iss 1 (Winter 1990), pp. 51–69.

Linz, Juan, and Alfred Stepan. *Problems of Democratic Transition and Consolidation*. Baltimore: The Johns Hopkins University Press, 1996.

Lipset, Seymour Martin. "Some Social Requisites of Democracy: Economic Development and Political Legitimacy." *American Political Science Review* Vol. 53, Iss 1 (March 1959), pp. 75–80.

Mainwaring, Scott. "Presidentialism, Multipartism, and Democracy: The Difficult Combination." *Comparative Political Studies*. Vol 26, Iss 2 (1993), pp. 198–228.

Mainwaring, Scott. "Multipartism, Robust Federalism, and Presidentialism in Brazil." *Presidentialism and Democracy in Latin America*. Eds. Scott Mainwaring and Matthew Shugart. Cambridge: Cambridge University Press, 1997, pp. 55–109.

Mainwaring, Scott, and Matthew Shugart. "Juan Linz, Presidentialism, and Democracy: A Critical Appraisal." *Comparative Politics*. Vol 29, Iss 4 (1997), pp. 449–471.

Mazzuca, Sebastián. "Rentier Populism and the Rise of Super-Presidents in South America." *Reflections on Uneven Democracies: The Legacy of Guillermo O'Donnell*. Eds. Daniel Brinks, Marcelo Leiras, and Scott Mainwaring. Baltimore: Johns Hopkins University Press, 2014, pp. 89–105.

Metcalf, Lee Kendall. "Measuring Presidential Power." *Comparative Political Studies*. Vol 33, Iss 5 (June 2000), pp. 660–685.

Moore, Barrington. *Social Origins of Dictatorship and Democracy*. Boston: Beacon Press, 1966.

Morgenstern, Scott, John Polga-Hecimovich, and Sarah Shair-Rosenfield. "Tall, Grande, or Venti: Presidential Powers in the United States and Latin America." *Journal of Politics in Latin America*. Vol 5, Iss 2 (2013), pp. 37–70.

Mounk, Yasha. *The People Vs. Democracy: Why Our Freedom is in Danger & How to Save It*. Cambridge: Harvard University Press, 2018.

Negretto, Gabriel. *Making Constitutions: Presidents, Parties, and Institutional Choice in Latin America.* Cambridge: Cambridge University Press, 2013.

Neustadt, Richard. *Presidential Power and the Modern Presidents.* New York: The Free Press, 1990.

Nino, Carlos. "Hyperpresidentialism and Constitutional Reform in Argentina." *Institutional Design in New Democracies: Eastern Europe and Latin America.* Eds. Arend Lijphart and Carlos Waisman. Routledge: New York, 2018, pp. 161–174.

O'Donnell, Guillermo. *Modernization and Bureaucratic-Authoritarianism: Studies in South American Politics.* Berkeley: University of California Institute of International Studies, 1973.

O'Donnell, Guillermo. "Delegative Democracy." *Journal of Democracy.* Vol 5, Iss 1 (January 1994), pp. 55–69.

Palanza, M. Valeria. Lawmaking in separation of powers systems: On the choice of decrees vs. statutes. PhD thesis. Princeton University, 2009.

Palanza, Valeria. *Checking Presidential Power: Executive Decrees and the Legislative Process in New Democracies.* Cambridge: Cambridge University Press, 2019.

Pérez-Liñan, Aníbal, and Scott Mainwaring. "Cross-Currents in Latin America." *Journal of Democracy.* Vol 26, Iss 1 (January 2015), pp. 114–127.

Przeworski, Adam. *Democracy and the market: Political and economic reforms in Eastern Europe and Latin America.* Cambridge: Cambridge University Press, 1991.

Przeworski, Adam, and Fernando Limongi. "Modernization: Theories and Facts." *World Politics.* Vol 49, Iss 2 (1997), pp. 155–183.

Rose-Ackerman, Susan. "Hyper-Presidentialism: Separation of Powers Without Checks and Balances in Argentina and the Philippines." Faculty Scholarship Series. Paper 4155. 2011. http://digitalcommons.law.yale.edu/fss_papers/4155

Ross, Michael. "Does Oil Hinder Democracy?" *World Politics.* Vol 53, Iss 3 (April 2001), pp. 325–361.

Rueschemeyer, Dietrich, Evelyne Stephens, and John Stephens. *Capitalist Development and Democracy.* Chicago: The University of Chicago Press, 1992.

Rustow, Dankwart A. "Transitions to Democracy: Toward a Dynamic Model." *Comparative Politics.* Vol 2, Iss 3 (1970), pp. 337–363.

Scheppele, Kim. "Law in a Time of Emergency: States of Exception and the Temptations of 9/11." *University of Pennsylvania Journal of Constitutional Law.* Vol 6, Iss 5 (May 2004), pp. 1001–1083.

Seawright, Jason. *Party-System Collapse: The Roots of Crisis in Peru and Venezuela.* Stanford: Stanford University Press, 2012.

Shugart, Matthew, and John Carey. *Presidents and Assemblies: Constitutional Design and Electoral Dynamics.* Cambridge: Cambridge University Press, 1992.

Shugart, Matthew, and Scott Mainwaring. "Presidentialism and Democracy in Latin America: Rethinking the Terms of the Debate." *Presidentialism and Democracy in Latin America.* Eds. Scott Mainwaring and Matthew Shugart. Cambridge: Cambridge University Press, 1997, pp. 12–54.

Tsebelis, George. *Veto Players: How Political Institutions Work.* Princeton: Princeton University Press, 2002.

Varieties of Democracy. Codebook. July 2017.

Varieties of Democracy. Methodology. July 2017.

Weyland, Kurt. "Latin America's Authoritarian Drift: The Threat from the Populist Left." *Journal of Democracy.* Vol 24, Iss 3 (July 2013), pp. 18–32.

Weyland, Kurt, Raúl Madrid, and Wendy Hunter. *Leftist Government in Latin America: Successes and Shortcomings.* Cambridge: Cambridge University Press, 2010.

Zakaria, Fareed. "The Rise of Illiberal Democracy." *Foreign Affairs.* Vol 76, Iss 6 (1997), pp. 22–43.

2 Comparing Presidential Power in Theory versus Presidential Power in Practice in Argentina and Chile

In this chapter, I will provide an analysis of my dependent variable, presidential power, in my two cases. I will make two distinct arguments, namely that (a) presidential power in practice was always stronger in Argentina than in Chile since democratization, and (b) there has been some variation in presidential power in Argentina (based on a fluctuation in my second independent variable, the size of a president's party in congress).

In Parts I and II, I will describe formal and informal presidential power in Argentina, whereas in Parts III and IV, I will discuss formal and informal presidential power in Chile. For each country, I will first detail the constitutional power that presidents have. Then, I will discuss presidential power *in practice* and identify the discrepancy between formal presidential powers and presidential powers in practice. I will show how whereas in formal terms the Argentine president is significantly constrained in a similar way as US presidents, the Chilean president has far greater powers. Nevertheless, I will illustrate how, in practice, whereas Argentine presidents have often wielded significant power to the point of hyperpresidentialism, Chilean executives have been far more restrained.

In my discussion of the *informal* power of Argentine and Chilean presidents in Parts II and IV, I will show how during most years, Argentine presidents were able to pass projects with relatively little opposition from institutions of horizontal accountability. I will show how institutions such as the court system and congress often simply rubber-stamped a president's proposals. On the other hand, in the case of Chile, I will show how presidents faced numerous hurdles in getting their projects enacted, and how they faced strong resistance from the legislative and judicial branches.

In analyzing my dependent variable, presidential power, in addition to the comparison between Argentina and Chile, I will also briefly analyze intra-country variation within Argentina. Although as I mentioned above Argentina is generally a case of hyperpresidentialism, there are moments when Argentine presidents became more constrained. I will analyze how while Peronist executives showed characteristics of hyperpresidentialism, non-Peronist presidents (namely Alfonsín, De La Rúa, and Macri) faced greater hurdles. I will attribute this intra-country variation

DOI: 10.4324/9781003142904-2

within Argentina to variation in my second independent variable, the size of the president's party in congress. Although there is some variation in presidential power in Argentina, presidential power has remained relatively constant in Chile (as there have been few variations in my three independent variables). As I mentioned above, note that despite the variation in presidential power in Argentina, in absolute terms at all moments since 1990 presidential power in practice was stronger in Argentina than in Chile.

This chapter will lay the groundwork for Chapters 3–5, in which I will, respectively, discuss my first, second, and third independent variables that shaped presidential power in the two cases.

Part I: Formal Presidential Power in Argentina

Presidential powers are delineated in Argentina's constitution of 1853, which was reinstated in 1983 after the military dictatorship collapsed; it was later amended in 1994. The constitution of Argentina bears many similarities to that of the USA, and as Galan describes, the Founding Fathers of the republic

> drafted it essentially along the lines of the US Constitution, responding to the Argentine traditions and needs, and in the frame of a Civilian legal system. Like the US model the Argentine Constitution provides for a strict separation of powers among the three branches of government, the Executive, Congress and the Judiciary.[1]

Like the USA, Argentina is a federal state and is divided into 23 provinces and the capital city, the Autonomous City of Buenos Aires. Similarly, Argentina possesses a bicameral legislature, composed of the Chamber of Deputies and the Senate. Senators are elected for six-year terms, and each province along with the Autonomous City of Buenos Aires is entitled to three seats (for a total of 72 seats). The Chamber of Deputies contains 257 seats, where each of the provinces is equivalent to an electoral district; within each district, deputies are selected for four-year terms based on a system of closed-list proportional representation. In the case of the Chamber of Deputies, every two years, half of the seats are up for reelection, whereas in the Senate, a third of seats are up for reelection every two years. There is severe malapportionment in the Argentine congress, and under-populated states get a disproportionate amount of representatives (this will be discussed in greater depth in Chapter 4).[2]

The judicial system in Argentina also bears similarities to that of the USA, with a Supreme Court (CSJN) that has the power of judicial review. Elias notes that:

> It must be noticed that in Argentina, each and every court, in every jurisdiction, enjoys the power of constitutional review over

legislation, executive decrees and administrative action generally. This power was not contemplated explicitly in the 1853 Constitution, but early on the laws organizing the judiciary provided for judicial review, and so did the Supreme Court, following in the footsteps of Marbury v. Madison. Today, the constitutional text explicitly recognizes the power of judicial review.[3]

Judges have tenure until the age of 75, and the constitution contains a provision that the salary of judges cannot be diminished. The Argentine Supreme Court has traditionally had five justices (1862–1990),[4] although it is important to note that in 1990, the size of the court was expanded to nine members, after which in 2006, it was changed back to five members. Supreme Court justices are nominated by the president (like in the USA) and must then be approved by a two-thirds vote in the Senate (note that before the 1994 constitutional reform, the threshold in the Senate was a simple majority). For lower-court judges, the process is slightly different than in the USA. A president can still nominate lower-level federal judges (who need to be confirmed by the Senate by a simple majority vote), but they must be taken from a shortlist of three candidates proposed by the Council of Magistrates (Section 99/4 of the constitution). The Council of Magistrates is composed of 13 members (made up of judges, legislators, one member of the academic community, and a representative of the executive branch) and is supposed to ensure judicial independence.

In a manner similar to the American president, the Argentine president possesses veto power over any piece of legislation that congress presents; to override the veto, congress would need a two-thirds majority in both chambers. Most importantly, one of the powers given to Argentine presidents is the ability to use the line-item veto.

Moving to the official proactive powers of Argentine presidents, section 99/3 of the Argentine constitution describes the president's role in lawmaking:

He takes part in the making of laws according to the Constitution, promulgates them and has them published. The Executive Power shall in no event issue provisions of legislative nature, in which case they shall be absolutely and irreparably null and void. Only when due to exceptional circumstances the ordinary procedures foreseen by this Constitution for the enactment of laws are impossible to be followed, and when rules are not referred to criminal issues, taxation, electoral matters, or the system of political parties, he shall issue decrees on grounds of necessity and urgency, which shall be decided by a general agreement of ministers who shall countersign them together with the Chief of the Ministerial Cabinet.[5]

The constitution severely curtails the lawmaking capabilities of the president ("The Executive Power shall in no event issue provisions of legislative nature"). Nevertheless, as I will discuss later, in practice decrees have been a critical tool through which Argentine presidents have wielded influence. Beginning in 1994, the constitution officially gave the president the power to issue Necessity and Urgency Decrees (NUDs) during "exceptional circumstances." After an NUD is approved, it must be sent to congress within ten days, where the body may vote to repeal the decree with simple majorities in both chambers.

In short, in this part of the book, I have outlined the constitutional foundations of the separation of powers in Argentina. Whereas the Argentine constitution bears many similarities to that of the USA and on paper establishes a system of strong checks and balances, I will show in the next part how in practice presidents have concentrated power at the expense of congress and the Supreme Court.

Part II: Hyperpresidentialism in Practice in Argentina

There is a vast gulf between Argentine presidential power in theory as described in Part I and presidential power in practice. Jones highlights this discrepancy when he writes that "a strict reading of the Argentine constitution would identify the Argentine president as comparatively weak in terms of legislative power...The reality of Argentine presidentialism between 1983 and 1994, however, was a much more powerful president (i.e. 'potentially dominant')."[6] Argentine presidents since democratization have been characterized by the term "decretazo" to imply their significant use of decree power. This difference between presidential power in Argentina in theory and in practice also came across in an interview with Ricardo Barrios Arrechea, the ex-governor of the Province of Misiones between 1983 and 1987, and a Federal Deputy during the 1990s. When asked to explain the reasons behind the hyperpresidentialism witnessed in Argentina (in practice) and specifically whether the constitution was to blame, he noted that "[the constitution] does provide controls and a division of powers. However, the Argentine culture is unique. The constitution is not the problem, but rather the type of society, the culture, and the history preceding the constitution."[7]

In this part, I will begin by discussing the two methods through which hyperpresidentialism can occur, namely either hyperpresidentialism through the use of decrees or hyperpresidentialism through the legislature. I will then discuss how the judiciary failed to restrain presidential power in Argentina. Finally, I will address the variation in presidential power in Argentina since the country democratized.

Hyperpresidentialism Through the Use of Decrees

There are two broad types of decrees that presidents can issue, non-usurpative decrees in areas that are pre-authorized by congress (this category also includes regulatory or administrative decrees), and usurpative decrees (known as NUDs, or Necessity and Urgency Decrees in Argentina) that received no congressional authorization whatsoever and change the law on topics normally reserved for congress. In comparing these two types of decrees, Eaton writes that these NUDs are "potentially more troubling for legislators...[and] they were not officially sanctioned by the constitution before its reform in 1994."[8] In an interview with Federal Deputy Martín Maquieyra, he also noted that "Argentina is so presidential because of the existence of NUDs...If NUDs did not exist, the system would be more normal."[9]

Before 1989, NUDs were a relatively rare occurrence in Argentina. There was, however, an enormous spike in the use of decrees after the transition from Alfonsín to Menem (see Table 2.1). What is particularly perplexing is that the spike in NUDs beginning with the Menem administration occurred during a time period when NUDs were not even formally incorporated into the constitution. NUDs only became an official part of the constitution in 1994. The precarious legal situation of NUDs before 1994 is described by Llanos, who writes that:

> The Argentine Constitution did not grant the Executive the power to enact decrees that became law at the moment of signature. In other words, the Constitution did not allow presidents to legislate by means of a decree. In effect, the Executive's decree powers involved other functions: regulatory decrees to implement existing legislation and administrative decrees to perform functions within the bureaucracy...Thus, the power to legislate unilaterally was not present in the Constitution, but it became in practice another resource available to Argentine presidents. As a matter of fact, during the twentieth century these decrees were rarely enacted, only under special circumstances of extreme economic or institutional crisis that demanded extraordinary solutions. The president's incursion into the sphere of legislative decisions, without demanding subsequent congressional approval, was a presidential prerogative in effect introduced during the democratic regime inaugurated in 1983...By asserting their right to issue 'necessity and urgency decrees'—as they are known in Argentina—Argentine presidents assumed prerogatives of legislation belonging to Congress.[10]

Until 1994, NUDs fell into the category of what Carey and Shugart term "paraconstitutional initiatives."[11] Jones calls the use of NUDs in the first years of Menem's presidency a "constitutionally questionable device" and notes that they only acquired some sort of legal recognition following the *Peralta* decision by the Argentine Supreme Court in 1990, which upheld a decree that was the basis for the *Plan Bonex* (decree 36/90).[12]

After the 1994 constitutional amendment, the next major change in the legislative framework of NUDs was in 2006 when congress modified the mechanism by which an NUD could be rejected. Prior to the 2006 reform, if congress overturned an NUD, then the president could veto the repeal legislation; the only way for congress to guarantee that the NUD would be repealed would be to gather a two-thirds majority. Under this old system, as long as the president's party had over one-third of *one* of the chambers of congress (and the party voted in a unified way), this would ensure that his NUD was safe from congressional action. Nevertheless, following the 2006 reform, the president could no longer veto congressional legislation to repeal an NUD. Now, rather than requiring one-third of either chamber, a president needs a majority in either of the chambers to ensure that an NUD is maintained. Nevertheless, as Professor Javier Zelaznik noted in an interview, "if one has a majority, like the Peronists, nothing changes. Things only change if a [president's] party does not have a majority."[13]

Although historically the frequency of the use of NUDs increased under Alfonsín, his decrees were a response to real emergencies. For example, the *Austral Plan* (implemented by decree) which created a new currency was a response to triple-digit inflation in 1983 and 1984. Nevertheless, it is still important to note that Alfonsín was constrained in his use of decrees, and in the *Rolón Zappa* ruling, the Supreme Court of Argentina rejected one of Alfonsín's decrees which would have reduced payments to pensioners. Chavez provides a contrast with Menem's presidency when she writes:

> Menem faced no such restrictions on his decree power...In his attempt to justify the decrees he argued that they treated urgent matters requiring immediate attention. In reality, his DNUs [NUDs] addressed issues such as donating cement to Bolivia, televising soccer games, and taxing movies. Furthermore, although Menem claimed that Congress was in recess when he issued the DNUs, he issued 38 percent of his DNUs when Congress was in ordinary session and 62 percent during extraordinary sessions.[14]

There was one particularly egregious instance when congress passed a law, yet the president vetoed the law only to propose the exact same law again but in the form of an NUD. By passing an NUD identical to a bill he vetoed, Menem was effectively trying to project his primacy over the legislative branch.[15]

Table 2.1 illustrates the historical use of decrees in Argentina.

Under Menem, only a fraction of NUDs were even communicated to congress, and in 1991 for example, of the 85 NUDs that Menem signed, only 21 were communicated to lawmakers.[16] Rubio and Goretti conclude that:

> Menem has exhibited a new style of decision making - discretionary, informal, sometimes arbitrary, and with a low commitment to the

Table 2.1 Historical use of necessity and urgency decrees in Argentina

1853– 1983	1983– 1989 Alfonsín	1989– 1999 Menem	1999–2001 De La Rúa	2002– 2003 Duhalde	2003–2007 Kirchner, Néstor	2007– 2015 Kirchner, Cristina
<20[a]	10	545	73	158	270	76

[a]And these decrees were truly only limited to emergencies. See Rubio and Goretti 2000; p.2

sanctity of formal political institutions — one resembling the style of old local leaders, or caudillos. Concurrently, Congress has lost legitimacy and political capacity, reducing its ability to act in reaction to presidential initiatives. All these developments were responses to public opinion and public demands for quick and effective policy making. The presidency was better prepared, both structurally and in terms of leadership capacity, to satisfy those demands than Congress, which faces formidable collective action problems. As a consequence, reactions against presidential decree authority have been isolated and uncoordinated.[17]

Upon coming to power during an economic crisis, President Menem implemented a radical neoliberal agenda, and throughout the 1990s, Argentina became a poster-child for the IMF's policies. Many of these neoliberal reforms were in fact done via decree, with minimal involvement of congress. Most notably, several public enterprises, including the national airline (*Aerolíneas Argentinas*) and the national phone company (*Entel*), were privatized by decree, bypassing the legislature.[18]

The plurality of decrees issued by Menem was in the realm of tax policy (21%). Despite the fact that constitutionally like in the USA only congress in theory has the authority to regulate taxes, in practice, between 1989 and 1993, Menem signed over 69 decrees related to taxation. For example, through NUDs, Menem created a tax on fuel, a tax on financial assets, various changes in the Value Added Tax (VAT), a tax on the exhibition of films (the "cinema tax"), etc.[19] Other important areas in which decrees were used included the regulation of salaries (especially during the 1989 hyperinflationary crisis, with 60% of the NUDs being devoted to salary regulation), public debt (especially during 1990), public agency reorganization (these NUDs were mainly aimed at reducing public expenditure), and deregulation of the economy.[20] The breakdown of Necessity and Urgency Decrees during Menem's first term in office (336 NUDs) is listed in Table 2.2.

It would be misleading to view the impact of Menem's decrees simply in terms of the total number of NUDs that he issued. Rubio and

Table 2.2 Breaking down Menem's NUDs during his first term in office[a]

Policy Area	1989	1990	1991	1992	1993	1994	Total
1. Taxes	2	7	23	17	21	2	72
2. Salaries	18	9	3	–	2	7	39
3. Public debt	5	14	5	3	1	1	29
4. Trade	–	–	–	5	3	2	10
5. Transport	–	–	3	8	7	3	21
6. Nation/ Provinces	–	–	–	4	1	1	6
7. Real estate privatization	–	3	6	3	7	3	22
8. Civil and political rights	2	–	2	1	–	3	8
9. Public agencies	1	11	7	5	5	3	32
10. Proceedings against state	–	–	5	–	–	–	5
11. Electric energy	–	4	1	2	1	–	8
12. Promotion of industry	–	3	3	1	1	–	8
13. Mega-NUD 435/90	–	7	5	–	2	–	14
14. Mega-NUD 1930/90	–	5	11	6	–	–	22
15. Mega-NUD 2284/91	–	–	4	3	1	–	8
16. Others	2	–	7	11	10	2	32
Total	30	63	85	69	62	27	336

[a]This table is recreated from Rubio and Goretti 1998; p.46

Goretti use the term "mega-NUD" to describe individual NUDs which contained several disparate parts (thus, one "mega-NUD" was a de facto series of multiple NUDs). For example, NUD 435/90 included 70 sections across 30 policy areas, including prohibiting the Central Bank from making up the Treasury's operating deficit, suspending payments to public contractors, changing the Value Added Tax Act, modifying taxes on capital, etc.[21] Another example of a mega-NUD was NUD 2284/91, whose main purpose was the deregulation of the economy. It contained numerous provisions which could have each been decrees in their own right (in fact, it either altered or completely repealed over 43 laws already on the books), including shutting down ten regulatory and audit agencies, reforms to the social security system, a repeal of rules that distorted market prices, the deregulation of professional practices, the transport of goods, and the sales of medicines.[22] Rubio and Goretti overall note that 80% of the economic policies throughout Menem's first term in office would not have been implemented had it not been for NUDs.[23]

Throughout the 2000s, after Menem was no longer in power, even though the use of Necessity and Urgency decrees declined, decrees continued to play an important role in modifying the budget. A series of laws called the *superpoderes* passed during the 2000s allowed the president's Chief of the Cabinet of Ministers (*Jefe de Gabinete*) to modify certain parts of the budget by decree *after* the budget passed in congress (note that technically this is not classified as an NUD). Presidents Néstor and Cristina Kirchner widely used these *superpoderes*. According to Luciana Díaz Frers, who at the time of the interview was a high-ranking member of the *Auditoría*:

> In the budgetary process there are various symptoms that show a concentration of power in the executive [relative to the legislature] that contrast with the role that the legislature should have...the executive power has become technically and politically hegemonic in the budgetary process.[24]

Overall, Delia Ferreira Rubio claims that the ability to modify the budget by decree "deinstitutionalizes the budgetary process and takes away the right of congress to decide the allocation of a large portion of public expenditure."[25]

Presidential control over the federal budget is not only proactive, but also reactive in the sense that presidents can decide to slash any expenditure they do not agree with through the line-item veto. Although a full veto of the budget is rare and occurred only once throughout the 1993–2003 decade, as Santiso writes, "[the president] amply vetoed specific provisions of most budget laws approved by parliament."[26] Although congress can in theory override the presidential veto, given the composition of congresses throughout the past three decades, this has been almost impossible to achieve.

Lastly, in a manner similar to NUDs, the line-item veto in Argentina for a very long time was used despite having no formal recognition. Jones makes the interesting observation that prior to the 1994 constitutional amendment, the line-item veto was in fact never expressly mentioned in the constitution. He writes that "the use of the line item veto, while not explicitly mentioned in the Constitution prior to the 1994 constitutional reform, was nevertheless a de facto power exercised by presidents, particularly since the 1960s."[27] Chavez adds that while Perón did give the line-item veto official legal status in the 1949 constitution, this constitution was short-lived as the 1853 constitution was reinstated in 1956 (which did not expressly provide for the line item veto). Despite the lack of specific constitutional provisions for the line-item veto, after 1956 it was given "tacit congressional acceptance...congress did not oppose the practice. Frondizi used the line-item veto seven times during his four years in office from 1958 until 1962."[28] In 1967, the Supreme Court approved the use of the line-item veto after the *Colella* decision, with the stipulation that it does not affect the "unity" and "coherence" of the law as originally passed by congress. In the case that congress wishes to override a line-item veto, both chambers would need a two-thirds majority.

In this section, I have described how various presidents in Argentina have used decree powers to govern unilaterally. I have claimed that whereas Carlos Menem excessively used decrees to pass laws in a variety of areas, decrees were also used during the administrations in the 2000s in order to make modifications to the budget without approval from congress. I have also described how for a significant part of Argentine history, these instruments did not even have constitutional recognition (as was the case with NUDs and line-item vetoes). In the following section, I will explain how hyperpresidentialism through the legislature worked in Argentina.

Hyperpresidentialism Through the Legislature

As I mentioned earlier, although the most obvious manifestation of hyperpresidentialism is the excessive use of decrees, it may also be characterized by the president's use of the legislature as a doormat for his/her projects. Normally, going through congress would be interpreted as a sign that institutions of horizontal accountability are strong, yet in the case of Argentina, this is not necessarily true because of the nature through which the president often dominated the legislative process and the control he/she had over congress. In this section, I will illustrate several scenarios in Argentina where even though a law was passed through congress (during periods of time when Peronist presidents faced a Peronist-dominated congress), there was often little to no debate, and no serious changes to the president's proposal were made. While it is normal in any political system that under unified government the legislature will be friendly toward a president's proposals, as I mentioned in Chapter 1, what is not normal is for congress to cease in its role as an institution of oversight. Nevertheless, as I will show, in Argentina, Peronist presidents faced few obstacles from Peronist-dominated congresses, and they were allowed to get away with numerous abuses of power.

Although Menem sometimes went through congress, he almost always chose to do this merely to grant greater legitimacy to a reform project, and he did this in a context in which he possessed near certainty that his reforms would pass. Even if he would have to sacrifice several minor concessions to legislators, the benefits of having gone through congress outweighed these tradeoffs. During the presidency of Menem, although many important aspects of his neoliberal reforms passed through decrees (especially privatizations), in the instances in which he did go through congress (notably for pension reform and the Convertibility Plan), the process often included little to no meaningful debate. Perhaps the most egregious example of such a law was the Convertibility Plan, which involved a major overhaul of the Argentine economy by pegging the Argentine Peso 1:1 with the US dollar. The executive branch presented the law to congress on March 20, 1991, and it passed both chambers of congress a week later and was signed into law on March 27, 1991. It is noteworthy that when the law was repealed in 2001 under President Duhalde, the repeal law was passed *in two days*: in a special session, the Chamber of Deputies debated the law and approved it the same day on January 5, 2002; the next day, it passed the Senate and was signed into law (Law 25561).

Although the process of pension reform was slightly more complicated and lengthy than the Convertibility Plan, the ultimate product was extremely close to what Menem had envisioned. During the passage process, there were numerous procedural irregularities, including the lack of quorums during committee votes.

It is important to note that in many cases where laws went through congress, the president could have gotten away with passing them through decrees. In fact, Menem used the possibility of passing a project through a decree as a "weapon" to force congressional action. For example, in the case of pension reform, Menem informed legislators that if they failed to pass the reform, he would later do so by decree anyway. Jones claims that:

> Decrees of urgent necessity provided the president with a very powerful tool with which to influence the legislative process...[The] president could use the threat of a decree as a way to pressure Congress to pass a bill. That is, the president could state that if Congress did not pass a bill, then he would implement it by decree, and thus Congress would miss any opportunity to influence the content of the bill.[29]

For a more detailed discussion of presidential dominance during pension reform in Argentina, see Berbecel 2018.

Although the use of decrees declined under the successive administrations of Néstor and Cristina Kirchner (especially under Cristina Kirchner who made very little use of Necessity and Urgency Decrees), the reason that this does not indicate a representative democracy is that their control over congress was extremely tight, and through vast majorities, they were able to pass many projects with little meaningful debate. As Federal Senator Ángel Rozas noted in an interview, "during the Kirchnerist period, the lights were off in congress, you had majorities in both chambers, and congress was merely the writing desk (*'escribanía'*) of the executive branch rather than a congress which served as a fundamental pillar of power of the republic."[30] When asked to elaborate on why congress was so weak during the period of the Kirchners, Rozas explained that:

> There was no debate. You could never change even a comma of what the executive would send...Whether desired by the governing party

or by the opposition, it was impossible to change the project. They were literally approved as they came, the budget and any other law, all without debate.[31]

Similarly, in an interview with Alfonso Prat Gay, who at the time of the interview was a Federal Deputy (he later became Minister of the Economy), he stated that "congress is merely a trampoline for the next project of the executive rather than a body which seriously represents the people."[32] Federal Deputy Mario Barletta (a top Radical party official who served as the President of the National Committee of the UCR) also added that "[Cristina Kirchner] would send a project to parliament and it would not be discussed or analyzed. The parliament was totally subordinate to the executive." Similarly, Federal Deputy Luis Pastori added that:

> Néstor Kirchner was able to generate hyperpresidentialism after coming to power in a situation of extreme weakness in the political system...Cristina Kirchner continued the presidency of her husband also with a strong personalist bias. Practically speaking, no changes, reforms or modifications could be made to projects coming from the executive branch, and they had to be approved the way they came.[33]

Whereas the above politicians opposed President Cristina Kirchner, even her allies admit that in Argentina there is a strong concentration of power in the president, including during her tenure. For example, Senator Abal Medina (who was the Chief of the Cabinet of Ministers for Cristina Kirchner between 2011 and 2013) noted in an interview that "there is a strong primacy in the executive," and when asked about the levers congress possesses to keep presidential power in check, he answered that "[congress] has very few."[34]

One of the mechanisms through which Cristina Kirchner was able to speed up the passage of key legislation in congress was through the use of special sessions. Normally, for a law to pass, it must first go through the appropriate congressional committee(s) and only then can be brought to a floor vote in the legislature. Holding a special session allows congress to skip the committee process and send the legislation directly for a vote in the chamber, thereby significantly shortening the passage process. The use of special sessions was a tool that was also significantly utilized by the Menem government, including during his first term.[35]

There are numerous examples of laws passed by Cristina Kirchner with little meaningful debate. For example, Cristina Kirchner in 2008 desired to nationalize the pension system, and although the law was first proposed to the Chamber of Deputies on October 21, 2008, it passed both houses in a month and received final approval by the Senate on November 20, 2008 (Law 26245). Other major laws that passed congress with little to no meaningful debate during the Cristina Kirchner administration involved the nationalization of *Aerolíneas Argentinas*, a law that sought to "democratize" the justice system (which in reality tried to pack the Council of Magistrates with members favorable to the president), a media law which sought to hurt a powerful independent media outlet that had been critical of her government (the *Clarín* Group), etc. Budgets, in particular, would pass extremely quickly under Cristina Kirchner's government with little to no hurdles in congress.

When Abal Medina was asked if there were any projects that Cristina Kirchner desired but could not get her party to approve, he replied with a terse "no."[36] Similarly, when asked more generally if there was any project that she would have desired that could not get through congress, he similarly replied "no."[37] A congress that gave the president everything she wanted was certainly not a serious institution of horizontal accountability. A similar concept is echoed by Rubio, who in an interview described that Cristina Kirchner

> was one of the most powerful presidents we have had who possessed absolute control over congress. She would send legislative projects to congress and they would be approved within a week. She did not need to use NUDs...Under the Kirchners, congress was transformed into a military base. Nothing was discussed, and things were approved in record time. Not even the governing bloc would discuss [the bill].[38]

In an interview with Miguel Iturrieta, an ex-Federal Deputy for the Province of Misiones (2005–2009) who served during the tenures of both Néstor and Cristina Kirchner (as a member of their coalition), he described the difficulty of passing a law as a member of congress compared to the executive branch. He claimed that "the system by which laws were approved was very authoritarian...a lot of the time the laws that were passed were those that had approval from the executive branch."[39] What is particularly striking with these comments is that Deputy Iturrieta *is from the same bloc as Néstor and Cristina Kirchner* and served as part of the PJ-FPV. He describes how executive proposals always had priority over proposals from members of congress and that there was a "subordination of the will of congress to the executive."[40] He related one instance in which he attempted to propose a law where he tried to limit benefits given to foreigners originating from Paraguay, yet stated that "nobody was listening to me."[41] Iturrieta details how lawmaking during the presidency of Cristina Kirchner was difficult for legislators, since on one hand, in order to get a bill passed, one required the support of the president. On the other hand, it was nearly impossible as a simple legislator to physically speak to the president, and as he claims:

> There lacked meetings between the president and deputies under Néstor and Cristina. With Néstor at least we had some friendly

encounters, but I never met with Cristina. With Néstor we would share rides when he would invite deputies on the presidential plane. The only time that I travelled with Cristina, she did not even stop to say hello to my group of deputies.[42]

Several interviewees explained to me that when the president does meet with legislators, it is usually only with high-ranking party officials.

In my interview with Mario Barletta, he neatly summarized that:

The executive has significant resources, comes to congress, and calls a meeting with legislators to discuss certain projects. One can raise his hand, but it is the executive that comes to congress to tell us what we need to do. The congress does not have the capacity to generate political proposals.[43]

In short, so far in this chapter, I have identified two forms that hyperpresidentialism took in Argentina, namely hyperpresidentialism through decrees and hyperpresidentialism through the legislature. Oftentimes, the determining factor in whether presidents would choose to exercise hyperpresidentialism through NUDs or through the legislature depended on their majority in congress. Barletta elaborates that:

When you have a parliament with a majority that permits you to undertake project, the laws conceived by the executive branch will be pursued by the legislative branch. Since you have a majority, you do not require the use of an NUD. On the other hand, when you have a legislature in which you lack a majority, you make greater use of both NUDs and the veto.[44]

The Weakness of the Judiciary in Constraining Presidential Power in Argentina

Just like congress failed to restrain the power of Argentine presidents, the judiciary similarly failed in its role as an oversight institution, especially during the tenure of Carlos Menem.

Under Alfonsín, the Supreme Court exercised some degree of independent oversight. For example, Alfonsín had been constrained by the Supreme Court in his use of decrees (as mentioned earlier, in the *Rolón Zappa* ruling the Supreme Court rejected one of Alfonsín's decrees that attempted to reduce payments to pensioners).

Under Menem, the Supreme Court became largely a rubber stamp institution. Notably, the Supreme Court failed to take any action on several Necessity and Urgency decrees of questionable legal foundation. Although in theory NUDs are meant only for situations of "necessity and emergency" as their name implies, this lawmaking tool has been used far more liberally. Many of Menem's NUDs were not urgent and should have gone through the congressional process. Although by 1991 the Argentine economy had recovered and was growing rapidly, Menem continued to pass NUDs that sometimes had nothing to do with serious state matters. For example, as was mentioned earlier, he signed an NUD that affected broadcasting rights for soccer games, an NUD regarding shipments of cement to Bolivia, etc. Whereas the Supreme Court should have reasonably ruled these decrees illegal, it stood silent.

The most controversial decision by the Supreme Court of Argentina which facilitated Menem's abuse of the Necessity and Urgency decree is the 1990 *Peralta* decision. As I mentioned earlier, before 1994, there was no constitutional basis for the president to issue Necessity and Urgency Decrees, yet through this decision the court in fact legitimized the president's use of a paraconstitutional device. Larkins argues that *Peralta* was "perhaps the most extreme example in which the court validated questionable acts by the executive and promoted a delegative version of democracy."[45] Helmke also notes that "by legitimizing the power of the executive to legislate, the [Peralta] decision was also widely seen as endangering the separation of powers on which the Argentine Constitution rests."[46] The *Peralta* decision was made in response to decree 36/90, where Menem froze bank accounts greater than approximately 600 dollars; this raised questions not only about the limits of presidential power (especially since constitutionally such an action could only be accomplished through a law by congress), but also about the protection of private property. Larkins writes that "the decree represented an extremely questionable grant of power to the executive to take on legislative functions and suspend certain constitutional rights."[47] Regarding the separation of powers, the court's opinion stated that "separation of powers should not be construed in such a manner to equal the dismemberment of the state." The court also established a precedent of "tacit approval" where the court essentially validated any proactive executive action (including decrees) which was not subsequently rejected by congress, essentially putting the burden on congress to explicitly *reject* a presidential proposal. In its opinion, the Court seemed to forget its primary role of upholding the constitution and the rule of law when it claimed that "the greatest value of the constitution is not in its written text...but rather in the practical, realistic work of finding the formula that harmonized interests, traditions, [and] contradictory and bellicose passions."[48] The opinion also claims that "the constitution should be interpreted in a way that does not contravene...the sovereign will of the Nation."[49] These statements are particularly noteworthy since the Court is effectively admitting that the written text of the constitution should not be the primary determinant of its decisions, but rather the more murky "will of the Nation" which the court evidently interpreted to mean the will of the president.

One of the most controversial powers which the Argentine Supreme Court would abuse to benefit the Menem government was the application of the *per saltum* legal device. Menem issued a decree privatizing *Aerolíneas Argentinas* (1024/90), yet a lawsuit was filed to block the privatization from taking place. A lower court ruled in favor of the plaintiffs, thus freezing the privatization process of the airline. Although normally the case should have been allowed to go through the court system, the Supreme Court decided to directly take control of the case rather than having it go through the regular chain of appeals. By taking control of lower-court cases, the Supreme Court not only committed itself to serving as a rubber stamp for the executive, but also to *rapidly* removing any judicial obstacles. Many legal experts believe that by applying the *per saltum* process, the Supreme Court directly violated the constitution of Argentina (which does not explicitly grant the *per saltum* power to the Supreme Court). As Chavez writes:

> The *Aerolíneas Argentinas* decision was the first time in Argentina's history that the Court used per saltum to bypass lower courts. The ruling [on *Aerolíneas Argentinas*] set a dangerous precedent that the Supreme Court could use per saltum to intervene in any case involving a "serious institutional matter," regardless of whether the case had first reached a lower court. The Buenos Aires Bar Association argued that the decision violated Article 101 of the Argentine Constitution, which "is clear in requirement that, except in cases of original jurisdiction, the Court will follow the appeal process according to rules dictated by congress."[50]

One of the most infamous cases where the Supreme Court demonstrated a lack of respect for the rule of law and the judges made clear that they intended to abuse the power of their office to help a sitting president was in the 1993 case of Banco Patagónico. In this case, the Court initially made a decision on October 8 which would have gone against the Menem government; nevertheless, this decision mysteriously "disappeared" from the court's official register, and it is alleged that Chief Justice Boggiano and Associate Chief Justice Barra took part in a plan where the decision was stolen and substituted with one more favorable to the Menem government.[51]

Similarly, the Supreme Court questionably intervened in various local elections to help candidates favorable to Menem. For example, in 1992, it overturned the decision of the Corrientes provincial Supreme Court that granted victory to a candidate for governor from the opposition *Pacto Autonomista Liberal* (PAL) party. This decision arguably violated Article 105 of the constitution, which protects provinces from federal intervention in the election of their officials.[52] Helmke tersely summarizes that "to protect Menem's interests, the [Supreme] Court was often willing to bend blatantly the rule of law."[53]

The perception that the Argentine Supreme Court failed to constrain President Menem is also illustrated in opinion polling. In a 1993 poll, 69% of respondents believed that the court's decisions were politicized, and 87% of respondents stated that they were not satisfied with the state of justice in the country.[54] The weakness of the judiciary in Argentina is summarized in an interview with Germán Bordón, a lawyer by training and a Deputy in the legislature of the Province of Misiones (*Cámara de Representantes*) who claimed that "the justice system is one of the greatest problems [in Argentina] and unfortunately, it has not fulfilled its role as an institution of horizontal accountability."[55]

Under the administration of Néstor Kircher, the Supreme Court regained a certain degree of legitimacy, and the court did occasionally make decisions that went against the government.

Perhaps one of the most important decisions where the court ruled a federal law unconstitutional was the case of the "Democratization of the Justice System" of 2013 (Law 26853) in which Cristina Kirchner wanted to both increase the composition of the Council of Magistrates (responsible for the appointment and firing of lower-level judges) as well as ensure that each member would be *democratically elected*. Because this move would obviously benefit the Peronist party to the detriment of both judicial autonomy and the opposition, the measure barely passed in the Chamber of Deputies by a vote of 130 in favor and 123 against, almost purely along party lines and with a barrage of accusations from the opposition. The measure easily passed in the Senate on April 27. As the regional newspaper *La Arena* reported, "the special session [of congress] happened amidst accusations between the Front for Victory and the opposition, which argued that this project would politicize the justice system."[56] Federal Deputy Elisa Carrió had very harsh words in particular against the law, and according to *La Nación*, she claimed that this is a "turning point between democracy and the tyranny of the majority."[57] She also warned that the law would usher in a "fascist, persecutory, and authoritarian state." Nevertheless, in a rare moment of judicial autonomy, the Supreme Court only two months later in June struck down the law in a near-unanimous vote (6-1). What was particularly notable was that even several Kirchner-appointed judges joined the majority, including Ricardo Lorenzetti, Elena Highton de Nolasco, and Carmen Argibay; Juan Carlos Maqueda, who had been appointed by Duhalde, also voted with the majority.[58] The effect of the Supreme Court striking down the law was that the Council of Magistrates would function as it did based on the prior law in place.

While decisions such as this prove that the Kirchner court was certainly not an "automatic majority" as with the Menem court, there were numerous other decisions in which the court sided with the administration in ways that bring its partiality into question. While even in advanced democracies such as the USA it can be expected that members of the Supreme Court will tend to favor laws made by the president/party that appointed them, some of the decisions of the Argentine Supreme Court, as well as the deliberation process, proved legally questionable.

For example, the court controversially sided with the administration of Cristina Kirchner in upholding a media law which sought to weaken the *Grupo Clarín* (a media outlet that had been critical of her administration). Justice Minister Germán Garavano described that there "were pressures" on the Supreme Court.[59] Additionally, the Supreme Court did not question a substantial part of the economic program imposed by post-2001 presidents in Argentina. In an interview with scholar Matteo Goretti who has written extensively about presidential power and the use of NUDs in Argentina, he noted that the Supreme Court's level of restraint on presidents was predicated on the level of popularity of the president, and that while Cristina Kirchner was popular, the Supreme Court avoided making decisions against her government. Goretti concludes that "the court was independent, yes, but the court did not limit [presidential] power. It only did it as Cristina was on her way out...."[60]

One of the most controversial decisions where the Court sided with Néstor Kirchner was to support the elimination of amnesty for certain military officials. Coming into office, Néstor Kirchner was determined to bring to trial members of the military who had been involved in human rights abuses. However, he faced significant legal hurdles because of two amnesty laws that had been passed under the Alfonsín administration. In 1986, President Alfonsín passed the *Ley de Punto Final* (Full Stop Law), which was complemented in 1987 by the *Ley de Obedencia Debida* (Law of Due Obedience). In addition to being passed by congress, there was also judicial precedent supporting amnesty, and for example, in June of 1987, the Supreme Court of Argentina affirmed that the Law of Due Obedience was constitutional.[61] Nevertheless, on June 14, 2005, the new Supreme Court declared the two amnesty laws unconstitutional. The decision was highly controversial, and two years prior to the Supreme Court ruling when the Senate voted to annul the amnesty laws, an article in The Economist claimed that "the annulment—a victory for President Néstor Kirchner, who had promised to get it—is certainly contentious, because the constitution does not seem to allow it."[62] The decision was also questionable given that one of the judges who voted to declare the amnesty laws unconstitutional in 2005 had previously voted to affirm the laws. The judge, Enrique Petracchi, explained his shifting position by claiming that "times had changed."[63] There continues to be a debate as to whether the action of the Supreme Court in Argentina was legal, with some individuals claiming that the decision to annul the amnesty laws was politically motivated to appease Néstor Kirchner.[64]

Another legally questionable decision by the Supreme Court during Néstor Kirchner's term in office was the decision to allow the "pesification" of dollar deposits. As I will discuss in Chapter 5, Argentina faced a severe economic crisis in 2001, which involved a freeze on the withdrawal of bank deposits (the *Corralito*). The Argentine peso, which had previously been pegged 1:1 to the US dollar, faced devaluation. Amidst this crisis, the Duhalde government decreed that all dollar deposits would be "pesified" (forcibly converted to pesos) at the rate of 1.4 pesos per dollar. Nevertheless, the exchange rate of dollars to pesos was around two pesos per dollar, effectively wiping out a portion of the deposits held by Argentines.[65] There were various lawsuits filed by depositors against the government, and in a Supreme Court decision on March 5, 2003, Decree 214/02 (through which Duhalde converted dollar deposits to pesos) was declared unconstitutional in a case involving the province of San Luis. Two of the main arguments that the Supreme Court brought up were that Duhalde's decree exceeded his legal presidential authority, and that the decree went against the property rights of depositors.[66] An article published shortly after this decision in the Inter-American Law Review claimed that:

> If the Court had bowed to political pressure and upheld the pesification decree, the Argentine government would have been pleased... Yet, a ruling in favor of pesification would have dealt a crushing blow to the hopes of Argentine depositors seeking to recover the value of their converted deposits, further enraging these weary citizens and confirming the widely-held belief that the Court lacks any independence from the country's political apparatus.[67]

Nevertheless, in May of 2003, Néstor Kirchner commenced his term in office and moved to change the composition of the Court. In a legally questionable decision issued on October 26, 2004, the new Supreme Court reversed the decision (in the *Bustos* case) it had issued less than two years earlier and now claimed that Duhalde's pesification decree had been constitutional.[68] It is difficult to view the Supreme Court's reversal of its own precedent as anything but the result of a lack of independence from the executive branch. Even though as described earlier the Supreme Court under Kirchner was more independent than the Supreme Court under Menem, this decision certainly reflects the Court's desire to please Néstor Kirchner.

While the Supreme Court during the Kirchner administration constrained the president to some, albeit a small degree, there was significantly less pushback from the lower-level judiciary, which as I will describe in the next chapter, suffered significant court-packing under Néstor and Cristina Kirchner. According to several sources familiar with the judicial system, many acts of corruption normally in the domain of the lower courts were not investigated.

In short, the judiciary in Argentina has not fundamentally fulfilled its constitutional role of checking presidential power. The courts were completely subservient to the executive branch under Menem, and while the

Supreme Court gained some independence starting with the Kirchner administration, the lower courts were highly politicized.

Is Argentina Truly a Hyperpresidential System?

It is important to note that there remains a debate in the literature about the extent to which Argentine presidents including Menem bypassed institutions of horizontal accountability.[69] Although many accounts state that congress and the judiciary were extremely weak, there is a group that claims that even under Menem, institutions of horizontal accountability were not as weak as they appear. Levitsky, for example, writes that:

> Even on the dimension of horizontal accountability, the Menem government's abuses were comparatively limited. To the extent that the delegative democracy label fits the Argentine case, it does so only for the 1989–90 period. President Menem did not routinely bypass parties or the legislature after 1990. The bulk of the government's post-1990 reform measures were approved by Congress, and most of these involved arduous negotiations with (and important concessions to) legislative leaders, governors, and business and labor leaders. Many reform bills, including those to privatize social security, natural gas, and petroleum, were modified heavily by the legislature. Others, such as labor law reform, were blocked entirely."[70]

Menem's strength declined even further during his second term, when a group of approximately 40 Peronist legislators "rebelled" by taking the side of Eduardo Duhalde and stalled several pieces of legislation proposed by Menem. Examples of legislation that were stalled for significant periods of time in the legislature included the privatization of airports and the postal system, although they did get approved eventually. Perhaps Menem's greatest loss was when in 1998 he attempted to run for a third term, yet a majority in congress (including in his own party) as well as his own appointed Supreme Court opposed the move. Furthermore, in 1999, the Court voted to curb the ability of presidents to issue executive decrees, a ruling which would also apply to the next president.[71]

Mariana Llanos in her piece on privatization also argues that the president's powers were not unlimited even during the 1990s, claiming that:

> The formulation and approval of the privatisation policy in Argentina was a highly institutional process, led by the Executive, in which Congress participated actively. Faced with the President's initiatives, Congress made use of its powers of approving, delaying, amending, and preventing the submission of legislation, during different stages of the reform process. However, these lawful features of the policy of privatisation do not contradict the mounting evidence of a President

who exercised legislative powers in an unilateral and discretionary way.[72]

She claims that "hyperpresidentialism" is not the correct term to use in the case of Argentina, but that this was rather a case of "limited centralism" in which although the president was the dominant actor, he was still subject to some degree of constraint.

Perhaps one of the most notable works that challenges the notion that Argentina was hyperpresidential is Kent Eaton's piece, Politicians and Economic Reform in New Democracies. He articulates his position when he claims that:

> Despite broad support for reform on the part of governing-party legislators, the Argentine legislature did not operate as a rubber stamp institution. Instead, careful analysis of the congressional record reveals that congress did modify legislation in sometimes important ways, both at the committee stage and on the floor of each chamber. The record also clearly suggests that most modifications were the result of attempts by legislators to defend or promote the interests of their provinces of origin.[73]

Despite the above claims, showing that congress had *some* power does not make the country a representative system. Even though Argentina exhibited fewer characteristics of hyperpresidentialism during Menem's second term, even by the most stringent standards, the beginning of his first term would qualify as hyperpresidential. To clarify, hyperpresidentialism does not imply that congress has no power whatsoever. Hyperpresidentialism merely occurs when significant power is concentrated in an executive; congress may still have some marginal power (enough to be an "inconvenience" for a president). A representative system, however, is reached only when congress is an equal partner with the president in lawmaking. I consider congress an "equal partner" when the notion is institutionalized into the minds of political actors, particularly those in the executive branch, that going through congress is the "only game in town." In other words, a president would not *even think* of passing a law without backing in congress and views congress as a serious obstacle that could derail an entire legislative project.

The role of congress only becomes significant if it can *credibly threaten to block the centerpiece of a reform* and if the executive faces more than just marginal constraints. The ability of congress to obtain concessions on the side is *not enough* for a political system to move away from the label of hyperpresidentialism. Rather, a country only moves away from this situation when congress becomes an equal partner in lawmaking and can obtain more than a few concessions on the side from the president. Congress and the judiciary under Menem were not effective veto players, and Larkins in a 1998 piece writes that "President Menem has enjoyed the virtual absence of any checks and balances capable of frustrating his policies for most of his term."[74]

Presidential Power in Theory versus in Practice: The Case of the "Jefe de Gabinete"

Another critical area where presidential power in practice differs from presidential power in theory is the role of the *jefe de gabinete* or the Chief of the Cabinet of Ministers. The *jefe de gabinete* is a position that is roughly comparable to that of Prime Minister in other countries, and some of the attributes of the *jefe de gabinete* include control over certain budgetary matters and serving as a liaison between the president and the legislature (for example, the *jefe de gabinete* must go before congress once every month). The full list of attributes of the *jefe de gabinete* is outlined in articles 100 and 101 of the constitution. The *jefe de gabinete* was created in the 1994 constitutional reform as a way to diminish hyperpresidentialism by dispersing power away from the president. Goretti claimed that "[the position of jefe de gabinete] was conceived as a way to moderate hyperpresidentialism, [but] it didn't work."[75] As Goretti describes, the main flaw in the constitutional design is that the *jefe de gabinete* does not need any type of congressional confirmation and responds "100 percent to the president."[76] A president can hire and fire the *jefe de gabinete* at his own will, and as the constitution describes, "on his own account, he appoints and removes the Chief of the Ministerial Cabinet."[77] The only mechanism for congress to be able to remove the *jefe de gabinete* is through an absolute majority vote in both houses of congress. Even though certain powers are shifted from the president to the *jefe de gabinete*, given that he is a political ally who can be replaced at will, the *jefe de gabinete* in practice serves as a pure rubber stamp and can be considered an extension of the presidency.

The Capture of the Central Bank by Argentine Presidents

Although in theory the Argentine central bank is "independent" from the executive branch, this institution in practice has been a rubber stamp for what the president desired.

The most important indicator of the Argentine Central Bank's inability to restrain presidential power was the fact that it printed money in excess. Normally, presidents desire expansionary monetary policy given the short-term economic benefits, and central banks, which have price stability as a goal, need to deny this request. For example, at one point, Chairman Powell of the US Federal Reserve raised interest rates despite objections from President Trump. Argentine presidents did not face such restrictions on monetary policy, and in recent years, the Central Bank has largely rubber-stamped whatever monetary policies Argentine presidents desired.

For example, central bank presidents under Cristina Kirchner significantly expanded the money supply in order to temporarily finance populist policies and boost the economy. In expanding the money supply, Argentine central bank governors forgot about their mandate for price stability and succumbed to pressures from incumbent presidents. This caused significant inflation, which, for the past decade, has been in the double digits and which has hurt long-term economic growth. Although inflation in 2000 in Argentina was virtually near-zero, by the end of Cristina Kirchner's term in office, the figure stood at over 30%, with some sources stating that it was as high as 40%.[78]

Variation in Executive Power in Argentina in Practice across Time

In discussing the case of Argentina, it is important to note that presidential power was not static, and that it experienced some volatility across time based on the variation in my second independent variable, the size of a president's party in congress (my first independent variable, rule of law, and my third independent variable, the presence of recent economic crises, experienced substantially less fluctuation across time).

Presidential power in Argentina can be roughly divided into six periods, which are illustrated in Table 2.3. Although the Argentine president was **always** stronger than the Chilean president, in some periods this strength was greater than in others due to the variation in the second variable.

Note that the above description of a president as *weak* only describes his/her power *relative to other presidents in Argentina* in the post-democratization period (they were still strong relative to Chilean presidents).

The graphs in Figure 2.1 illustrate the variation in legislative and judicial constraints in Argentina and Chile.

Several observations can be made in this analysis of intra-country variation in Argentina and Chile between 1990 and 2017. First, whereas there is some variation in legislative and judicial constraints in Argentina, there is virtually no variation in Chile. In the graphs in Figure 2.1, the lines representing Argentina fluctuate to a certain degree, whereas the lines representing Chile are largely flat. The reason for this is rooted in the variation of my second independent variable, the size of the president's party in congress. In Argentina since 1990, whereas Peronist presidents often benefitted from unified government or near-unified government, no non-Peronist presidents have enjoyed anything close to unified government. One can clearly discern the effect of whether or not a president had a working majority in congress as illustrated in Table 2.3, in the analysis of legislative and judicial constraints in Figure 2.1 (especially

Table 2.3 Comparing the strength of the various post-democratization
presidencies

	Alfonsín	Menem's first term	Menem's second term	De La Rúa	Duhalde, Néstor and Cristina Kirchner	Macri
Strength of president (relative to other presidents in Argentina)	Weak	Strong	Strong (but weaker than in his first term)	Weak	Strong	Weak
Presidential working majority in both houses of congress?	No	Yes	Yes, but less control than in first term due to a split within the PJ	No	Yes for most years of their tenures	No

legislative constraints). One can observe the following movements in an analysis of the shape of the line representing legislative constraints in Argentina: legislative constraints were low during Menem's first term in office when he held solid working majorities in congress (note that technically, Menem's PJ was just shy of a majority in the Chamber of Deputies. However, for all practical purposes, Menem did have a solid majority based on the almost guaranteed support of legislators from smaller parties, including regional parties); during Menem's second term in office, legislative constraints increased slightly, as a split emerged in the PJ (with the emergence of a camp led by Eduardo Duhalde, Menem could rely less on his working majority in congress); during the De La Rúa presidency, legislative constraints increased sharply as he did not possess a majority in both chambers of congress; in the period following De La Rúa, legislative constraints fell as Duhalde and the Kirchners benefitted from strong working majorities in congress; finally, after 2015, there was a sharp rise in legislative constraints given the fact that Macri no longer possessed the majorities which Cristina Kirchner enjoyed.

The first independent variable, institutional strength, is relatively constant across time, and there is little variation in either Argentina or Chile. As I will show in Chapter 3, institutions in Argentina have consistently been weak, whereas in Chile they have been strong. More generally, it is very difficult to rapidly improve the strength of state institutions, and if

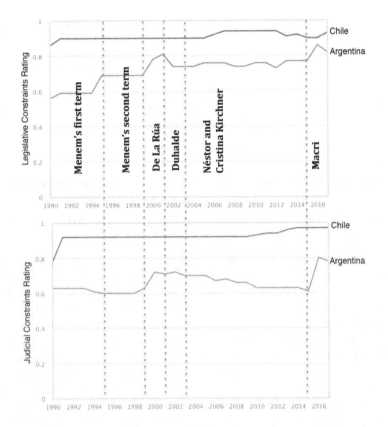

Figure 2.1 Varieties of Democracy Legislative Constraints on the Executive and Judicial Constraints on the Executive scores across time for Argentina and Chile.

changes occur, they usually take a protracted period of time (you cannot either destroy or ameliorate a country's institutions overnight).

On the opposite end, of the three independent variables, the one which will exhibit the greatest year-to-year fluctuation is the size of the president's party in congress. Given the regularity of elections, the degree to which the president can expect to be supported in congress can change regularly from one year to the next.

The third independent variable, the existence of recent economic crises, exhibits what I call "moderate" fluctuation. By "moderate" fluctuation, I refer to the fact that although economic crises generally occur at long intervals from each other, when they do occur, they can have a profound impact. In this sense, the fluctuation caused by economic crises year-to-year is less than that caused by the size of the president's party in congress (which changes very regularly), but significantly more than the

Institutional strength	The existence of recent economic crises	The size of the president's party in congress
Very little year-to-year change	There is occasionally a year-to-year change. Though economic crises happen much more rarely than elections, when they do occur, economic crises can have profound effects on presidential power.	Frequent year-to-year changes

Least variation ────────────────────────────▶ **Most variation**

Figure 2.2 Comparing the potential variation in my three independent variables.

variation in institutional strength, which changes very slowly over time. From 1990 to 2019, there were no economic crises in Chile. In Argentina, there was a severe economic crisis in the 2001–2002 period, and while legislative and judicial constraints do indeed fall in 2002, it is difficult to conclude whether this is due to the economic crisis, the fact that the president once again had a working majority in congress, or both. It is also difficult to study the fluctuation in my third independent variable since it is not clear for how long an economic crisis will affect presidential power. While in this book I do establish that economic crises can increase the power of presidents who are not blamed for the downturn, it is unclear how one economic crisis affects presidential power in each subsequent year (for example, how will an economic crisis impact presidential power in the first year after the downturn vs. the fourth year?). Unlike majorities in congress where it is simple to isolate the effect of the independent variable in each year, in the case of crises, it is difficult to assess year-over-year fluctuations.

Figure 2.2 illustrates the degree to which my three independent variables exhibit fluctuation.

Summary

In short, in this part, I have attempted to provide evidence for why I refer to Argentina in the post-democratization period as "hyperpresidential." While I have attempted to show how presidential power in practice was very strong vis-à-vis institutions of horizontal accountability such as congress and the judiciary, I have also suggested that there was some variation in presidential power in Argentina based on changes in the size of the president's party in congress. In Parts I and II of this chapter, I also showed how although the Argentine president is restrained in theory, these restraints evaporate when analyzing presidential power in practice.

Part III: Formal Presidential Power in Chile

Despite the fact that Argentina has witnessed a significantly greater degree of hyperpresidentialism than Chile, the Chilean president is considered by many to be endowed with far greater formal powers. Payne attempts to numerically compare the powers of the Argentine and Chilean presidents, and Table 2.4 is drawn from data in his piece.

Siavelis summarizes some of the constitutional powers of Chilean presidents when he writes:

> In brief, the 1980 Constitution provides the president exclusive initiative in all matters relating to taxation and the creation of new public agencies and employment therein. Presidential exclusive initiative also applies to any bills creating or changing the terms of entitlement programs and social security, and any proposals dealing with collective bargaining procedures. The national budget proposed by the president automatically becomes law in 60 days if Congress fails to approve it. The president also has the right to declare legislation urgent in any phase of its consideration and to declare extraordinary sessions of Congress, during which only initiatives of the executive branch may be considered (Constitutional Articles 62–64).[79]

The first constitutional provision that gives great power to Chilean presidents is urgencies, which provide the president control over the legislative agenda by allowing him/her to prioritize bills in congress. Based on Article 71 of the constitution as well as the *Ley Orgánica*, there are three levels of urgency which a president can use to try to force a decision on a bill. The first level, simple urgency (*simple urgencia*) mandates that a bill must be voted upon within 30 days. The second level, extreme urgency (*suma urgencia*) mandates that a bill must be voted upon within ten days. Finally, the third level, immediate discussion (*discusión inmediata*) mandates that a bill must be voted on within three days. Siavelis notes that "presidential urgency has been interpreted as an important tool in the arsenal of the Chilean president."[80]

Another powerful tool in the arsenal of the Chilean president is the power of exclusive initiative, which, according to Article 62 of the Chilean constitution, extends to the following areas: proposing the budget (and,

Table 2.4 The constitutional strength of executives in Argentina and Chile in several areas[a]

	Decree	Budget	Total proactive power	Veto	Partial veto	Exclusive initiative	Total reactive power	Power to convoke plebiscite	Total legislative power
Argentina	0.33	0.45	0.38	0.85	0.85	0.00	0.48	0.50	0.47
Chile	0.33	0.73	0.50	0.85	0.85	0.67	0.77	1.00	0.68

[a]Payne 2007; p.96

very importantly, any law that involves spending), taxation, "creating new public services or remunerated employment," retirement payments, pensions, the minimum wage (including in the private sector), regulating collective bargaining, amending social security laws, etc. The constitution states that if a president proposes modifications in these areas, "the National Congress may only accept, reduce or reject the services, employment, salaries, loans, benefits, expenditures and other related proposals made by the President of the Republic."[81] In other words, congress cannot propose any laws in these areas and may only reject proposals by the executive. In another book,[82] Siavelis notes that the interpretation of these areas of exclusive initiative has traditionally been very broad, and they affect legislation which might at first appear to be unrelated to any of these domains. For example, in 1993 a senator proposed a bill that would allow women to decide when they wanted to take maternity leave, since the existing law specified a particular time period before and after the birth of the child when this was permitted (the new law would give the woman greater choice over the timing of the maternity leave). Nevertheless, this seemingly straightforward piece of legislation was ruled unconstitutional because it incurred into the area of "social security" over which the president possessed exclusive initiative. Because of the numerous areas in which Chilean presidents possess exclusive initiative, as per Table 2.4, Payne assigns Chile a score of 0.67 in this category of executive power. In Argentina, the president has few powers of exclusive initiative and thus receives a score of 0 on this criterion.

In terms of veto power, in a manner similar to Argentina, Article 70 of the Chilean constitution provides that the president may reject any bill of which he/she disapproves and can send it back to the originating chamber of congress. If, however, both of the Chambers insist on passing the legislation and achieve a two-thirds majority, the veto would be overridden. Chilean presidents also possess the line-item veto.

The reason why the Chilean constitution overall gives the president so much power is rooted in the process through which it was adopted. The Chilean constitution currently in force was drafted in 1980, replacing the previous one that had been written in 1925. The dominant force in writing the constitution was the military junta led by Pinochet, who was extremely skeptical of the legislature and wanted to centralize power in the executive branch (it is important to mention that one of the key constitution-writers was lawyer Jaime Guzmán, a close advisor to Pinochet). In their piece, Nef and Galleguillos claim that:

> The policymaking functions of the future legislature were made extremely limited, especially when compared with those enjoyed before the 1973 military coup. Formerly a proactive, engaging, and dynamic institution, Congress was now to be transformed into a paper tiger... The new political system became, at least on the surface, one of

unrestricted presidentialism. Most matters of importance remain in the privilege of the president, as indicated in Articles 62 and 64 of the Constitution.[83]

Constitutional Tribunal and Supreme Court

Unlike in the USA and Argentina, constitutionally the top layer of the judiciary in Chile is divided between the Supreme Court and the Constitutional Tribunal. The Supreme Court's responsibility is to act as a final court of appeals for civil and criminal matters but does not possess the power of judicial review, whereas the Constitutional Tribunal does have the power of judicial review over laws. Article 82 of the constitution states that the Constitutional Tribunal has the power:

> 1. To exercise control of the constitutionality of the constitutional organic laws prior to their promulgation, and of the laws that interpret some precept of the Constitution; 2. To resolve on questions regarding constitutionality which might arise during the processing of bills or of constitutional amendment[s] and of treaties submitted to the approval of Congress; 3. To resolve on questions which should arise over the constitutionality of a decree having the force of law.

Note that starting when Pinochet took power in 1973, the Constitutional Tribunal ceased to exist, and there remained only the Supreme Court as per the Constitution of 1925 (note that although in 1970 Law 17,284 created a Constitutional Tribunal, it was dissolved along with the congress when the military junta took power). The Constitutional Tribunal would be revived in 1980 under the new constitution.

The Chilean president has significantly more limited appointment powers than the Argentine president for judges on the high courts. For the Supreme Court, Chilean presidents must choose between a shortlist of nominees pre-determined by the Supreme Court itself. For the Constitutional Tribunal, the president only has control over three of the ten members (the rest are appointed by either the Supreme Court, the Senate, or the Chamber of Deputies). The appointment mechanism for Chilean judges and how it encourages judicial independence (by lessening the control of the president over the selection process) will be described in further detail in Chapter 3.

In deciding the constitutionality of laws, the Constitutional Tribunal has two legal options. The first, and more uncommon method used is to declare an entire law as unconstitutional; the second and far more frequent method is to declare that parts of the law are inapplicable to certain individuals/organizations. The distinction between these two situations is that although a law may be constitutional in many cases, courts could find particular cases in which the law does not apply (*inaplicabilidad*). The

Chilean Constitutional Tribunal exercises its capacity as a veto player not only by declaring laws unconstitutional/inapplicable after they are passed but also ex-ante *before bills become the law*. In order to declare an *existing* law unconstitutional, a supermajority of eight out of ten members is needed, whereas to declare an existing law inapplicable, or to declare unconstitutional a law that has *not yet been implemented*, a simple majority of six out of ten is required (in case of a tie vote, the president of the Tribunal casts the tie-breaking vote). Constitutionally, organic laws always need ex-ante approval by the Constitutional Tribunal (i.e., approval before they become law). Organic laws are a set of laws that are of special importance because many of them deal with the functioning of organs of the state, including the electoral system, political parties, the judiciary, the *Ministerio Público* (the equivalent of the US Department of Justice), and the Constitutional Tribunal. Even during the passage of a regular law (which unlike an organic law does not need ex-ante approval), in what is called a *requerimiento*, deputies and senators can voluntarily petition the Constitutional Tribunal to verify if certain aspects of a law under debate are legal (as noted above, to prevent a law from passing, only a simple majority of six out of ten members of the Tribunal must rule against the law). The Bachelet government during her second term in office had an especially high number of *requerimientos* from the different legislators.[84] Although the absolute number of *requerimientos* is low, those that do arrive before the Constitutional Tribunal touch upon very important "hot potato" issues. According to Federal Deputy Felipe de Mussy, "there is a culture whereby the Constitutional Tribunal is reserved for the most important or extreme cases... *Requerimientos* are reserved only for the most important topics."[85] Also, unlike the US Supreme Court, the Chilean Constitutional Tribunal cannot pick and choose which cases it decides to review. According to Professor Valeria Palanza, an expert on presidential power and checks and balances, the Constitutional Tribunal

> can easily turn into a veto point. It's very powerful. It's like one more legislature in the process that can veto legislation. If they do, it's not like a presidential veto that can be overridden, [since] it's simply unconstitutional. It's a very powerful actor...The composition of the Constitutional Tribunal ends up being key.[86]

As I will later describe, in terms of the strength of the judiciary in practice, unlike in Argentina where the courts for a long time simply rubber-stamped laws proposed by the executive, the two top courts in Chile have maintained significant independence and have actively challenged presidential proposals.

Although the Supreme Court of Chile does not perform judicial review, it can still constrain the president through the contentious-administrative route. If the president violates certain aspects of the constitution and abuses the constitutional rights of other Chileans, the victims may be able to file a motion called a *recurso de protección*.

The Contraloría

One of the most important institutions in Chile that serves as a counterweight to the executive is the Comptroller General or *Contraloría General.* The *Contraloría* was first created in 1927 under the advice of Princeton University economics professor Edwin Kemmerer. Unlike Comptrollers General in other countries, the Chilean *Contraloría* serves both as an audit organization that ensures that public finances are spent according to the law as well as a presidential oversight organization that is charged with reviewing the legality of presidential decrees.

In the early 1940s, the *Contraloría* became an autonomous organization within the government, meaning that it does not respond to either congress or the executive branch. In essence, the *Contraloría* in Chile can be seen as a third veto player to the presidency (in addition to congress and the judiciary), and in an interview with Luis Cordero (a lawyer who is an expert on the *Contraloría*), he claims that "the *Contraloría* was born as an institution meant to control the public administration, but also an institution to control presidentialism."[87] He later claims that "in Chile one of the things that explains why the president cannot abuse power is the existence of the *Contraloría*."[88]

The method through which the *Contraloría* controls presidential power is that it has the legal authority to review presidential decrees. Before a presidential decree becomes law, the *Contraloría* must provide ex-ante approval (with minor exceptions called *decretos exentos* which I will discuss below). After an executive submits their decree to the *Contraloría*, the institution has two choices: it can either approve it in a process called *toma de razón* or it may deny the decree (called *representación*). The denial of the decree may be for two reasons, either because of unconstitutionality or illegality. Whereas unconstitutionality is used for cases where the decrees violate the constitution, illegality is used in cases where the decrees violate a given law (that is not part of the constitution). In an interview with the head of the *Contraloría*, Jorge Bermúdez, he described that in recent years, the *Contraloría* has become more and more strict and that the approval rate for decrees has fallen.[89]

The only type of decree not subject to control by the *Contraloría* is the *decreto exento* ("exempt decree"). Note that in order to be exempt, the *Contraloría* must explicitly state through a resolution (Resolution 1600 of 2008, formerly Resolution 520 of 1996) that it will not verify the legality of decrees in certain areas. The basis for *decretos extentos* is that Article 63 of the constitution gives a list of topics that are matters of law (that can only be made by congress), but if a certain topic is not part of Article 63, then the president can rule unilaterally on that subject. For presidents, the problem is that the list of 20 areas in Article 63 is extremely broad, and what particularly lowers presidential power and broadens the authority of congress is subsection 20, which states that laws will include "every other norm of a general and obligatory character, that establishes the essential bases of a juridical order."[90] This subsection has traditionally been viewed very broadly by courts and has significantly limited the scope of executive action even in areas such as regulatory decrees.[91]

As mentioned earlier, in addition to serving as a check on presidential power, the *Contraloría* also serves an auditory purpose to make sure that government expenditures are legal. If during the course of an investigation the *Contraloría* finds that a certain government agency misused funds (this is not necessarily corruption, but can also include the use of money for any purpose other than what was specifically mandated by law), the public employees who disbursed the money become personally liable. A court system exists within the *Contraloría* to determine whether certain individuals are guilty and misused funds. After an initial finding by a judge working for the *Contraloría*, a public employee accused of misusing funds can appeal to a panel of three members. Note that this process runs parallel to the Chilean judicial system.

To summarize, the *Contraloría* is one of the main roadblocks responsible for making sure that the president does not exceed his/her power with regard to decrees. On the other hand, in Argentina, the review of decrees is delegated to a bicameral committee in congress (this bicameral commission in cases of unified government was often stacked with supporters of the president). While an organization does exist in Argentina called the *Auditoría General de la Nación* (abbreviated AGN) which has some similarities to the Chilean *Contraloría*, as I will discuss in the next chapter, the AGN's authority is significantly more curtailed, and it has often lacked independence from presidents in power.

Short Summary

In short, in this part of the book, I have noted how the Chilean president possesses very broad powers (significantly broader than Argentina's executive) through prerogatives such as exclusive initiative and urgency provisions. I have also discussed the theoretical checks and balances that exist through the legislature, the judiciary, and the *Contraloría*. In the following part, I move beyond the constitutional foundations of executive/legislative/judicial powers and illustrate how the relationship between these institutions played out *in practice* in Chile. I will show how since 1990, Chile has not witnessed any episodes of unchecked presidentialism.

Part IV: No Hyperpresidentialism in Practice in Chile

In Argentina, I illustrated how despite strong constitutional constraints, executives have often governed in a hyperpresidential manner. The situation is the opposite in Chile, and as I will show, despite the strong

Table 2.5 Approval rate for presidential initiatives in Chile between 1990 and 1993[a]

Presidential initiatives	With urgency	Without urgency	Total
Approved	240 (64%)	164 (62.6%)	404
Pending withdrawn	135 (36%)	98 (37.4%)	233
Total	375	262	637

[a]This table is recreated from Siavelis 2002; p.94

aforementioned theoretical powers of the Chilean president, in practice, he/she works closely with congress and is constrained by various institutions.

Quantitatively, the lack of hyperpresidentialism in Chile first becomes evident through an analysis of approval rates of executive initiatives that were proposed to congress between 1990 and 1993. Table 2.5 taken from Siavelis shows these trends.

Overall, what these trends show is that a sizeable proportion of executive initiatives overall (whether urgent or not) do not pass congress. Of the 637 executive initiatives in congress, only 404 were approved (slightly less than two-thirds).

Whereas Argentine presidents have consistently abused decree authority, decrees of the NUD-type have been virtually inexistent in Chile since democratization. Although Chilean presidents do frequently use decrees called *decretos con fuerza de ley*, unlike NUDs, these decrees are in areas *pre-authorized by congress*, and by using them, the president is not trampling over the legislature's authority. There are no cases of decrees where the president actually made laws normally reserved for the legislature. According to Rodrigo Egaña, who at the time of the interview was the National Director of the Civil Service, although the president has significant power, "he is a co-legislator with the parliament…[and] has practically no power to dictate legal norms [by decree]…If he wants to initiate a reform, he requires the consent of parliament."[92] Similarly, Professor Miguel Ángel Fernández, who at the time of the interview was the Director of the Public Law Department at the Pontificia Universidad Católica de Chile (he was subsequently appointed to the Constitutional Tribunal), claimed that "in Chile [Argentine-style] Necessity and Urgency Decrees do not exist, and the president cannot dictate them even in special or extraordinary circumstances…the constitution does not permit Necessity and Urgency Decrees."[93] Similarly, Carlos Carmona, a Minister on the Constitutional Tribunal, in an interview when asked about the ability of presidents to issue decrees claimed that:

It is difficult to find a case where there is no law or which is not a topic that must be governed by law. As a result, for almost 30 years of democracy the president has governed with the backing of congress.[94]

Several other interviewees familiar with constitutional law affirmed the inexistence of an NUD-like instrument.[95] The few instances where Chilean presidents signed *decretos de emergencia* that had some semblance to NUDs were reserved for emergency situations and were extremely limited in their scope (for example, a decree was issued in 2008 in response to the failure to fund the Santiago transportation system and a decree was issued after the 2010 earthquake). Unlike Argentine NUDs, the emergency decree in Chile does not allow the president to actually enact legislation and only authorizes him/her to spend additional money to tackle the crisis (up to 2% of the budget, as described in Article 32, Section 22 of the constitution). Theoretically, the president cannot govern by decree legally even during a catastrophe like a war.[96] The last time in Chile that NUD-like instruments were used was during the military period when Pinochet would issue what was called the *decreto ley* (abbreviated DL), an instrument that ceased to be used once democracy was restored. Figueroa claims that:

> A D.L. is an executive decree that regulates a topic that normally would be regulated by a statute, that is, regular legislation, but without the authorization of the Congress. A D.L. is generally regarded as possessing the same binding authority as a valid statute.[97]

Unlike in Argentina where presidents issued decrees despite their inexistent constitutional foundation (recall that decrees were not explicitly recognized until the 1994 constitutional amendment), in Chile, the lack of decree power in theory translated into a lack of decree power in practice. Cordero notes that although NUD-like instruments were used during the military period, they have not existed during "conditions of [democratic] normality."[98] According to Mario Venegas, a Federal Deputy in Chile, governing by decree would be considered taboo for a president, and he claims that:

> It is supposed that democracy means negotiation. A president could use decrees, but the cost would be very big. Many people would go against this president...In this sense, here [in Chile] there is respect between the executive and legislative branches.[99]

Journalist Fernando Paulsen also claims that the Chilean congress "is a real congress, and the president cannot govern by decree."[100]

Similarly, another constitutional tool that has been underutilized by Chilean presidents is veto power, which has been used extremely rarely since the return to democracy (recall that the Chilean president possesses the line-item veto).[101]

What is particularly remarkable in the case of Chile is that throughout the three decades since democratization, informal restraints against presidential abuses have been so strong there have been few *attempts* by executives to expand their powers. In performing interviews in Chile, I posed to over 20 interviewees the question of whether they believed that *any* of the presidents since democratization tried to abuse power. Not a single interviewee answered positively, and everyone concurred that no president has attempted to stretch the limits of their power. The answers did not depend on political affiliation, and neither the right nor the left accused the other side. Gaspar Rivas, a National Deputy (Independent), when asked whether there were differences between the desire of the left versus right to concentrate power responded "no" and claimed that "when they got to power, all presidents have been significantly presidential."[102] José Luis Cea, the former president of the Chilean Constitutional Tribunal, claimed in an interview that "in the past 25 years in terms of scandalous [abuses of presidential power] there is no example, and even if there were attempts, they were immediately halted either by the Constitutional Tribunal...or in congress."[103] He also claims that during the particular period of time that he was a minister in the Constitutional Tribunal, which overlapped with part of President Lagos's term:

> I had a good relationship with Lagos. He never tried [to abuse power], and I would never have accepted. We were not subordinated to the executive. My duties were clear, and we did not accept pressures from anyone...There was never an excess [of presidential power], nor a scandalous abuse by the president.[104]

Overall he says that Chile enjoys the "universal application of the separation of powers with breaks and counterweights."[105] Coming from José Luis Cea, this claim is particularly significant considering that he was squarely in the conservative wing of the court, having been appointed by the right-leaning National Security Council in 2002 (whereas Lagos was part of the leftist *Concertación*). This sentiment is also echoed by Federal Deputy Venegas, who when asked if in the past 25 years there was any presidential abuse of power, replied:

> I would say not. We have transitioned after the dictatorship toward a process of democratic consolidation that would prevent this. There is a republican culture that would eliminate not only the possibility, but also the temptation for a president to abuse power. Here, we have controls.[106]

Using Impeachment (or the Threat of Impeachment) to Constrain the Executive Branch

One of the most important ways through which the Chilean congress has actively checked presidential power is through its willingness to use what is known as the *acusación constitucional* or "constitutional accusation" (this is also known as the *juicio político* or "political judgment"). This is equivalent in the USA to an impeachment hearing and is conducted when congress believes that a certain minister has overstepped their constitutional authority or has committed legally questionable actions. It is important to note that this mechanism is not limited to members of the executive branch and can also be used to impeach judges, high-ranking officials of the *Contraloría*, etc. It is the lower house in Chile which conducts investigations and decides whether they warrant impeachment proceedings, and it is the upper house which would conduct a trial. This mechanism has regularly been used since democratization for impeachments, with over 20 constitutional accusations from 1990 to the present (including against Pinochet in 1998). Egaña notes that the threat of impeachment proceedings is a strong deterrent against presidential abuses of power. He claims that "risking a *juicio político* is extremely grave, since it can result in the removal of a president."[107] The bar for starting an impeachment proceeding is not high, and like in the USA, requires a simple majority of the lower house. Although in the Senate a two-thirds majority is required to impeach the president, the bar is significantly lower for all other public officials, with only a majority required.[108] Even if the impeachment process does not end in an actual impeachment, it can still hurt a presidency.

An example of an impeachment was Harald Beyer, a former Education Minister under Piñera (during his first term in office). Remarkably, the Education Minister under the first Bachelet government, Yasna Provoste, was also impeached by congress. Congress also began proceedings against the former Justice Minister of President Bachelet, Javiera Blanco, as well as the former Health Minister, Carmen Castillo. These cases are especially remarkable since Bachelet's coalition possessed a majority of the seats in congress during the time of the investigations, indicating that congress conducts investigations in a bipartisan manner. Although the Chamber of Deputies eventually did not move forward on the impeachments of Ministers Blanco and Castillo, it was willing to investigate them and force them to testify (*interpelación*). Ángel Fernández notes that although impeachment is not common, it does happen and is a real possibility. Table 2.6 includes all constitutional accusations from 1990 to 2018.

Similarly, congress in Chile frequently makes use of investigative committees to investigate the president. Investigative committees can also call witnesses for interrogation. When asked to name the most important indicator demonstrating that the president is constrained by congress, Deputy Rivas discussed

the possibility of the congress to investigate actions of the president through investigative committees, especially if there is an act of corruption or irregularity. There also exist tools for impeachment proceedings to remove an authority figure including the president of the republic when they contravene the constitution.[109]

Table 2.6 Constitutional accusations from 1990 to 2018[a]

	Date charges brought	Resolution	Position	Name(s)
1	16 May 1991	11 Jun 1991	Ministro de Transportes	Señor Germán Correa
2	17 Dec 1992	20 Jan 1993	Ministros de la Excma. Corte Suprema y Auditor General del Ejército	Ministros Señores Cereceda, Beraud y Valenzuela Auditor Señor Torres Silva
3	31 May 1994	17 Jun 1994	Ex Ministros de Minería y Hacienda	Señores Hales y Foxley
4	04 Sep 1996	01 Oct 1996	Ministros de la Excma. Corte Suprema	Señores Ortiz, Zurita, Navas y Álvarez
5	04 Jun 1997	19 Jun 1997	Ministro de Educación	Señor José Pablo Arrellano Marín
6	02 Jul 1997	26 Jul 1997	Presidente de la Excma. Corte Suprema	Señor Jordán
7	15 Jul 1997	08 Aug 1997	Ministro de la Corte Suprema	Señores Jordán, Zurita, Aburto y Faúndez.
8	17 Mar 1998	09 Apr 1998	General	Augusto Pinochet Ugarte
9	13 Oct 1998	26 Oct 1998	Ex Ministro de Obras Públicas	Señor Ricardo Lagos Escobar.
10	29 Aug 2000	13 Sep 2000	Ministro de la Exma. Corte Suprema	Señor Luis Correa Bulo.
11	19 Jun 2002	10 Jul 2002	Intendente de la Región Metropolitana	Señor Marcelo Trivelli Oyarzún.
12	20 Mar 2003	02 Apr 2003	Ministro de Economía, Fomento y Reconstrucción	Señor Jorge Rodríguez Grossi
13	16 Dec 2003	13 Jan 2004	Intendente Subrogante de la Quinta Región y Gobernador de la Provincia de Valparaíso	Señor Ivan De La Maza Maillet
14	03 Nov 2004	17 Nov 2004	Ministro de Justicia	Señor Luis Bates Hidalgo
15	22 Jun 2005	19 Jul 2005	Ministros de la Excma. Corte Suprema	Señores Domingo Kokisch Mourgues, Eleodoro Ortiz Sepúlveda y Jorge Rodríguez Ariztía
16	11 Mar 2008	17 Apr 2008	Ministra de Educación	Señora Yasna Provoste Campillay
17	15 Jun 2010	01 Jul 2010	Intendenta de la Región de Atacama y Gobernador de la Provincia de Copiapó	Señora Ximena Matas Quilodrán y Señor Nicolás Norman Garrido
18	09 Aug 2011	31 Aug 2011	Ministro del Interior y Seguridad Pública	Señor Rodrigo Hinzpeter Kirberg
19	11 Apr 2012	02 May 2012	Ministro del Interior y Seguridad Pública	Señor Rodrigo Hinzpeter Kirberg
20	02 Apr 2013	18 Apr 2013	Ministro de Educación	Señor Harald Beyer Burgos
21	19 Aug 2014	09 Sep 2014	Ministro de la Excma. Corte Suprema	Señor Héctor Carreño Seaman
22	12 Nov 2015	09 Dec 2015	Ministra de Salud	Señora Carmen Castillo Taucher
23	16 Aug 2016	06 Sep 2016	Ministra de Justicia y DD.HH.	Señora Mónica Javiera Blanco
24	29 May 2018	20 Jun 2018	Ministro de Salud	Señor Emilio Santelices
25	23 Aug 2018	13 Sep 2018	Ministros de la Excma. Corte Suprema	Señores Enrique Dolmestch Urra, Manuel Antonio Valderrama Rebolledo y Carlos Guillermo Künsemüller Loebenfelder

[a] Source: Chilean Chamber of Deputies

The Limited Control of the President Over His/Her Own Cabinet

One of the examples that best illustrates the weakness of the Chilean president vis-à-vis congress is the fact that presidents have surprisingly limited control in practice over cabinet appointments, which in virtually all presidential systems are the exclusive and sacred domain of the president. In Chile, as I will discuss in Chapter 4, in order to please members of their coalition, Chilean presidents dole out cabinet positions to each party. As a result, the president has limited control over the selection of their ministers, in favor of the parties in congress needed to pass his/her legislative program.

The Lack of Practical Power of Exclusive Initiative

Earlier, exclusive initiative was identified as a powerful tool of the executive branch; although on the surface this constitutional prerogative would provide significant power to Chilean presidents, like with the case of urgencies, what can be observed is that *in practice* presidents do not benefit as much as would be expected. For example, despite the power of exclusive initiative in areas such as the budget, in practice, legislators have significant influence, and the process is often one of intense negotiation between the executive and legislative branches. Siavelis, for example, writes that:

> Scholars of budgetary politics have noted that although deputies are barred from formal consultation on the budget, in reality members have a good deal of informal input in its formulation state. Their influence continues during negotiations in legislative conference committees of the two houses and in negotiations outside formal congressional institutions. Presidents routinely consult with legislators of their own parties and members of the coalition to reinforce coalition unity and ensure that the budget is acceptable to coalition partners. More importantly, informal negotiation has also been central to securing the votes of the opposition to pass budgets, even though presidents do not necessarily need these votes. During negotiations on most budgets, the Concertación's various ministers of finance have met and negotiated with opposition leaders.[110]

Siavelis's argument was similarly echoed by Guillermo Pattillo, who played a key role in DIPRES, the organ in Chile within the executive branch responsible for drafting the budget (he was the *subdirector* of DIPRES). When asked whether congress had any influence in the drafting of the budget, he replied that:

> Normally, it is necessary to negotiate with congress certain elements of the budget. During my three years, congress asked for several

items to be modified. Congress cannot do it directly but can condition the passage of the budget on these modifications. In the end, congress and the committees that analyze the budget have a power that is not small, although the law gives them significantly less power. They cannot raise spending, but could reduce it, except in areas of permanent spending...In the negotiation process they ask that certain parts of the budget be shifted around, or else they will not give their approval.[111]

Similarly, Professor Raúl Letelier who specializes in Public Law in Chile claimed in an interview that:

The president has exclusive initiative in various areas...The problem is that there is no point in having exclusive initiative if you have a congress that will not approve [the law]. Exclusive initiative is a good power, but under these circumstances it has deteriorated.[112]

He goes on to claim that in practice, legislators *do* informally propose projects that require spending, and while the president can theoretically reject these projects (since members of congress do not have the right to initiate spending legislation), in practice, the president goes on to propose legislation that incorporates the provisions desired by these legislators. Therefore, whereas legislators cannot formally propose spending, in practice they have the leverage to convince the president to author the bills they desire.[113] A similar concept is described by Egaña, who notes that:

If there is any element of a law that involves spending...the legislator can propose it to the executive and if the executive thinks it is a good idea he can propose it [himself]. Many of the presidential proposals are in fact suggestions by members of parliament.[114]

Similarly, Paulsen claims that "[a legislator] redacts a law, passes it to the president, and if the president agrees with it, sends it as though it was his/her initiative."[115]

In an interview with a Federal Deputy in Chile who desired to remain anonymous, when I asked him where the power of congress comes from if only the president can propose spending, he replied, "saying no. When congress says no, if the executive wants something to be approved, they have to present something that is able to at least muster a majority."[116]

In an interview with Senator Patricio Walker, who served as president of both the Chilean Senate and the Chamber of Deputies, he described that when Piñera was attempting to reform a law that would have increased maternity leave in Chile, the president and congress differed in the additional time they wanted to give (congress wanted to give more time). Ultimately, Walker claims that congress threatened not to pass the project, and that as a result, maternity leave was extended by a greater amount of time than the president wanted.[117]

The Lack of Practical Power of Urgencies

Regarding the urgency provisions through which presidents can mandate votes within a designated period of time, their effect is limited.

From the data in Table 2.5, it is evident that there is, in practice, no significant difference between the approval rate for initiatives tagged with urgency versus without urgency (as I mentioned earlier, there are three types of urgencies, *simple urgencia, suma urgencia,* and *decisión inmediata*). Although it is not possible to definitively conclude that marking a bill as urgent has no effect (since perhaps the president merely marks as urgent bills which have less of a chance of passing, and leaves less divisive initiatives without urgency), statistically bills marked as urgent do not have significantly higher passage rates.

With regard to the speed of passage, in theory congress must vote on legislation designated as *simple urgencia, suma urgencia,* and *discussión inmediata* within, respectively, 30, 10, and 3 days. However, the completion rates within these time frames are merely 17%, 45%, and 75%, respectively.[118] In an interview with Federal Deputy Felipe de Mussy, he attributed much of this delay to the slow passage process in the Senate.[119] In practice, the executive is often flexible with deadlines and grants several time extensions if congressional leaders desire. Despite urgency being an important tool at the disposal of the president, Siavelis notes that because of the fact that presidents were flexible and that congress often failed to abide exactly by the deadlines, "urgencies form a part of the overall equation of constitutional executive dominance that has yet to come into play."[120] Arbelaez and Tanaka similarly argue that "in practice, the Chilean president has not exercised presidential urgency powers in a strict and inflexible manner as expected in the constitution. The president has more incentives to cooperate with other parties...."[121] Deputy Venegas similarly described that the main tool that Chilean legislators have at their disposal to get around urgency provisions is the threat of rejecting a law. Venegas claims that:

> When the president tries too much to rush a project, we tell him/her that we might vote against it. It is better for the president to give us 2–3 days more rather than having the initiative rejected. He pressures us with the urgency, we pressure him with the threat of voting against it.[122]

In describing his personal experiences with urgencies, Sebastián Soto (a professor of constitutional law and a former top-ranking official in the

Piñera administration who served as the head of the juridico-legislative division between 2010 and 2014) claimed that:

> In reality if urgencies are not respected, nothing happens. Those who have the power to push the commission to approve, reject or discuss a project are either the president of the commission or the chamber president (*presidente de la sala*). I can place an urgency, but if the committee president does not want to take up the project, there is no way to force him. Oftentimes when we would mark a project as urgent, we would call the committee president, ask him what he thought of the project, and there was a dialog. If he did not agree, there was no way to force him to modify the committee's agenda... This happened to us, and while we would mark a project as urgent, the president of the committee would say no.[123]

Similarly, Senator Patricio Walker claimed that:

> there is no punishment [for not complying with urgencies]. What happens frequently is that...urgencies prioritize the passage of certain laws in congress, but given that there is no punishment, the specific time frame is not necessarily the one established by the executive.[124]

At first glance, it would appear that Chilean presidents have underutilized their constitutional powers because they are "nice" and value the role of other institutions of horizontal accountability. Nevertheless, the underutilization of power by Chilean executives is not an altruistic, noble gesture, and as I argued in the first chapter, presidents will generally try to maximize their power relative to the other veto players in a political system. For example, Francisca Moya described in an interview that Chilean presidents would ideally like to maximize their regulatory powers in areas where the constitution does not mandate a law.[125] Similarly, when discussing decree authority in Chile, Palanza argued that "presidents would use it more if they could."[126]

Paulsen also claims that "currently, congress is stronger than the president...[In the case of current President Bachelet] the president is the weakest state figure. The judiciary and the legislature are stronger."[127] Carlos Huneeus, an academic and expert on the Chilean presidency, added that "historically, the congress in Chile has been powerful. It is a powerful institution...It is clear that there is no hyperpresidentialism."[128]

An Examination of the Strength of Congress and the Judiciary Through the Significant Executive Initiatives Rejected

One of the clearest ways in which it is possible to assess that the Chilean congress and judiciary have been independent and stood up to the executive is looking at presidential initiatives that were rejected. Earlier in this chapter, I noted in detail how Argentine presidents for most of the post-democratization period have been able to get their projects approved with few obstacles from congress or the judiciary. As I will show, the Chilean president has had far greater problems in this regard.

The first case of a major project where congress asserted its authority was tax reform. Although tax reform was enacted in 2014, it was at first rejected by congress, and the version that was approved was substantially different from that desired by Bachelet. Alejandro Olivares described that "in the end, the tax reform did not come out exactly as the government had wanted, and an intermediate form emerged with significantly less reach than before."[129] Similarly, *The Wall Street Journal* describes that "the approval [from congress] came after the executive branch watered down proposals that angered the business sector and opposition politicians."[130] Ultimately, tax reform was approved unanimously in congress, but only after having gone through various amendments.

Significant concessions also had to be made in the case of health reform in Chile under Lagos. In his desire to expand health coverage across Chile, Lagos proposed the creation of a Solidarity Fund (FS) which would have included money from both the state-run portion and the private-run portion of the Chilean healthcare system. The debate in congress was fierce, and there was dissent *even among Lagos's own coalition.* Although in the end the reform was approved (termed "AUGE"), the solidarity fund, a critical pillar of the reform, had to be scrapped. The Christian Democratic Party was split on the creation of the Solidarity Fund, and in the end, the majority of legislators from the party opposed it. As well, the reform was significantly more bare-bones than Lagos had envisioned, and although Lagos had initially hoped that the plan would provide universal coverage for 56 critical conditions, coverage would be gradual with 25 illnesses covered in 2005 and all 56 being covered only in 2007.[131] As well, the passage process dragged on for three years, and although Lagos initially proposed the reform in 2001, the AUGE law was only approved in 2004 (Law 19966).

Another notable case of a reform where the president suffered defeat was labor reform under Bachelet. Despite having to make numerous concessions because of opposition even from members of her own coalition, after the bill passed the congress, the most critical parts of it were rejected by the Constitutional Tribunal in a 6-4 decision. Two of the key provisions that were rejected included a measure that would prohibit companies from negotiating with entities not legally recognized as unions, as well as a measure that would have prohibited companies from extending benefits obtained through collective bargaining to employees not part of the union (in effect, the ruling struck down part of the law based on the fact that it violated the "right-to-work" principle).[132] Francisca Moya summarizes Bachelet's legislative difficulties when she claims that:

In the case of both projects [the labor reform law and the tax law], there was a big difference between how the project entered [congress] and exited. In the case of the tax reform, the project changed in the Senate because the Senate opted for a more conservative formula... in the case of the labor reform, it changed a lot in congress, and went twice to the constitutional tribunal.[133]

What differentiates Chile from many of the countries in the region is that the letter of the law is actually followed, and once the Constitutional Tribunal rules against the government, in practice the law never goes into force. After the Constitutional Tribunal struck down the labor reform law, the governing coalition removed in June from the bill the parts declared unconstitutional and let the rest pass (although of course the signature elements of the bill were missing).[134] Another prominent example of when the Constitutional Tribunal rejected a presidential initiative was the case of the morning-after pill. Michelle Bachelet had signed a law that would allow minors between 14 and 18 to obtain the morning-after pill over the counter, yet the Tribunal ruled that they required a medical prescription.

Congress notoriously rejected a project by the executive branch in the case of the *Transantiago* transportation system in the capital city in 2007. Bachelet had asked congress to approve a 92 million dollar project to finance the *Transantiago*, but it was rejected in the Senate; the Chamber of Deputies then decided to instead pass a project with a symbolic two dollars in funding. The failure to pass legislation financing the *Transantiago* was so notorious that the Argentine newspaper *La Nación* called it "the worst defeat of the *Concertación* since the center-left coalition got to power in 1989."[135] Ultimately, Bachelet used an emergency decree in order to finance the *Transantiago* (recall that the president is permitted under the constitution in cases of an emergency to spend a sum of money up to 2% of the budget). Even though Bachelet used an emergency decree, it would be incorrect to equate this action to an NUD by a president like Menem, as this was just a decree to authorize extra spending.

Also, Bachelet during her time in office attempted to reform the educational system, and although she eventually did get reforms through congress, they were modest in comparison to what she would have wanted. To provide some context about the educational reform, there were student protests in both 2006 and 2011 (the 2006 protests were informally called the "Penguin Revolution"). The basis for these protests was an educational system that was overly expensive and based on vouchers; critics also argued that the voucher system resulted in sharp socioeconomic inequality. At the university level, attending college was traditionally very costly and resulted in students having to take out large amounts of debt (*annually*, a university education costs between $6,000 and $15,000[136]). Educational reform under Bachelet in fact included several separate

reforms meant to alter education at all three levels; collectively, these reforms fell short of expectations, and Bachelet was unable to deliver all
that she would have wanted. One of the first bills to pass was a law that
sought to end profit-making and certain selective admissions practices by
private schools receiving state subsidies (these schools are roughly comparable to charter schools in the USA). Although the law was approved
in early 2015, it had faced an eight-month battle in congress and con-
fronted opposition not only from the rightist parties in congress but also
from sectors within the Christian Democratic Party (part of Bachelet's
coalition). According to Reuters, in the negotiation process in congress,
"though the government's center-left political bloc has a majority in Congress, it does not have enough votes to ram the education reform through
and will need to negotiate and likely make concessions to the center-right
opposition."[137] Ultimately, the law did not have the transformative impact that many had hoped, since it essentially continued the voucher system in Chile. Critics also point to several loopholes that allow charter
schools to get around selectivity regulations that provide opportunities
for earning profits.[138] According to the Buenos Aires Herald, "Chilean
students consider that Bachelet's measure still falls short of their expectations and continue to take to the streets in protest."[139]

   On December 26, 2015, Bachelet signed into law another bill that would
provide free university education to a large percentage of students. After
facing significant hurdles in congress, the Constitutional Court struck
down one of the parts of the bill, claiming that the tuition-free scheme in
the law discriminated against several privately-run universities. The law
was altered to comply with the ruling, and ultimately, after the bill passed,
there were protests on the street as many considered that the bill was too
modest. According to the bill, 70% of students would have free university
education by 2018, and only by 2020 would it be free for all students.[140]
In an interview with Lucas Sierra, the Vice President of the left-leaning
Chilean think tank, *Centro de Estudios Públicos (CEP)*, he claimed that
"education was an important campaign promise [for Bachelet] which did
not go well for her."[141] Notably, she promised a free education system, but
by the end of her term, it was only free for approximately 60–70% of university students. As well, many of the improvements were in education
at the university level as opposed to the primary and secondary levels.
Alejandro Olivares also summarized the problems Bachelet faced in getting educational reform passed when he claimed that it will be difficult
to reconcile the interests of the left and right given that "the right wants
vouchers, and the left wants a system of gratuity at state universities."[142]

   During his tenure in office, Piñera presented various education reform
proposals which were rejected by congress. Similarly, Piñera presented
a project to congress to extend maternity leave which also suffered significant changes in the legislature. Also, Piñera shortly after being
elected president in 2010 proposed the legalization of civil unions for

gay couples. Although the bill did ultimately pass, the process took *more than four years*, and Piñera faced considerable opposition from the UDI party within his own coalition. Ironically, the passage of the bill took so long that it was ultimately signed into law by Piñera's successor, Michelle Bachelet. Similarly, Piñera wanted a reform of the Chilean electoral system, but also failed to achieve this.

During the last part of her second term in office, Bachelet desired pension reform. Although her personal long-term goal included establishing a public pension system that would compete with the current system of private pensions, in August 2016, she proposed more modest reforms whose centerpiece would involve raising the required contributions from employers and independent workers in order to be able to provide higher payouts for retirees.[143] She sent this bill to congress several months later in April of 2017. Nevertheless, she was unable to get it passed into law before her term in office expired in March of 2018. The difficulties in getting pension reform through congress are summarized in a *Reuters* article (written before her term expired) which stated that:

> Her governing coalition is severely divided…[and] debate on complex bills can take years in Chile. Earlier in April, Chile's finance minister said divisions in the government might make any pension reform impossible, and earlier this week, a major education bill pushed by Bachelet failed in committee.[144]

Professor Ivan Obando who specializes in public law and political science summarizes the influence of the Chilean congress when he claims that "the Chilean congress functions like that in the United States…Congressional committees are very powerful, and introduce modifications to legislative projects. Legislative projects do not leave congress in the way that the president proposed."[145] Similarly, Soto concurred that "the Chilean congress would change many legislative projects. The projects were negotiated… This government even with [coalitional] majorities in both chambers had to change legislative projects."[146] Many Chileans refer to the informal negotiation process over laws as taking place in the "kitchen" of a member of congress.

Just as important as the projects by Bachelet that were rejected or modified in congress are the projects which she did not try to propose throughout her time in office because of the fear of the divisions that it would create within her own coalition. Senator Walker claimed in an interview that "Bachelet left toward the end of her presidency two projects which were the most controversial within her coalition. One of them is constitutional reform…and in second place she has delayed but will present the gay marriage law."[147]

Another case which shows the limits of the Chilean president's power was the failed attempt by the first democratically-elected president in the post-democratization period, Patricio Aylwin, to change the composition of the Supreme Court. Aylwin tried to pack the court because he had grown frustrated that it refused to condemn many human rights abuses by the military, at one point claiming that the court showed "moral cowardice"[148] (Aylwin unsuccessfully tried to get a 1978 amnesty law declared as unconstitutional[149]). Although as Helmke notes President Aylwin would have liked to reshape the composition of the Court (which was conservative), the justices were well insulated from political pressure.[150] Unlike in Argentina where Menem was able to pack the Supreme Court, the situation in Chile went in the opposite direction.

Aylwin's court-packing plan held remarkable similarities to the process that Menem used, and involved both trying to expand the size of the court, as well as trying to impeach judges. In 1993, Aylwin tried to add four members to the Supreme Court and thus change its composition from the then-17 members to 21. Unlike in Argentina where such a plan was successful, it failed in Chile. It is important to note that the expansion of the size of the court as proposed by Aylwin would have had a significantly smaller impact than Menem's court-packing plan (while Aylwin desired an expansion from 17 to 21 members, Menem expanded the court from 5 to 9 judges).

In addition to the failed effort to expand the size of the court, there was an attempt under the Aylwin administration to also impeach three justices. Fiss claims that "although Aylwin's effort to increase the size of the Supreme Court came to naught, oddly enough, a more troublesome remedy—impeachment—proved more viable."[151] Whereas Menem and Néstor Kirchner in Argentina successfully used impeachment to get rid of unfriendly justices (judges were either impeached or resigned prior to impeachment proceedings), impeachment had very limited effects in Chile. Of the three justices that were subject to impeachment proceedings, only one of them was ultimately impeached.

Therefore, whereas in Argentina Menem successfully manipulated the composition of the court, Aylwin failed and only managed to get one justice impeached. As well, another critical difference was that there was significantly more bipartisanship in the process in Chile, and as Fiss notes, "the decision to remove [judge] Cereceda critically depended on the support of three senators from a conservative faction...Note should be taken of the fact that Cereceda was widely disliked."[152]

The Judiciary as a Check During the Military Period

Remarkably, the judiciary in Chile has served as a check on the president's power not only during the democratic period but also during the military dictatorship under Pinochet. Several important decisions by the Chilean Constitutional Tribunal and Supreme Court serve as a testament to this.

First, in 1974, one of the first acts of the Chilean Supreme Court after the military coup was to assert its authority to conduct judicial review in a decision that mirrored *Marbury v. Madison* in the USA. In particular, the Supreme Court exerted its authority to review military decrees (the Decreto Ley, DL). In July of 1974, the Supreme Court of Chile decided to review D.L. 449, "Federico Dunker Briggs." The case itself was not particularly noteworthy and merely revolved around the legality of the government setting rent controls on urban real estate. In the end, the Court ruled in favor of the government, *yet at the same time asserted its authority to be able to review future decrees and assess their constitutionality.* As Barros writes in referencing several anti-government decisions made by the Chilean Supreme Court, "a few months after its warning in 'Federico Dunker Briggs,' the Supreme Court made good on its threat to declare unconstitutional decree-laws that contravened the constitution...Thus, as the Court ruled, the constitution would supersede the Junta's decree laws."[153] As Barros notes, the military was not happy that the Court was exercising judicial review, and later passed DL 788, which attempted to restrain the power of the Supreme Court. In effect, DL 788 would have placed the Junta above the law and made it difficult for the Supreme Court to invalidate any decree. Ultimately, a significantly watered-down version of DL 788 was passed, and while there is mystery surrounding why the Junta chose to weaken DL 788, Barros suggests that:

Had this decree-law [in the initial form] gone into effect, it would have made a shambles of the Supreme Court's claim to uphold the supremacy of the constitution and undermined the military's relatively cordial relations with the court. A sharp break with the Supreme Court likely would also have had immediate political impact on the military's civilian base of support. The court had played a key role in the legal struggle against the Allende government and any move against the judiciary could have turned important sectors of the centrist and conservative political class away from the regime. What considerations led to the shift are unclear. The available archival materials contain no documentation of what transpired between the initial presentation of this draft decree law and the eventual promulgation of D.L. No. 788.[154]

Regarding the other Chilean high court, the Constitutional Tribunal demonstrated independence from the executive branch during the Pinochet era when it issued five rulings against the dictator that helped usher in the period of democracy. These five rulings were handed out between 1985 and 1987, and helped restore the party system, freedom of expression and opinion, the dissemination of a free news media, the creation of a court to oversee the plebiscite, as well as the lifting of all states of emergency and siege. The Constitutional Tribunal showed great courage, and remarkably even Pinochet himself accepted these rulings.[155] One particularly noteworthy judge was Eugenio Valenzuela Somarriva, who tipped the balance of the court against Pinochet. What is especially interesting about this judge is that he had been appointed by the National Security Council, and can thus be considered to have been close ideologically to Pinochet. Nevertheless, unlike Menem's judges, he put the law before his ideological affiliation. The strength of the Constitutional Tribunal is described by former Constitutional Tribunal Minister José Luis Cea, who claims that:

> The Constitutional Tribunal was independent, and thanks to the jurisprudence of the Tribunal, Chile was able to recover its democracy...[Resolutions dictated between 1985 and 1987] were dictated with courage by the Tribunal, which thought it unacceptable to continue with the dictatorship. Those five rulings were respected by Pinochet, who did not want to go against them.[156]

Robert Barros describes the one possibly most significant decision the Constitutional Tribunal made during this period on September 24, 1985 (called *Sentencia Rol No. 33*). This decision sought to regulate the plebiscite that would be held in Chile, by ruling unconstitutional part of Pinochet's law, the *Tribunal Calificador de Elecciones* (TRICEL), which aimed to create a special electoral court. In describing the importance of this 4-3 ruling where Valenzuela Somarriva was in the majority, Barros writes that:

> The Constitutional Tribunal's ruling was a political bombshell. Not only would an independent organ oversee the plebiscite and adjudicate complaints regarding any alleged improprieties committed in its execution, but the organic constitutional laws regulating ART. 18 would also have to be in force if the constitutionality of this event were not to be open to challenge. This was a far broader oversight of the plebiscite than was discussed within the Junta's joint commission. For, pursuant to the court's sentence, the TRICEL would not only oversee the act of the plebiscite – something which all four services apparently were willing to accept. It would also oversee a system of voter registration and voting counts which, according to the court's public sentence, would now have to be in place for any plebiscite to satisfy the terms of the constitution. Significantly, there is every reason to suspect that at the time of the Tribunal Constitucional's sentence, the executive had not committed itself to the use of electoral registries, and it is incontrovertible fact that no bill had been presented to provide for them even on an ad hoc basis by this date.[157]

Barros describes that after this decision, the Constitutional Tribunal continued to play a strong role in monitoring and determining the legality of procedures related to the plebiscite.[158] Ultimately, Barros concludes that:

> In subsequent rulings the court consistently struck provisions that restricted free political competition or provided opportunity for arbitrary intervention in the political process. In this process, the fact that the constitution contained a full bill of rights emerged as a decisive limit upon the military government. Since Chapter 2 guaranteed such rights as equality before the law, equal protection of the law, due process, and freedom of association, as well as political rights, the constitutional court could strike as unconstitutional any precept that violated these norms. In the remaining period leading up to the plebiscite, the constitutional court repeatedly did so when it reviewed the remaining political organic laws. The court struck any number of articles that would have established inequalities or enabled arbitrary restrictions of rights at the different stages of the political electoral process – from party formation and registration, internal party organization, voter registration, electoral and plebiscitary campaigns, the convocation of elections and plebiscites, to voting and the qualification of elections.[159]

The Role of the Contraloría in Restricting Chilean Presidential Power in Practice

In practice, the Chilean president has faced resistance not only from the courts but also from the *Contraloría*. Cordero described the strong role of the *Contraloría* as a check on presidential power when he stated:

> For many years, what has happened is that the *Contraloría* has objected for reasons of legality [to decrees] with a certain degree of regularity. In the Chilean institutional system, you have a relation where every day the executive passes decrees and the *Contraloría* makes observations. In the institutional system of Chile, it is not abnormal that the *Contraloría* asks the executive to adjust a decree. There is a relationship of normality between the *Contraloría* and the president and his ministers. Every month there are objections to decrees.[160]

The capacity of the *Contraloría* to restrain presidential power in practice can be seen as far back as the military period. In 1977, at the peak of the military's power, Pinochet desired to call a plebiscite and issued the appropriate decree. Nevertheless, the decree was rejected by the *Contraloría* in a critical juncture which set a precedent for the strong supervisory role that this organization would later have on presidents. At the helm of the *Contraloría* was Héctor Humeres, who had been in this position for over a decade since 1967. After rejecting the decree, Humeres resigned and was replaced by Sergio Fernández who rapidly approved the plebiscite. Nevertheless, Humeres's action set an important precedent, as he preferred to immediately resign from his position rather than accept political pressure. Although many argue that Humeres was fired for his action, this is not entirely correct since at the time of the ruling against Pinochet, Humeres had *already* applied for retirement, although the rejection of Pinochet's decree prompted the administration to accelerate his application.[161] One of the recent heads of the *Contraloría* of Chile, Patricia Arriagada, declared in an interview that:

> Perhaps he who brought the most and set in stone the independence of the *Contraloría* was Héctor Humeres, who refused to accept a decree sent by the executive at the time, and then left. I believe that this symbolizes the independence the *Contraloría* always had, whatever the government in power.[162]

It is important to mention that the *Contraloría* also objected to many of Allende's decrees that would allow the state to intervene in industries. Professor Ruiz-Tagle, a specialist in constitutional law, describes that "during the Allende [presidency], the *Contraloría* was much more aggressive."[163]

In the post-democratization period, it has been a common occurrence that the president desires to pass a decree and the *Contraloría* asks that changes be made. The *Contraloría* regularly finds faults with presidential decrees, yet almost always is willing to work with the executive branch to remedy the problems. Alicia De la Cruz, a specialist on the *Contraloría*, adds that oftentimes, the *Contraloría* in fact even encourages ministers from the executive branch to send a team to work with the *Contraloría* to help make the decree legal, implying that the relationship is not one of antagonism but of cooperation.[164] One of the symbolic acts that shows the weight of the *Contraloría* is that when members of the executive and the *Contraloría* negotiate changes to a decree, it is the presidential staff that goes to the offices of the *Contraloría* rather than vice versa.[165]

The result is that there is a constant back-and-forth between the executive branch and the *Contraloría*.[166] One case study that illustrates the institutional strength of the *Contraloría* and the high level of respect that presidents have given it is the case of the *decreto de insistencia* ("decree of insistence"). As described earlier, the *Contraloría* can reject a decree because it is either unconstitutional or illegal. Whereas unconstitutional decrees contravene some aspect of the constitution, illegal decrees contravene *a law or a regulation* (that is not part of the constitution). If a decree is ruled unconstitutional by the *Contraloría*, there is no legal means

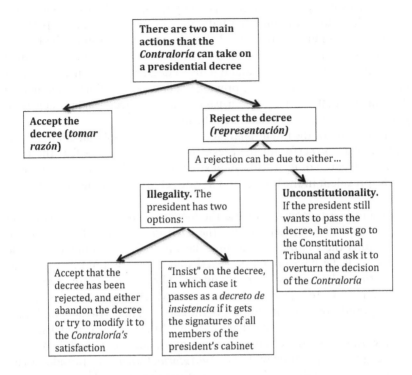

Figure 2.3 The acceptance/rejection of a decree by the *Contraloría*.

of appeal other than the Constitutional Tribunal. Note that in practice, Chilean presidents in recent history (as of 2017) have never appealed a decision ruled unconstitutional by the *Contraloría* to the Constitutional Tribunal (despite the fact that the *Contraloría* regularly declares decrees unconstitutional).[167] Similarly, in an interview with Juan José Romero Guzmán, a Minister on the Constitutional Tribunal, he claimed that in all the years he has been on the court, he has never seen such a case.[168] Nevertheless, if a decree is rejected because of illegality, then the president has a tool at his disposal called the *decreto de insistencia* where he can "insist" that the decree be passed. If the president obtains the signatures of all members of his cabinet, a decree ruled illegal by the *Contraloria* is allowed to go through.

On the surface, the *decreto de insistencia* would seem to be a useful tool for Chilean presidents who may be at odds with the *Contraloría* over certain decrees. Nevertheless, as several interviewees noted, as of 2017, this decree was used *only once* since the return of democracy.[169] This one time was under Aylwin in the early 1990s, when he wanted to fire the president of a state university, yet she refused to leave. Aylwin then signed a decree which was subsequently rejected as being illegal by the *Contraloría*, yet Aylwin chose to insist, and eventually the university president left office.

Soto in an interview recounted that, in March of 2010 (while he was serving as the head of the juridico-legislative division), a minister called him and explained that he wanted to use a decree of insistence given that the *Contraloría* had ruled the previous decree illegal. Soto explained to the minister that the decree of insistence had not been used for nearly 20 years, and the minister abandoned the idea.

One reason for the intentional lack of usage of a tool that could potentially be very powerful for the president is that executives fear the *Contraloría*. Because of its institutional strength, it is able to cause problems for the president in the future, and as Soto claimed in an interview:

> There is a reason not to use the [decree of insistence]. This would mean pitting yourself against the *Contraloría*. Nobody wants to go against the *Contraloría* because the *Contraloría* can make your life difficult. Perhaps not on this particular decree, but in future decrees or through the mechanism of audits....The *Contraloría* receives thousands of decrees from the government, which are reviewed ex ante as opposed to ex post on the part of the courts. There is a lot of dialogue. The *Contraloría* may say that a certain phrase is illegal, and discusses it with the executive. Things are not black and white, and there is the need for cooperation with the *Contraloría*. Otherwise, presidents run the risk of retaliation [on the part of the *Contraloría*].[170]

This sentiment is echoed by Professor Ivan Obando, who argues that "if the *Contraloría* rules that a decree is illegal, the president can insist, but will suffer the consequences of a political crisis and a possible impeachment."[171] As the head of the *Contraloría* Jorge Bermúdez described in an interview, "in such a legalistic country [as Chile], [insisting on an illegal decree] does not look good."[172]

The only time in modern history when decrees of insistence were truly abused was during the Allende presidency. In this period, there was significant antagonism between Allende and the *Contraloría*, with the body ruling many of his decrees illegal. To get around the *Contraloría*, Allende used the decree of insistence to force them through. Ultimately, the tension that existed between the *Contraloría* and Allende was one of the many factors that ultimately contributed to the coup against Allende. The head of the *Contraloría* Jorge Bermúdez describes that the negativity associated with the end of Allende's presidency is one reason why many presidents refrain from trying to bypass the *Contraloría*.[173]

In addition to fearing the *Contraloría* itself, presidents fear the congressional backlash that would result from defying the *Contraloría*. Presidents who are perceived as trying to skip over the *Contraloría* can be seen as tyrannical and may be subject to a constitutional accusation, in which they or their ministers risk impeachment.[174] Since democratization, there have never been moments of strong antagonism between the *Contraloría* and the executive.

In addition to decrees of insistence, there are many other decree types that the president has not abused, and the *Contraloría* deserves significant credit for this. The first is the *decreto con fuerza de ley* in which congress gives the president the power to enact decrees in certain delimited areas. This has some resemblance to the *superpoderes* in Argentina, but has not been abused by presidents. Another type of decree is regulatory decrees to implement laws that have already been passed by congress. The third type of decree common in Chile is the administrative decree (*decreto de reglamento autónomo*), which concerns matters within the executive branch (e.g., the hiring and firing of presidential staff). The fourth type of decree that empowers the president in Chile is the *decreto de emergencia económica* ("economic emergency decree"), which allows him/her during a period of emergency to spend money that is not authorized in the budget (Article 32/20: "public calamities, external aggression, internal commotion, grave harm or danger to the national security or the exhaustion of resources designated to maintain services which cannot be paralyzed without serious detriment to the country"). Note, however, that as described earlier, this emergency spending cannot exceed 2% of the total expenditures in the budget. All of these types of decrees are overseen by the *Contraloría*, which ensures that the president does not overstep his/her authority.

Recently, there have also been several high-profile cases in which the *Contraloría* served as a check on the executive branch through the auditory mechanism. Bermúdez for example discussed the case of a presidential project called the "20 20 20" hospital plan where the Health Ministry wanted to have 20 new hospitals built, 20 under construction, and 20 in planning. The project involved a bidding process for construction companies, yet in several instances, this project was done poorly; the *Contraloría* blocked these projects, and they were not undertaken. Another example of a case where the *Contraloría* went against the president is an audit that it conducted within the Ministry of Finance related to *Codelco*, the state-owned copper company.[175]

The Ability of the Central Bank to Resist Presidential Pressure

Earlier in this chapter, I described how the Argentine central bank, despite its legal mandate for price stability, was successfully pressured by the president to pursue an expansionist monetary policy, causing significant long-term inflation. This has not been the case in Chile.

Since the return to democracy, the central bank has often been at odds with the elected administrations, yet unlike in Argentina where presidents encroached upon the independence of the institution, the Chilean

Central Bank was able to resist pressure from the executive branch. Boy-lan in her book describes some of the conflicts that occurred between the Central Bank and various administrations when she writes:

> The manifest tension between the policy objectives of democratic governments and the autonomy of the central bank is further revealed by looking at the nature of various conflicts that arose between the two over the course of the 1990s...While [Central Bank President] Zahler wanted to keep interest rates at their currently high levels, [Finance Minister] Aninat urged the central bank to ease its relentlessly tight monetary policy to facilitate renewed growth...The Frei government felt inordinately restricted by the central bank in its ability to pursue a more aggressive growth-oriented policy agenda. But perhaps the best support in favor of the argument that the central bank legislation was a constraint on incoming governments is the fact that dissatisfaction with its contents persisted well into democratic rule.[176]

The Lack of Variation in Presidential Power in Chile

In the discussion of Argentina, I described how the country has experienced some variation in terms of presidential power in practice. I attributed this variation to the differing size of the president's party in congress; whereas Peronist presidents often had strong working majorities in congress that permitted them to concentrate power, non-Peronist presidents did not benefit from unified government. In Chile, there has been significantly less variation in presidential power over time, as there have been few changes in my three independent variables. Chile since democratization has always had strong institutions and has never experienced a sharp economic contraction; similarly, as I will discuss in Chapter 4, presidents have *never* held party majorities in Chile since 1990. Given that there has been little variation in Chile on the three independent variables that I will introduce in the following three chapters, it should not be a surprise that there has also been little variation in presidential power in practice.

Summary

In this part, I have tried to demonstrate how whereas Chilean presidents on paper have significant power, in practice presidents have been remarkably constrained. The difference between presidential power in theory versus in practice in Chile is neatly summarized by Soto, who claimed that:

> Formally, in Chile the president has very strong powers. However, in practice these powers are significantly reduced for two reasons.

First, there are many tools in the constitution that although they seem strong, are not very efficient. Urgencies are an obvious example, since although they seem strong, they are in reality not that powerful. Second, the way politics is done in Chile is through consensus and dialog. No president wants to have a confrontation with congress...Chile is balanced between the president and congress through informal means. I worked intimately for a president and ministers, and members of parliament had power. They would call you on the telephone and you had to reply. They would ask you for something and you had to do it. Fundamentally, they have power to threaten, to prevent, and to annoy.[177]

President Aylwin appropriately referred to the Chilean style of cooperation between the different branches of government as "the politics of consensus" (*la política del consenso*).[178] At the end of the interview, Soto reiterated the difference between presidential power in theory versus on paper and stated that the perspective of someone on Chilean presidential power

depends on whether that person is speaking based on political experience or based on textbooks. If that person makes the claim based on textbooks it is pure theory. In Chile, constitutionalists write from the stratosphere. They say that Chile is hyperpresidential, but when you look at the real world, things change.[179]

Similarly, José Luis Cea described that "political life often alters constitutional features. A constitution could say something, but political behavior could lead to completely different situations."[180]

Chapter Summary

In short, in this chapter, I have attempted to illustrate how while Argentina has been a case of hyperpresidentialism, in Chile, presidents were constrained. I began my discussions of Argentina and Chile with a description of constitutional presidential powers (i.e., presidential powers in theory). I then discussed how much power presidents wielded in practice, and this greatly differed from what one would expect based on an analysis of the text of the constitution. Whereas Argentine presidents in theory have been significantly constrained by the constitutions, as I tried to show, for a significant part of the post-democratization period, Peronist presidents acted in a hyperpresidential manner. On the other hand, whereas theoretically Chilean presidents are less constrained by the constitution, they have been restrained in practice.

In this chapter, I have conducted not only a comparison between Argentina and Chile but have also tried to analyze the variation across time within Argentina. While the Legislative Constraints on the Executive and

Judicial Constraints on the Executive data by Varieties of Democracy show that Argentina has consistently been more hyperpresidential than Chile since the return of democracy, there has been significant fluctuation in Argentina over time. I concluded that most of the intra-country variation comes from changes in the second independent variable, the size of the president's party in congress (the other two variables exhibit significantly less variation).

In the next three chapters, I will explore how these three independent variables operated in both Argentina and Chile. I will show in Chapter 3 how Argentine institutions exhibited significant weakness since democratization, whereas Chilean institutions have been remarkably strong. I will then elaborate in Chapter 4 on how Argentine Peronist presidents for many years in the post-democratization period have enjoyed working majorities in congress, whereas Chilean presidents have never held party majorities. Afterward in Chapter 5, I will explain how Argentina since democratization has been significantly more plagued by economic crises than Chile.

Notes

1 Galan 2015; p.264.
2 Snyder and Samuels 2004.
3 Elias 2015; p.24.
4 Law 23774 of 1990 and Law 26183 of 2006 affected the size of the Supreme Court. For a listing of members, see Corte Suprema in the "References" section.
5 Constitution of Argentina.
6 Jones 1997; p.285.
7 Author's interview with Ricardo Barrios Arrechea (Ex-Governor of the Province of Misiones, 1983–1987, and Federal Deputy during the 1990s).
8 Eaton 2002; p.253.
9 Author's interview with Martín Maquieyra (Federal Deputy, PRO).
10 Llanos 2002; p.20.
11 Carey and Shugart 1998; p.14.
12 Jones 1997; p.285.
13 Author's interview with Javier Zelaznik (Professor specializing in legislative politics).
14 Chavez 2004a; p.70.
15 Author's interview with Delia Ferreira Rubio (Lawyer and scholar with a deep knowledge of Necessity and Urgency Decrees).
16 Rubio and Goretti 1998; p.52.
17 Rubio and Goretti 1998; p.58.
18 Rubio and Goretti 1998; p.40.
19 Rubio and Goretti 1998; pp.48–49.
20 Rubio and Goretti 1998; p.45.
21 Rubio and Goretti 1998; p.47.
22 Rubio and Goretti 1998; p.48.
23 Rubio and Goretti 1998; p.36.
24 Author's interview with Luciana Díaz Frers (a high-ranking member of the *Auditoría*).

25 *Chequeado* September 28, 2012 (the article cites Delia Ferrira Rubio).
26 Santiso 2008; p.254.
27 Jones 2001; p.162.
28 Chavez 2004a; p.68.
29 Jones 1997; p.288.
30 Author's interview with Ángel Rozas (Senator and ex-governor of Chaco, UCR).
31 Author's interview with Ángel Rozas (Senator and ex-governor of Chaco, UCR).
32 Author's interview with Alfonso Prat Gay (Former Federal Deputy).
33 Author's interview with Luis Pastori (Federal Deputy (Misiones), UCR).
34 Interview with Senator Abal Medina (Senator and Former Chief of Cabinet of Ministers for President Cristina Kirchner).
35 Author's interview with Orlando Gallo (Ex. Federal Judge in Mercedes Province during the military period, ex-Federal Deputy 1991–1995 (Party: Movimiento para la Dignidad y la Independencia)).
36 Author's interview with Juan Manuel Abal Medina (Senator and Former Chief of Cabinet of Ministers for President Cristina Kirchner).
37 Author's interview with Juan Manuel Abal Medina (Senator and Former Chief of Cabinet of Ministers for President Cristina Kirchner).
38 Author's interview with Delia Ferreira Rubio (Lawyer and scholar with a deep knowledge of Necessity and Urgency Decrees).
39 Author's interview with Miguel Iturrieta (Ex-Deputy for Misiones 2005–2009, PJ-FPV bloc).
40 Author's interview with Miguel Iturrieta (Ex-Deputy for Misiones 2005–2009, PJ-FPV bloc).
41 Author's interview with Miguel Iturrieta (Ex-Deputy for Misiones 2005–2009, PJ-FPV bloc).
42 Author's interview with Miguel Iturrieta (Ex-Deputy for Misiones 2005–2009, PJ-FPV bloc).
43 Author's interview with Mario Barletta (Federal Deputy (Santa Fe), ex-president of the UCR, 2011–2013).
44 Author's interview with Mario Barletta (Federal Deputy (Santa Fe), ex-president of the UCR (2011–2013)).
45 Larkins 1998; p.434.
46 Helmke 2005; p.135.
47 Larkins 1998; p.434.
48 Supreme Court of Argentina *Peralta* Decision; p.1515.
49 Supreme Court of Argentina *Peralta* Decision; p.1515.
50 Chavez 2004a; p.47 (This provides an excellent account of specifically how the court violated the rule of law to benefit Menem).
51 Larkins 1998; p.430.
52 Chavez 2004a; pp.47–48.
53 Helmke 2005; p.147.
54 Larkins 1998; p.429.
55 Author's interview with Germán Bordón (Lawyer and UCR Deputy in the Misiones Provincial Legislature, *Cámara de Representantes*).
56 *La Arena* April 26, 2013.
57 *La Nación* April 26, 2013.
58 *Clarín* June 18, 2013.
59 Author's interview with Germán Garavano (Justice Minister of Argentina).
60 Author's interview with Matteo Goretti (Political scientist who coauthored a piece on decrees with Delia Ferreira Rubio).
61 Roehrig 2009; p.732.

62 *The Economist* September 4, 2003.
63 Roehrig 2009; p.738.
64 Author's interview with Juan Carlos Neves (A retired member of the navy, and secretary-general of the political party, *Nueva Unión Ciudadana*).
65 Jacobs 2003; p.402.
66 International Law Office. April 25, 2003.
67 Jacobs 2003; p.394.
68 Smulovitz 2006; p.72.
69 See notably Eaton 2002 and Calvo 2014.
70 Levitsky 2005; p.80.
71 Helmke 2003; p.223.
72 Llanos 2001; p.96.
73 Eaton 2002; pp.130–131.
74 Larkins 1998; p.426.
75 Author's interview with Matteo Goretti (Political scientist who coauthored a piece on decrees with Delia Ferreira Rubio).
76 Author's interview with Matteo Goretti (Political scientist who coauthored a piece on decrees with Delia Ferreira Rubio).
77 Constitution of Argentina Section 99 Article 7.
78 *USA Today* April 1, 2014.
79 Siavelis 2002; p.84.
80 Siavelis 2002; p.95.
81 Constitution of Chile Article 62 Section 6.
82 Siavelis 2000.
83 Nef et al. 1995; p.118.
84 Author's interview with Francisca Moya (Employee in the Ministry General Secretariat of the Presidency which is responsible for the relation between the executive and legislative branches).
85 Author's interview with Felipe de Mussy (National Deputy, UDI).
86 Author's interview with Valeria Palanza (Professor specializing in presidential decrees in Latin America).
87 Author's interview with Luis Cordero (Lawyer and expert on the *Contraloría*).
88 Author's interview with Luis Cordero (Lawyer and expert on the *Contraloría*).
89 Author's interview with Jorge Bermúdez (Head of the *Contraloría* in Chile).
90 Constitution of Chile, Article 63, subsection 20.
91 Author's interview with Francisca Moya (Employee in the Ministry General Secretariat of the Presidency (which is responsible for the relation between the executive and legislative branches)).
92 Author's interview with Rodrigo Egaña (National Director of the Civil Service).
93 Author's interview with Miguel Angel Fernández (Professor and Director of the Public Law Department at the Pontificia Universidad Católica de Chile).
94 Author's interview with Carlos Carmona (Minister on the Constitutional Tribunal of Chile).
95 For example, this was discussed in the author's interview with Sebastián Soto (Head of the Juridical Legislative Division during the previous Piñera administration).
96 Author's interview with José Luis Cea (Former Minister of the Constitutional Tribunal).
97 Figueroa 2013; p.397.
98 Author's interview with Luis Cordero (Lawyer and expert on the *Contraloría*).
99 Author's interview with Mario Venegas (National Deputy, Christian Democrat).
100 Author's interview with Fernando Paulsen (Journalist and TV presenter).

101 Author's interview with Pablo Ruiz-Tagle (Specialist in Constitutional Law).
102 Author's interview with Gaspar Rivas (National Deputy, Independent).
103 Author's interview with José Luis Cea (Former Minister of the Constitutional Tribunal).
104 Author's interview with José Luis Cea (Former Minister of the Constitutional Tribunal).
105 Author's interview with José Luis Cea (Former Minister of the Constitutional Tribunal).
106 Author's interview with Mario Venegas (National Deputy, Christian Democrat).
107 Author's interview with Rodrigo Egaña (National Director of the Civil Service).
108 See Articles 48 and 49 of the Constitution.
109 Author's interview with Gaspar Rivas (National Deputy, Independent).
110 Siavelis 2006; p.49.
111 Author's interview with Guillermo Pattillo (Associate Director (*subdirector*) of DIPRES during the previous Piñera administration (DIPRES is the executive organ charged with drafting the budget)).
112 Author's interview with Raúl Letelier (Professor specializing in Public Law).
113 Author's interview with Raúl Letelier (Professor specializing in Public Law).
114 Author's interview with Rodrigo Egaña (National Director of the Civil Service).
115 Author's interview with Fernando Paulsen (Journalist and TV presenter).
116 Author's interview with a Deputy who desired to remain anonymous (their ideology is to the right of the political spectrum).
117 Author's interview with Patricio Walker (National Senator (ex-president of the Chamber of Deputies, and ex-president of the Senate), Christian Democrat).
118 Siavelis 2002; p.96.
119 Author's interview with Felipe De Mussy (National Deputy, UDI).
120 Siavelis 2002; p.96.
121 Arbelaez and Tanaka 2012; p.361.
122 Author's interview with Mario Venegas (National Deputy, Christian Democrat).
123 Author's interview with Sebastián Soto (Head of the Juridical Legislative Division during the previous Piñera administration).
124 Author's interview with Patricio Walker (National Senator).
125 Author's interview with Francisca Moya (Employee in the Ministry General Secretariat of the Presidency).
126 Author's interview with Valeria Palanza (Professor specializing in presidential decrees in Latin America).
127 Author's interview with Fernando Paulsen (Journalist and TV presenter).
128 Author's interview with Carlos Huneeus (Professor specializing in Chilean politics).
129 Author's interview with Alejandro Olivares (Professor and Political Scientist).
130 *The Wall Street Journal* September 11, 2014.
131 Huber and Stephens 2012; p.182.
132 *Reuters* April 27, 2016.
133 Author's interview with Francisca Moya (Employee in the Ministry General Secretariat of the Presidency).
134 *Voa News* July 6, 2016.

135 *La Nación* November 22, 2007.
136 *Buenos Aires Herald* December 26, 2015.
137 *Reuters* October 21, 2014.
138 *NACLA* March 3, 2015.
139 *Buenos Aires Herald* May 30, 2015.
140 *Buenos Aires Herald* December 26, 2015.
141 Author's interview with Lucas Sierra (Vice president of the think tank, *Centro de Estudios Publicos*, CEP).
142 Author's interview with Alejandro Olivares (Professor and Political Scientist).
143 *Reuters* August 10, 2016.
144 *Reuters* April 13, 2017.
145 Author's interview with Ivan Obando (Professor specializing in Public Law and Political Science).
146 Author's interview with Sebastián Soto (Head of the Juridical Legislative Division during the previous Piñera administration).
147 Author's interview with Patricio Walker (National Senator (ex-president of the Chamber of Deputies, and ex-president of the Senate), Christian Democrat).
148 Author's interviews with Carlos Carmona and with Lucas Sierra.
149 Prillaman 2000; p.146.
150 Helmke 2005; p.164.
151 Fiss 1993; p.75.
152 Fiss 1993; p.76.
153 Barros 2004; p.98.
154 Barros 2004; p.101.
155 Author's interview with José Luis Cea (Former Minister of the Constitutional Tribunal).
156 Author's interview with José Luis Cea (Former Minister of the Constitutional Tribunal).
157 Barros 2004; p.299.
158 Barros 2004; p.302.
159 Barros 2004; p.302.
160 Author's interview with Luis Cordero (Lawyer and expert on the *Contraloría*).
161 Barros 2004; p.111.
162 *Diario Uchile* April 18, 2015.
163 Author's interview with Pablo Ruiz-Tagle (Specialist in Constitutional Law).
164 Author's interview with Alicia De La Cruz (Specialist on the Chilean *Contraloría*).
165 Author's interview with Alicia De La Cruz (Specialist on the Chilean *Contraloría*).
166 Author's interview with Luis Cordero; this informal process is also corroborated in an interview with Ruiz-Tagle.
167 Author's interview with Jorge Bermúdez (Head of the *Contraloría* in Chile).
168 Author's interview with Juan José Romero Guzmán (Minister on the Constitutional Tribunal).
169 Author's interview with Rodrigo Egaña (National Director of the Civil Service) and author's interview with Sebastián Soto (Head of the Juridical Legislative Division during the previous Piñera administration).
170 Author's interview with Sebastián Soto (Head of the Juridical Legislative Division during the previous Piñera administration).
171 Author's interview with Ivan Obando (Professor specializing in Public Law and Political Science).

172 Author's interview with Jorge Bermúdez (Head of the *Contraloría* in Chile).
173 Author's interview with Jorge Bermúdez (Head of the *Contraloría* in Chile).
174 Author's interview with Alicia De La Cruz (Specialist on the Chilean *Contraloría*).
175 Author's interview with Jorge Bermúdez (Head of the *Contraloría* in Chile).
176 Boylan 2001; p.130.
177 Author's interview with Sebastián Soto (Head of the Juridical Legislative Division during the previous Piñera administration).
178 Author's interviews with Sebastián Soto and with Francisca Moya.
179 Author's interview with Sebastián Soto (Head of the Juridical Legislative Division during the previous Piñera administration).
180 Author's interview with José Luis Cea (Former Minister of the Constitutional Tribunal).

Bibliography

Arbelaez, Harvey, and Rie Tanaka. "Opacity in Latin America: Argentina and Chile: A Case Study Comparison." *Transparency and Governance in a Global World.* Eds. Jay Choi and Heibatollah Sami. Bingley: Emerald Group Publishing Limited, 2012, pp. 337–377.

Barros, Robert. *Constitutionalism and Dictatorship: Pinochet, the Junta, and the 1980 Constitution.* Cambridge: Cambridge University Press, 2004.

Berbecel, Dan. "The Politics of Policy Stability: Explaining the Levels of Volatility in Economic Policymaking in Argentina and Brazil between 1990 and 2010." *Canadian Journal of Latin American and Caribbean Studies/Revue canadienne des études latino- américaines et caraïbes.* Vol 43, Iss 1 (2018), pp. 18–46.

Boylan, Delia. *Defusing Democracy: Central Bank Autonomy and the Transition from Authoritarian Rule.* Ann Arbor: The University of Michigan Press, 2001.

Carey, John, and Matthew Shugart. *Executive Decree Authority.* Cambridge: Cambridge University Press, 1998.

Chavez, Rebecca Bill. *The Rule of Law in Nascent Democracies: Judicial Politics in Argentina.* Stanford: Stanford University Press, 2004.

Chilean Chamber of Deputies. Acusasiones Constitucionales Finalizadas.

Corte Suprema. Listado Histórico de Ministros.

Eaton, Kent. *Politicians and Economic Reform in New Democracies: Argentina and the Philippines in the 1990s.* University Park: The Pennsylvania State University, 2002.

Elias, José Sebastián. "Judges and Democracy in Argentina: An Elite in Search of Legitimacy." *Fair Reflection of Society in Judicial Systems-A Comparative Study.* Ed. Sophie Turenne. Cham: Springer, 2015, pp. 23–40.

Figueroa, Dante. "Constitutional Review in Chile Revisited: A Revolution in the Making." *Duquesne Law Review.* Vol 51 (Spring 2013), pp. 387–419.

Fiss, Owen. "The Limits of Judicial Independence." *The University of Miami Inter-American Law Review.* Vol 25, Iss 1 (Fall 1993), pp. 57–76.

Galan, Alejandra Rodriguez. "Judicial Rulings with Prospective Effect in Argentina." *Comparing the Prospective Effect of Judicial Rulings Across Jurisdictions.* Ed. Eva Steiner. Cham: Springer International Publishing, 2015, pp. 263–284.

Helmke, Gretchen. "Checks and Balances by Other Means: Strategic Defection and the 'Re-Reelection' Controversy in Argentina." *Comparative Politics*. Vol 35, Iss 2 (2003), pp. 213–228.

Helmke, Gretchen. *Courts Under Constraints: Judges, Generals, and Presidents in Argentina*. Cambridge: Cambridge University Press, 2005.

Huber, Evelyne, and John Stephens. *Democracy and the Left: Social Policy and Inequality in Latin America*. Chicago: The University of Chicago Press, 2012.

Jacobs, Becky. "Pesification and Economic Crisis in Argentina: The Moral Hazard Posed by a Politicized Supreme Court." *The University of Miami Inter-American Law Review*. Vol 34, No 3 (Summer 2003), pp. 391–434.

Jones, Mark. "Evaluating Argentina's Presidential Democracy: 1983–1995." *Presidentialism and Democracy in Latin America*. Eds. Scott Mainwaring and Matthew Shugart. Cambridge: Cambridge University Press, 1997, pp. 259–299.

Jones, Mark. "Political Institutions and Public Policy in Argentina." *Presidents, Parliaments and Policy*. Eds. Stephan Haggard and Mathew McCubbins. Cambridge: Cambridge University Press, 2001, pp. 149–182.

Larkins, Christopher. "The Judiciary and Delegative Democracy in Argentina." *Comparative Politics*. Vol 30, No 4 (July 1998), pp. 423–442.

Levitsky, Steven. "Argentina: Democratic Survival amidst Economic Failure." *The Third Wave of Democratization in Latin America*. Eds. Frances Hagopian and Scott Mainwaring. Cambridge: Cambridge University Press, 2005, pp. 63–89.

Llanos, Mariana. "Understanding Presidential Power in Argentina: A Study of the Policy of Privatisation in the 1990s." *Journal of Latin American Studies*. Vol 33, Iss 1 (February 2001), pp. 67–99.

Llanos, Mariana. *Privatization and Democracy in Argentina: An Analysis of President-Congress Relations*. New York: Palgrave, 2002.

Nef, Jorge, and Nibaldo Galleguillos. "Legislatures and Democratic Transitions in Latin America: The Chilean Case." *Legislatures and the New Democracies in Latin America*. Ed. David Close. Boulder: Lynne Rienner, 1995, pp. 113–136.

Payne, J. Mark. "Balancing Executive and Legislative Prerogatives: The Role of Constitutional and Party-Based Factors." *Democracies in Development: Politics and Reform in Latin American Countries*. Eds. J. Mark Payne, Daniel Zovatto, and Mercedes Mateo Díaz. Washington, DC: Inter-American Development Bank, 2007, pp. 81–116.

Prillaman, William. *The Judiciary and Democratic Decay in Latin America: Declining Confidence in the Rule of Law*. Westport: Praeger, 2000.

Roehrig, Terence. "Executive Leadership and the Continuing Quest for Justice in Argentina." *Human Rights Quarterly*. Vol 31, No 3 (August 2009), pp. 721–747.

Rubio, Delia, and Matteo Goretti. "When the President Governs Alone: The Decretazo in Argentina, 1989–93." *Executive Decree Authority*. Eds. John Carey and Matthew Shugart. Cambridge: University of Cambridge, 1998, pp. 33–61.

Rubio, Delia Ferreira, and Matteo Goretti. "Executive-Legislative Relationship in Argentina: From Menem's Decretazo to a New style?" Annual Conference, Argentina 2000: Politics, Economy, Society and International Relations. Oxford. May 15–17, 2000.

Santiso, Carlos. "Keeping a Watchful Eye? Parliaments and the Politics of Budgeting in Latin America." *Legislative Oversight and Budgeting: A World*

Perspective. Eds. Rick Stapenhurst, Riccardo Pelizzo, David Olson, and Lisa von Trapp. Washington, DC: The World Bank, 2008, pp. 243–266.

Siavelis, Peter. *The President and Congress in Postauthoritarian Chile: Institutional Constraints to Democratic Consolidation.* University Park: The Pennsylvania State Univesrity Press, 2000.

Siavelis, Peter. "Exaggerated Presidentialism and Moderate Presidents: Executive-Legislative Relations in Chile." *Legislative Politics in Latin America.* Eds. Scott Morgenstern and Benito Nacif. Cambridge: Cambridge University Press, 2002, pp. 79–113.

Siavelis, Peter. "Accommodating Informal Institutions and Chilean Democracy." *Informal Institutions and Democracy: Lessons from Latin America.* Eds. Gretchen Helmke and Steven Levitsky. Baltimore: The Johns Hopkins University Press, 2006, pp. 33–55.

Smulowitz, Catalina. "Judicialization of Protest in Argentina: The Case of Corralito." *Enforcing the Rule of Law: Social Accountability in the New Latin American Democracies.* Eds. Enrique Peruzzotti and Catalina Smulovitz. Pittsburgh: University of Pittsburgh Press, 2006, pp. 55–74.

Snyder, Richard, and David Samuels. "Legislative Malapportionment in Latin America: Historical and Comparative Perspectives." *Federalism and Democracy in Latin America.* Ed. Edward Gibson. Baltimore: The Johns Hopkins University Press, 2004, pp. 131–172.

Supreme Court of Argentina. Luis Arcenio Peralta y Otro v. Nacion Argentina (Supreme Court Decision Opinion). December 27, 1990, pp. 1513–1564.

3 The Impact of the Strength of State Institutions on Presidential Power

The first independent variable that is at play in determining the degree of presidential power in practice and the emergence of hyperpresidentialism is the differing levels of the strength of state institutions. In this chapter, I will contrast the strength of state institutions in Chile to their weakness in Argentina; whereas in Chile these institutions ensure that the president does not exceed his/her constitutional powers, in Argentina these institutions have failed to fulfill their mandates to restrain executive abuses. In Part I, I will begin with an analysis of the five most important institutions in Argentina that are theoretically supposed to constrain presidential power (yet fail to do so in practice). In Part II, I will discuss six important Chilean institutions that have shown considerable strength and an ability to restrict presidential power.

One of the critical issues that I wanted to address before beginning this chapter is that there is a fine line between this first independent variable, institutional strength, and my dependent variable, presidential power in practice. For example, a discussion of the historical lack of independence of the judiciary from the executive branch could at the same time be interpreted to describe both the weakness of the judiciary as an institution and the strength of the president. Similarly, a discussion of how congress rubber-stamped executive proposals in Argentina could be interpreted in terms of either the institutional weakness of congress or as one of the examples of hyperpresidentialism in the country. Given this issue, I want to explicitly detail how I differentiate between institutional weakness and presidential power (and by extension between Chapter 2 which discussed the dependent variable, presidential power, and this chapter which will discuss the independent variable, institutional strength).

For the purposes of this book, my understanding of the dependent variable, presidential power, is *limited specifically to an analysis of the degree to which presidents were "checked" by institutions of horizontal accountability.* In Chapter 2, I included a comprehensive discussion of how congress and the judiciary in Argentina often rubber-stamped presidential proposals, whereas in Chile, these institutions put up significantly more resistance. On the other hand, in the discussion of my first independent variable, institutional strength, that is to follow in this chapter,

DOI: 10.4324/9781003142904-3

the emphasis *will not be on analyzing instances in which presidents were "checked" by these institutions.* Rather, the emphasis will be limited to studying the intrinsic strength/weakness of these individual institutions. *Although it is a fine line, the strength/weakness of an institution is a different concept from whether or not it checks presidential power.*

In this chapter when discussing state institutions, I analyze four primary factors: the prestige of these institutions in society, the degree of independence of these institutions from the executive branch (i.e., whether these institutions were packed with allies of the president), the technical capacity of these institutions (e.g., whether or not they are properly staffed and whether they have the funds to perform their duties), and the degree to which the institution respects established rules and norms. These are all indicators of institutional strength. Notably, in this chapter, I will *not* go into significant detail about the degree to which these institutions actually restrained presidents. For example, in my discussion of the judiciary, whereas in this chapter I will discuss how Argentine courts have suffered from court-packing attempts and lacked independence from the executive branch, I do not go into detail about their rubber-stamping of presidential proposals. Whereas the court-packing in Argentina illustrates institutional weakness and is thus part of the realm of my first independent variable that will be discussed in this chapter, how this court-packing translated into restrictions (or lack of restrictions) on the actual behavior president was already highlighted in my discussion of the dependent variable in Chapter 2. To elaborate further, the distinction is that whereas a weak court that lacks independence because it was packed by the president is likely to rubber-stamp presidential proposals, in theory this court could still fulfill its constitutional duty and restrain presidential power. While Chapter 2 focused on the latter part (the degree to which institutions actually restrained presidential power), this chapter will focus on the former (the degree to which the institution is strong or weak).

Exploring the Causal Relationship Between the Dependent Variable in Chapter 2 and the First Independent Variable in Chapter 3

It is my hope that by the end of this chapter it will be clear why the diverging outcomes in terms of presidential power in Argentina and Chile (identified in Chapter 2) are related to the degree of institutional strength in a country. Institutions that possess characteristics such as independence from the executive branch, strong prestige in society, strong technical capacity, and a high degree of respect for established rules/norms are more likely to challenge the executive branch. Whereas a court with impartial judges will probably challenge an illegal decree by a president, a court where judges lack independence from the executive branch (for example, because of a history of court-packing) is more likely to act as a mere rubber stamp. Similarly, institutions that lack prestige in society will serve as significantly less of an impediment to a president than institutions that are highly respected. Prestige also involves the degree to which institutions *respect themselves*. For example, an institution led by individuals who believe in its mission will be in a stronger position to constrain the executive branch than an institution led by individuals who see the president as being above any established institutional

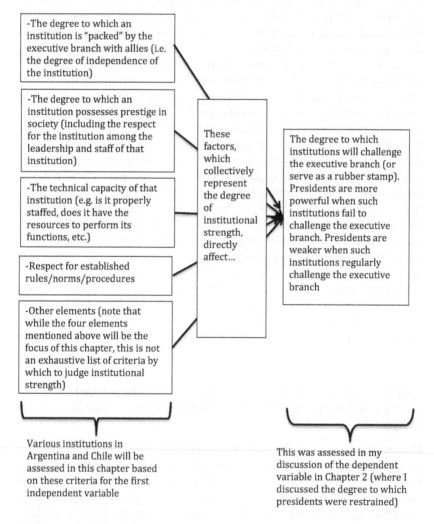

Figure 3.1 Operationalizing the variables and examining the relationship between the first independent variable, institutional strength, and the dependent variable, presidential power in practice.

norms. Additionally, institutions that have a higher technical capacity are in a stronger position to constrain presidential power than those with a weak technical capacity. By "technical capacity," I refer to whether or not an institution has the resources to carry out its main objectives. For example, does congress have the tools necessary to independently analyze a budget and verify the claims made by the president? Do legislators have the money to hire experts to study various pieces of legislation? Are institutions such as the Chilean *Contraloría* or the Argentine *Defensor del Pueblo* properly staffed? Finally, it is very difficult for the executive branch to go around institutions that adhere to longstanding rules and procedures; however, if rules/procedures are weak, it is easier for presidents to convince these institutions to "bend the rules."

I will use the above criteria (independence from the executive, prestige, technical capacity, and respect for established rules/norms) as the prism through which institutions in Argentina and Chile will be examined in this chapter. Note that this is not an exhaustive list of criteria by which to judge institutional strength. Figure 3.1 attempts to visually illustrate the relationship between this first independent variable and the dependent variable identified in Chapter 2.

Part I: Argentina—A Case of Severe Institutional Weakness

The main Argentine institutions whose weakness will be discussed in this part are congress, the judiciary, the *Auditoría General de la Nación* (AGN), the *Defensor del Pueblo* (DDP), and the Central Bank. Collectively, these institutions bear the main responsibility for checking executive power in the country.

Institutional Strength in Argentina in General

The most important numerical indicator illustrating that institutions are weak in Argentina is the score that the country received on the Corruption Perceptions Index (CPI). Ever since the CPI was first created in 1995, Argentina has performed poorly relative to other countries not only in the world but also in the region (though it notably improved under the Macri presidency). In Table 3.1, I note Argentina's score on this index since 1995, along with its global ranking.

The Judiciary

The Argentine judiciary has displayed significant institutional weakness since democratization. The popular narrative of the decline of the Argentine Supreme Court as an institution that defends the rule of law starts with Perón's purging of the body beginning in 1947. Nevertheless,

Table 3.1 Illustrating Argentina's weak
institutional capacity through
its low rankings on the
Corruption Perceptions Index[a]

Year	Score	Ranking
1995	5.24	24/41
1996	3.41	35/54
1997	2.81	42/52
1998	3.00	61/85
1999	3.00	71/99
2000	3.50	52/90
2001	3.50	57/91
2002	2.80	70/102
2003	2.50	92/133
2004	2.50	108/146
2005	2.80	97/159
2006	2.90	93/163
2007	2.90	105/180
2008	2.90	109/180
2009	2.90	106/180
2010	2.90	110/178
2011	3.00	100/183
2012	35	102/198
2013	34	106/198
2014	34	107/198
2015	32	106/198
2016	36	95/198
2017	39	85/198
2018	40	85/198
2019	45	66/198

[a]I would like to thank Elizabeth Sanchez
Flores for helping me compile this data

as Morgenstern and Manzetti describe, the actual decline of the Supreme
Court came earlier, following the 1930 coup:

> In Argentina, prior to the 1930 coup, the Supreme Court was gener-
> ally regarded as a rather professional and independent institution.
> Indeed, according to Miller 1997:232, between 1860 and 1929 the
> Court was a stabilizing political influence and a soother of political
> passions in a way that even the U.S. Supreme Court probably did
> not. Yet, the 1930 Argentine Supreme Court's decision to treat the
> authoritarian government created that year as one whose credentials
> could not be judicially questioned began to erode its prestige, as well
> as showing that the court was unwilling to counter executive abuse.[1]

The approval of the military coup by the Supreme Court can thus be considered the first major act since the 1853 constitution that weakened the

legitimacy of the body in the eyes of the population, as the Court essentially can be said to have abandoned its commitment to the rule of law.

The independence of the Supreme Court was further reduced as mentioned earlier in 1947 with the rise of Perón. As Gallo and Alston claim:

> After the impeachment of four out of five Supreme Court justices in 1947 and the subsequent new constitution in 1949, Argentina has never been able to return to cultivating a belief in a system of checks and balances...Successive military and civilian governments appointed their own Supreme Court justices in order to accomplish their political goals.[2]

Fast-forwarding to the post-democratization period, some argue that the Argentine judiciary between 1983 and 1989 was relatively clean and transparent. In his piece, Larkins claims that:

> Though not all-powerful, the Argentine judiciary that operated between 1983 and 1989 enjoyed notable degrees of impartiality and insularity and possessed fairly broad authority to regulate the legality of official acts. The Supreme Court was comprised of justices with diverse ideological and party backgrounds: having a homogenous court was not a top priority for President Alfonsín.[3]

Others disagree however that the Alfonsín Court was independent and nonpoliticized. Despite the high degree of professionalism of Alfonsín's Supreme Court appointees and the fact that the Court occasionally invalidated federal laws, some scholars suggest that the members of the Court did not come from both sides of the aisle and that the justices were either friends of Alfonsín, or anti-Peronists. Kapiszewski writes that:

> Concerning justices' ties to the sitting president or his party, one Alfonsín appointee was a close friend of the president, another was considered his 'man on the Court,' and most were strong anti-Peronists. Moreover, renowned Argentine legal scholar Carlos Nino has suggested that all were 'close friends of the administration.'[4]

Attempts to manipulate the Supreme Court became blatantly evident with President Menem's assent to power. Menem did not want to be bound by the previous judges chosen by Alfonsín and attempted to restructure the body as soon as he got to power. At first, he tried to offer both inducements and threats to the five sitting justices to resign. Among the inducements included ambassadorships and other prestigious posts, and among the threats included impeachment by the legislature. Nevertheless, at first, only Chief Justice Caballero chose to resign. Seeing that the other justices would not resign, Menem tried to expand the size of the court from five to nine. Menem decided to propose this as a bill in congress; Law 23,774 as it was called, passed quickly, although there were allegations of fraud in the voting process. Rubio and Goretti write that:

> The opposition protested alleged procedural irregularities in the study, floor debate, and approval of the bill with no success. The most serious charge was that when the vote took place, the Chamber of Deputies lacked a legal quorum. Radical Party representatives had decided not to stay on the floor. According to some reports electronic control devices that determine the existence of a quorum were turned on not by representatives but by imposters. There was no article-by-article vote on the bill, as Chamber rules required, and the bill was approved in its final form in only forty-two seconds.[5]

It is also notable that the above session during which impostors voted was intentionally scheduled to take place before dawn. Overall, Chavez concludes that "Menem used unconstitutional means to ensure the passage of the expansion law."[6]

Justice Bacque resigned to protest this attempt to destroy the independence of the judiciary. Helmke notes that the Peronist Senate rapidly approved the bill in September, and that although there was a delay in the Chamber of Deputies, the law ultimately passed in 1990. She also notes that there were numerous procedural irregularities:

> Following the passage of the bill, the opposition alleged that irregular procedures were used to get the bill through. For example, when the vote took place there was not a legal quorum present in the Chamber of Deputies.[7]

The quality of Menem's judges was extremely questionable. The first nominee, Julio Nazareno, was a justice on the Supreme Court of the province of La Rioja from which Menem originated, and had worked in Menem's law office. The second justice, Mariano Cavagna Martínez, was a close friend of Menem's brother, Eduardo Menem, and famously claimed "I am and always will be a Peronist." The third nominee, Rodolfo Barra, claimed that "my only two bosses are Perón and Menem." Antonio Boggiano was also appointed, and he had been one of Menem's advisors. Julio Oyhanarte was another one of Menem's appointees; he helped draft the government's response to *Acordada 44*. *Acordada 44* was the Supreme Court's official resolution that served as a denunciation of Menem's court-packing scheme, and Oyhanarte helped draft the Menem administration's rebuttal to the Court's criticism. Another justice Menem appointed, Eduardo O'Connor (the brother-in-law of one of Menem's advisors), had been the head of the Argentine Tennis Association, and his last publication in a legal journal had been in 1968 (over 20 years prior). Finally, Ricardo Levene had also been known for having deep ties to the PJ and served as an advisor to one of Menem's undersecretaries. Although congress in theory could have blocked Menem's candidates, Chavez notes the weakness of the body when she writes that:

> In order to ensure Senate approval of his nominees, Menem did not abide by a transparent selection process when he appointed four justices following his 1990 expansion of the Court. The speed of congressional proceedings impeded a thorough evaluation of the candidates. On April 18, 1990, only one day after announcing the expansion, Menem submitted his list of nominees to the PJ-controlled Senate. The two UCR representatives on the Senate Appointment Committee were absent from the hearing during which the PJ Committee members unanimously approved Menem's candidates. When the Committee's approval reached the floor, the Senate approved the list in a secret session only seven minutes long with no UCR senators in attendance.[8]

Another salient example of when congress broke procedural rules in order to help Menem further pack the court was the 1995 appointment of Adolfo Vázquez, a "close friend."[9] Chavez details what happened when she writes:

> The approval process for Vázquez lacked transparency and was replete with irregularities. By the time of the Vázquez appointment, the 1994 Constitution was in effect, which increased the Senate approval requirement for Supreme Court justices from a majority to two-thirds. Menem foresaw difficulties in securing the necessary two-thirds after December 10 when new opposition senators would take their seats. Thus, the PJ attempted to delay the entrance of UCR senators. When that strategy failed, the PJ violated Senate rules to rush the approval process. According to Senate rules, judicial nominees must be open for citizen consideration for seven days. The PJ violated this rule in order to hold the Senate vote before December 10.[10]

Larkins writes that immediately after Menem's appointment of the new justices, the Supreme Court began to overturn numerous legal precedents that had been unfavorable to the agenda of the government. The subservient nature of the Supreme Court which Menem had created is neatly encapsulated by an order that Menem gave to Vázquez after his appointment: "I selected you for your career, for your rulings, and especially for your position on cases against the state. Never allow the state to lose a case."[11] Indeed, the Menem court complied, and he rarely lost any significant cases before the Supreme Court during his tenure in office.

Menem's attempt to stack the judiciary was not limited solely to the Supreme Court. He was able to get four of the five members of the *Tribunal de Cuentas* to resign (the *Tribunal de Cuentas* was responsible for ruling on the legality of government expenditures). Menem also packed the Court of Cassation, and the scheme was so egregious that even Menem's own justice minister (Carlos Arlanián) resigned in protest.[12]

Although in the 1993 *Pacto de Olivos* Menem committed to improving the independence of the judiciary, this is questionable considering his appointment of Vázquez to the court in 1995.

More generally, after court-packing occurs in any country, this sets off a vicious cycle which leads to the long-term decline in capacity of this institution as a veto player. In other words, one act of court-packing will likely lead to more acts of court-packing in the following years. Political actors come to expect that the Supreme Court is not an independent institution, and they are thus incentivized to try to change its composition. Incoming presidents begin to believe that given the history of court-packing, it is their "natural right" to be able to select members of the High Court. At the beginning of his term, in response to criticism that he was trying to pack the court by expanding its size, Menem on a talk show argued, "why should I be the only president in fifty years who hasn't had his own court?" On the flip side, congress and other political actors do not have strong incentives to firmly oppose court-packing schemes in countries where this is perceived as the norm. Given that the composition of the court is so volatile, the opposition knows that when it comes to power eventually, it will be able to alter the Court in the opposite direction with the same ease as the current president. In other words, there is no point in using up political capital to fight to prevent the president from packing the court, given that there is no sense of permanence. In short, once court-packing occurs in a country (as was the case in Argentina after Perón's scheme), given the decreased prestige of the institution, it will be more likely that future political actors will modify the composition of the court, setting off a vicious cycle.

Nevertheless, in systems without any recent instances of court-packing, the opposite occurs, and it is precisely for this reason that there was such a high level of contention among US political actors in 2016 when a vacancy arose on the Supreme Court; unlike in Argentina, American political actors know that the composition of the Court is permanent.

After Néstor Kirchner assumed power, some of the most partisan judges either resigned or faced impeachment, and the judiciary did regain a certain level of independence. The size of the Court was gradually reduced back to its traditional size of five members (recall that Menem had expanded the court from five to nine members). It maintained seven members until 2014 when two judges retired, after which it reached its current legal composition of five. Unlike Menem, Kirchner did not select political cronies to the Supreme Court. Whereas some of Menem's judges lacked the necessary basic qualifications, the judges Kirchner chose were all qualified for the position. The current Justice Minister of Argentina, Germán Garavano in an interview described that "Kirchner tried to design a more serious court with a certain degree of independence and initially it functioned with a dose of independence."[13] Nevertheless, it is important to note that although Kirchner's court was substantially more qualified and independent than Menem's court, Néstor and Cristina Kirchner still enjoyed a "majority." For example, three of the five members of the current court (as of the time of writing of this book) were appointed by either Néstor Kirchner or Eduardo Duhalde (Ricardo Lorenzetti, Elena Highton de Nolasco, and Juan Carlos Maqueda). Garavano noted that during the Kirchner administrations "there was pressure from the government on the Supreme Court in various areas in order to try make the court functional and favorable [for the administration]."[14] On the surface, however, Kirchner's Supreme Court was certainly more serious than Menem's court, and as I noted in Chapter 2, there were a select few important decisions when the Supreme Court did rule against the government.

While the court-packing at the level of the Supreme Court has received the most attention (and for good reason), court-packing has also taken place in lower-level courts. Under the administration of Néstor Kirchner, a reform was made to the Council of Magistrates that increased the control of the executive branch over this body and weakened its independence. The reform was enacted in 2006 and decreased the size of the Council from 20 to 13 members; according to The Economist, this reform gave the executive a "veto."[15] President Kirchner effectively had a "veto" because out of these 13 appointees, the president controlled five, and as a result, he was in a position to deny a quorum for the deliberation of any judicial candidate unfriendly to the executive branch.[16] It is important to mention that while Néstor Kirchner was president when the law was passed, it was actually Cristina Kirchner who conceived of the project (she was a senator at the time).[17] This was a critical reform, since as mentioned earlier, the Council is responsible for the hiring and firing of the lower-level judiciary (although the president still nominates lower-level judges, he can only select from a shortlist proposed by the Council). The lower-level judiciary is critical since, like in the USA, federal judges can strike down or maintain federal laws, and this is especially important for presidential control in the area of administrative law. In an interview with Raúl Madueño, an ex-Federal Judge who served in the *Cámara Federal de Casación Penal* (he was part of the panel of judges who found Menem guilty in 2013 in a trial), he described that "what significantly helps to restrain the decisions of the executive in its role as an administrator is the contentious-administrative [part of the justice system]."[18] In addition to packing the lower-level judiciary with Kirchner loyalists, another effect of the changes on the Council of Magistrates was to silence unfriendly judges. Given that the Council can also remove judges, Justice Minister Garavano claimed that "this put pressure on the lower-level judiciary...There was an intention to imitate Venezuela under Chávez and Peru under Fujimori." Interim judges (*jueces interinos* or *jueces subrogantes*) were especially vulnerable to pressure from the executive, as a significantly lower threshold was required in the Council of Magistrates to impeach them (normally, a two-thirds majority is required to impeach a regular judge, but only a simple majority is required to impeach an interim judge). Controlling the lower-level judiciary was also important since these are generally the courts that investigate acts of corruption.

Even though Néstor Kirchner did partially increase the independence of the Supreme Court, this reform was undermined by his politicization of the lower-level courts, which ex-provincial deputy and lawyer Esteban Lozina calls "lamentable."[19] Similarly, Professor Ricardo Biazzi (the ex-Minister of Education of Argentina) claims that Kirchner's decision to influence the lower-level judiciary through the reform of the Council of Magistrates effectively annulled and "threw to the devil" all the positive advances made regarding the Supreme Court.[20]

In addition to the questionable independence of the Argentine judiciary at all levels, the Argentine judiciary is further undermined in its mission to enforce the rule of law by its extreme inefficiency. According to lawyer Germán Bordón:

> There are several cases that are being investigated based on complaints filed 8–10 years ago. A short time ago, there were even sentences handed out for crimes committed by employees of Menem who was president between 1989 and 1999. The problem of the justice system is one of the most lamentable problems [in Argentina], and the body does not fulfill its role as an institutional check.[21]

Congress

Congress is one of the institutions in Argentina which has encouraged hyperpresidentialism and failed to constrain leaders. In this section, I will justify why the Argentine congress is a weak institution and show how presidents have been able to concentrate power as a result of this weakness. I will characterize the Argentine congress as a body that lacks prestige and technical capacity, where resources are severely lacking, and where individual legislators have little influence.

One of the factors crippling the Argentine congress is the low reelection rate (only 20% in the Chamber of Deputies). There are three primary reasons why having a low reelection rate weakens the institutional capacity of any legislature. First, in the context of high turnover, there is simply no time for members of congress to develop the skills and experience necessary to be an effective legislator. Second, given that legislators will be in office for such a short period of time, they have no incentive to invest in congressional rules and procedures. Finally, if a legislator knows that his/her chances for reelection are slim, they have little incentive to perform well, since the ultimate reward, reelection, is off the table (they also face little punishment for poor performance).

The Argentine congress has also exhibited a strong lack of prestige that made it difficult to challenge presidents. There are several reasons for the lack of prestige of legislators. First, many Argentines do not know the names of the *diputados* representing them. *Diputados* are elected based on *listas sábanas* or closed-list systems where one votes for a party list rather than for a specific individual. With minor exceptions, such as high-profile members of congress (who are almost always at the top of the list), voters generally do not recognize the names of most of the candidates, who are often selected with significant input from the governor. This leads to a sharp disconnect between the voters and the legislators who are supposed to represent them. As a result of this disconnect, individual legislators rarely get personally rewarded for significant accomplishments during their tenures, and on the flip side rarely get punished and held accountable for failing to properly perform their duties. This impression of congress was echoed in an interview with Luis Jacobo, the former Education Minister in the Province of Misiones, who claimed that "if you ask someone on the street the name of their legislators, they will not know. Legislators in this country are highly discredited figures...Through closed lists, people vote without looking at what is inside."[22]

The lack of importance of individual legislators also comes across in the negotiation process that takes place for voting on bills. In an interview with Senator Abal Medina, when I explained to him how American presidents negotiate with individual legislators in congress through a variety of formal and informal mechanisms, he replied that this does not happen in Argentina and stated that "parliamentary negotiations are made [only with top congressional leaders] such as the president of the Chamber of Deputies." Common legislators are shut out of the negotiation process on larger bills, which further weakens the strength of congress as a whole.[23]

More generally, legislators lack prestige because they lack *individual initiative*. By individual initiative, I refer to the fact that there is relatively little space for individual legislators to make a difference. Legislators largely follow what party leaders and governors tell them, leaving them little incentive to even read the bills that they decide to vote on. In an interview with Senator Ángel Rozas who in the past served as the Governor of the Province of Chaco, when asked about whether he had control over the senators and deputies from his province, he replied that "in general terms yes, because when lists for deputies and senators were made the governor had a lot of influence. As a result, there remains a strong relationship between governors, senators, and deputies."[24] Jones et al. also mention this point when they write that:

> In Argentina, where local party bosses dominate the construction of the local party list, legislators' ability to independently pursue a legislative career is substantially curtailed...Within this institutional context, legislators have little incentive to work hard to improve their visibility in the eyes of the voters and no incentive to develop legislative policy expertise.[25]

Goretti also claimed in an interview that "individually, legislators do not have a lot of power, especially legislators from the minority bloc."[26] Federal Deputy Maquieyra concurred that generally, individual legislators have "little independence"[27] from party leadership.

Earlier in this chapter, I mentioned that institutional prestige was a critical component of institutional strength. I also described in detail how the Argentine congress grossly violated rules and procedures in order to appoint Menem's nominees to the Supreme Court (including the use of impostors to falsify a quorum). On this criterion, a congress which would be willing to so blatantly violate procedural norms illustrates not only the lack of institutionalization of the body but also the lack of respect by legislators for the institution they serve (how can an institution be described as prestigious if even its own members show such little respect for its rule and procedures?).

Direct violations of rules and procedures occurred particularly frequently during the Menem administration. In Menem's 1990 bill that helped him pack the Supreme Court, Orlando Gallo (at the time a Federal Deputy) described that "there was a falsification in the case of the vote to raise the number of members of the Court...the quorum was falsified. They used congressional employees [as imposters] and the opposition did not initially realize this, only afterward."[28] While this example of Menem's court-packing scheme (which I addressed in more detail earlier in this chapter) is perhaps the most egregious example of congress flouting rules and procedures in order to illegally help the president, there are numerous other examples throughout modern Argentine history. For example, in the case of the privatization of the pension system under Menem, it is alleged that despite not having a quorum at a committee meeting, the signatures of several members of the committee were forged.[29]

The lack of respect for procedural norms and the rule of law in the Argentine congress can also take on a particularly dark character in the form of outright corruption. Corruption exists within all major political parties in Argentina, and one of the most embarrassing instances of corruption occurred during the De La Rúa administration, when De La Rúa's coalition, the *Alianza*, became embroiled in corruption scandals in the Senate which ultimately led to the disintegration of the coalition. More recently, there are several cases where legislators took bribes in order to pass legislation. For example, in a law regarding labor flexibilization, according to a source familiar with the passage process, "senators and deputies were paid to vote for the law that the executive sent."[30]

Additionally, instances of corruption can make congress more vulnerable to blackmail from the executive branch. For example, when attempting to prompt congress to pass the State Reform Law to grant Menem broad powers to reform the economy (including conducting privatizations), Menem threatened to expose cases of corruption that had taken place under Alfonsín.[31] In this specific case, the lack of adherence to norms/procedures became especially visible when voting on the State Reform Law was supposed to take place. Even though the chamber lacked a quorum for the vote, like in the case of the aforementioned court-packing bill, several congressional employees entered the chamber and impersonated some of the legislators who were absent, providing a "quorum" for the vote to take place. Despite the serious procedural irregularities, congress failed to take action to punish Menem or prevent the law from passing.[32]

On several occasions, Argentine legislators have also shown a propensity to take the rule of law hostage in order to have their demands met. For example, during the 1980s, Alfonsín attempted to pass a labor reform law called the *Mucci* bill, and although it passed in the Chamber of Deputies, it failed in the Senate by one vote. The purported reason for the decisive vote against the bill had to do with the demands of a senator to remove a federal judge. Alfonsín refused to begin the removal process for that judge, and as a result, that senator voted to sink Alfonsín's bill. This instance is illustrative of a congress that does not value the rule of law and judicial independence.

Another example of the weak commitment of congress to established norms is that laws are sometimes passed which contain technical mistakes and which do not go together well with other legal norms in place. Orlando Gallo described the case of a bankruptcy law that was passed during his time in office. He claimed that "the bankruptcy law was not discussed. I remember because I wanted this law to be discussed. It left the committee without being discussed because Minister Cavallo wanted to pass it. After leaving the committee, it was voted upon."[33] He describes that while numerous technical errors were evident to the lawmakers who were lawyers by profession, these errors were never corrected.

An additional piece of proof of the lack of commitment of the Argentine congress to established rules and norms is that it has failed to appoint a national Ombudsman (approving an Ombudsman is part of the institutional prerogative of congress). Although the role of the Ombudsman and the Office's importance will be discussed later in this chapter, it is important to note that the national Ombudsman is an important figure in restraining government abuses of power, including those coming from the executive branch.

The institutional weakness of congress is further accentuated by the lack of resources of the body. In an interview, Senator and former Vice President Julio Cobos described that "the resources of the legislative system are minimal."[34] Most strikingly, Argentine legislators lack a budget with which they can perform research on laws and hire technical personnel; only high-ranking legislators who have leadership roles within their respective chamber and their committees get access to technical personnel. Although all Argentine legislators do have staff in their offices, these employees are, in fact, provided by and work for congress; they are not employees of the legislator. As well, these staff members are not technical personnel and generally perform administrative functions (answering the phones, scheduling, etc.). According to Federal Deputy Alicia Soraire:

> We do not have a budget...I [get technical advice from] a professor from the University of Belgrano. I have another person who is a friend. They are doing this because of friendship, but I do not pay them. If I wanted to hire you to explain to me what is going on in the United States, I would not have any money to pay you. We do not have a fund which we can draw on, and we do not manage money here.[35]

Soraire also described that of the resources available for legislators, many of them are controlled by the president of the congressional chamber to which the legislator belongs. Although legislators do have access to a research organization called the *Dirección de Información Parlamentaria* or *DIP*, this service merely helps legislators gather information (e.g., a legislator might ask the DIP to compile together all laws related to a certain topic); the DIP performs very limited analysis and does not create models to assess the impact of laws, and cannot be seen as the equivalent of the US Congressional Budget Office.

The overall institutional weakness of congress, especially under Peronist presidents, is described by Garavano, who claimed that under Peronist presidents "congress did not function like a congress...they used congress to consolidate power."[36]

The Auditoría General de la Nación

Another institution in Argentina which should normally serve as a check on the executive branch yet is crippled by institutional weakness is the *Auditoría General de la Nación* (AGN). The AGN is an audit organization under the control of the legislature, responsible for creating reports to be sent to congress about how public funds are managed, the functioning of the executive branch and various ministries, the implementation of government programs, and the functioning of the civil service. Note that although technically the AGN reports to congress, in an interview with AGN director Oscar Lamberto, he claimed that the relationship "is not that of a superior and subordinate, but rather is collaborative."[37] The AGN emerged out of the old *Tribunal de Cuentas* (which transformed into the AGN after the 1994 constitutional reform), but its scope goes beyond analyzing how money is spent. As Lamberto describes, "before the *Auditoría* you had the *Tribunal de Cuentas* which was restrained to the financial realm and functioned like a court. The Auditoría has a much larger scope...related to the functioning of the state."[38] The AGN was granted "functional autonomy" by the 1994 constitution (Section 85), and was meant to have the capacity to serve as an independent check on various centers of power of the state, especially the executive branch.

Despite the constitutional attempt at creating an independent organization, Rose-Ackerman notes that "in practice, however, the Audit Office does not operate as independently of the executive branch as the 1994 reformers might have hoped."[39] The main reason for the lack of independence of the AGN is that the composition of its leadership is made to reflect the composition of congress. Given that Peronist presidents including Cristina Kirchner enjoyed vast majorities in congress, the result was that the majority of the top leaders of the AGN were Peronists who did not seriously challenge her. More specifically, the leadership of the AGN is made up of seven auditors (one of the seven auditors is the president of the AGN). The president of the AGN is chosen by the principal opposition group (in the case of Cristina Kirchner, this meant that the president of the AGN was a Radical); three of the auditors are selected by the Chamber of Deputies, and the remaining three are selected by the Senate. Parties that have majorities in these chambers will be able to choose the majority of these six remaining auditors, so even if the president of the AGN is chosen by the opposition party, if a Peronist president has vast majorities in both chambers, Peronists can still effectively control the leadership of the organization. Note that the president of the AGN does not have any special voting powers relative to the other auditors and is considered *primus inter pares*. Between 2002 and 2015, although the president of the *Auditoría* was a Radical, four out of the seven auditors were Peronists (the Radicals were able to select merely the president, one auditor in the Senate, and one in the Chamber of Deputies due to their minorities in congress), and this caused partisanship to seep into the day-to-day functioning of the AGN. This partisanship goes beyond the top leadership of the AGN, since these seven auditors then select a group of second- and third-tier leaders below them, thus also politicizing the lower levels of the organization.

Rose-Ackerman summarizes that "the ruling party has used its authority to curtail the powers of the Audit Office. As a result, the Office does not function as a strong check on executive power."[40] One example she provides was a scandal in 2009 where a firm with ties to Néstor Kirchner allegedly overcharged the government in a contract for the construction of power lines in the province of Santa Cruz. Supposedly, the Peronist auditors attempted to suppress the report, yet in this case their effort was unsuccessful due to a strong reaction from civil society. Generally, however, the Peronist majority on the AGN has managed to successfully prevent the publishing of reports that would have been detrimental to the president. In a separate interview, ex-Federal Judge Madueño describes that the corruption in Santa Cruz under both Kirchner administrations was "disgraceful."[41]

The partisanship in the AGN is further reinforced by the fact that it cannot conduct any investigations without the direct or indirect authorization of congress. At the beginning of every year, the AGN must propose an annual plan delineating the areas where it wants to perform audits, and that plan must be approved by congress. If during the course of that year the AGN wanted to pursue any investigation outside of that plan, it must seek prior approval from the congress. Therefore, even if the leadership of the AGN was fully independent, the organization still would not be able to pursue cases that threaten the interests of the majority party in congress.

The weakness of the AGN is related not only to its lack of independence from Peronist presidents with majorities in congress but also to the fact that it only has power to analyze events after the fact (*ex-post*). The AGN cannot investigate an action that a president is currently taking and can merely publish reports about actions that have already happened (although exceptions are sometimes made, the AGN must generally wait for a minimum of one year from the occurrence of an event in order to start an investigation). As Raúl Allende, the Head of the Press Department at the AGN claimed in an interview, "if Macri were to buy 200 train carriages, we have to wait a year before investigating whether this is good or bad."[42] While it is true that a negative future report by the AGN can be a deterrent to presidents and other organs of the state that desire to abuse their power (since this can lead to embarrassment or even prosecution in the future), the fact that this process occurs only after the fact makes the AGN a weak veto player. This problem is further exacerbated by the length of time that it takes to write up the reports (*informes*), with some coming out even three years after the fact. Many of these reports were also traditionally written in extremely technical language that was difficult for a layperson to understand, and for the first period of the AGN's existence, these reports were not made public (they would only go to a parliamentary committee and remain there). Furthermore, even after reports were issued by the AGN, Federal Deputy Patricia Giménez notes that they are not "binding,"[43] with the AGN being unable to actually force an agency to enact any changes (only congress can do this). Díaz Frers summarizes that the reports by the AGN "did not inspire fear"[44]; as a result, executives who desired to abuse power did not view the organization as a serious institution of horizontal accountability.

It is a pity that the AGN has suffered from partisanship and limitations in the types of cases it could investigate, since the body truly has the ability to enact change and hold institutions accountable when it desires to do so. For example, after a train collision in Buenos Aires in 2012 where 51 passengers were killed and over 700 were injured, the AGN launched a series of investigations. Ultimately, the AGN released five reports which got to the bottom of the root cause of the accident (one of the conclusions was that the state had paid subsidies to individuals who failed to invest money into the railway, leading to poor maintenance). Similarly, the AGN has shown a willingness to try to become more accessible to the public through both a simplification in the way that reports are written (reports now include an executive summary with language accessible to laypersons) as well as the inclusion of all reports on the internet so that they are publicly available. Additionally, the AGN has begun the practice of trying to provide three-minute video summaries of its investigations in various areas to make them more accessible to the public.[45] Regarding the time that it takes to complete a report, there is currently a push to try to get it down to only nine months.[46]

Despite the strong potential of the AGN to enforce the rule of law and act as a counterweight to abuses by the executive branch, it has largely failed in its mission, and this is echoed by politicians from across the ideological spectrum. For example, Federal Deputy Martín Maquieyra (from Macri's PRO party) in an interview decried both the fact that the AGN performs only an ex-post analysis as well as the fact that the majorities held by the Peronists in congress spilled into the AGN and prevented it from being a neutral arbiter. He claims that during the administration of Cristina Kirchner, "there were topics [the AGN] was not allowed [by congress] to investigate."[47] On the other side of the aisle, Federal Deputy Alicia Soraire (from Kirchner's FPV) when asked whether the AGN was truly independent from the executive replied that "lamentably, no."[48] Similarly, Kirchnerist Senator Abal Medina, when asked about the effectiveness of the AGN, replied that "the *Auditoría* only has ex-post control.

Congress does not have the institutional capacity to correctly follow the functioning of the executive branch."[49] One of the most damning assessments about the AGN was given by Justice Minister Garavano, who described it as follows:

> You had an independent and serious auditor, Leandro Despouy, who worked very hard yet was consistently at war with the Kirchnerist majority in congress which tried to restrict the functional autonomy of the *Auditoría*...There are many topics being investigated today where the *Auditoría* did not publish any reports, and these abuses were evident and should have been identified earlier. If the *Auditoría* had had a more proactive attitude, this would have allowed us to gather evidence earlier and stem the corruption in the public administration, especially public works...The *Auditoría* could not go this far because of restrictions [by the Peronist congress].[50]

The Defensor del Pueblo

One of the greatest failures of the Argentine congress has been its inability to appoint a national Ombudsman or *Defensor del Pueblo*. The *Defensor del Pueblo* (to be abbreviated as DDP) in Argentina is one of the most important institutions designed to ensure the rule of law, yet unfortunately has been almost completely debilitated in recent years. The DDP's mission is to protect the fundamental rights of Argentine citizens and ensure that organs of the state, including executive organs, are not abusing power. The DDP performs important investigatory functions, and if it believes that an injustice has been committed, it is able to file a civil action on behalf of the aggrieved parties. For example, if residents of a certain city believe that a state-owned utility company is overcharging them, they may ask the DDP to investigate the matter, and the DDP has the further option to begin a trial against the utility company. Note that the DDP only has power to initiate court action in civil matters and can only refer criminal matters to the *Procurador General de la Nación*. Even though the DDP cannot formally prosecute individuals in criminal trials, it can serve the critical function of gathering information to later be used by prosecutors. The functions of the DDP are detailed in Article 86 of the Argentine constitution, which states:

> The Ombudsman is an independent authority created within the sphere of the National Congress operating with full autonomy and without receiving instructions from any other authority. The mission of the Ombudsman is the defense and protection of human rights and other rights, guarantees and interests sheltered under this Constitution and the laws, in the face of deeds, acts or omissions of the

Administration; as well as the control of public administrative functions. The Ombudsman has capacity to be a party in a lawsuit.[51]

The DDP was initially created by a presidential decree and then enshrined into law through Law 24,284. The Constitution of 1994 later explicitly recognized the DDP in Article 86. Formally, the DDP is outside of the three branches of government and is functionally autonomous. The main requirement of the DDP is to prepare a report once a year to be studied by a permanent bicameral commission in congress dealing specifically with the DDP (although it must prepare a report, given that it is functionally autonomous, the DDP does not have to respect the orders of congress). The DDP has jurisdiction throughout all of Argentina, yet the scope is limited to matters that relate to areas that touch upon *national* laws (for matters at the provincial or city-level, the case can be referred to local public defenders' offices). As well, the DDP has no jurisdiction to investigate the army or judiciary, although notably, it may investigate the executive.

As Juan Pablo Jorge, a lawyer working in the technical and legal division of the DDP describes, the organization can play a significant role in restraining executive power and ensuring that the rule of law is respected. He claims that "we can recommend that certain actions by the president be halted or modified...We can go to the court system in order to limit an action by the executive."[52] He further describes that there were "various times"[53] when the DDP took actions against the executive. Although initially the DDP was conceived as an institution which would try to deal with day-to-day problems people faced as opposed to high-level abuses of power by the president, some heads of the agency have taken more bold steps to constrain high-level abuses, to the chagrin of presidents.

Although in theory the DDP should be a powerful institution of horizontal accountability, in recent years, it has been severely weakened. The main reason for the destruction of this institution is that congress refused to appoint a leader to be in charge of the agency. The last *Defensor del Pueblo* that was appointed to lead the organization was Eduardo René Mondino, whose term ended in December of 2008. Since 2009, congress has failed to appoint a head to lead the organization. Initially, it was run by an "adjunto" (roughly comparable to a vice president), but after the *adjunto*'s term in office expired, a caretaker administrator took over (currently, the name of this figure is Juan José Böckel). It is important to note that the DDP under the current caretaker administration cannot perform the basic functions described in the constitution. Although the DDP can still perform investigations, until a new leader is appointed, it cannot initiate civil trials, thus leaving it powerless to take any actions against abuses that it uncovers.

The weakening of the Ombudsman's office was a particularly strong blow to checks and balances in Argentina, since as Rose-Ackerman writes, "the Ombudsman is arguably the most significant state agency overseeing the executive."[54] Rose-Ackerman describes that the DDP was extremely efficient, and claims that:

> The Ombudsman can initiate investigations in order to uncover actions of the national administration that amount to an illegitimate, defective, irregular, abusive, arbitrary, discriminatory, negligent, or seriously incompetent exercise of their functions, including those that might affect diffuse or collective interests. He must also pay special attention to behavior that shows a systematic and general failure of the administration, and promote mechanisms to eliminate or reduce them. The Ombudsman's powers allow him to investigate actions that judges cannot evaluate. Indeed, according to the political question doctrine elaborated by the Supreme Court, judges cannot assess the opportunity, merit, or convenience of a decision made by the political branches of government. In contrast, the Ombudsman can issue warnings, recommendations, or reminders of the duties of public officials and propose new measures.[55]

The decapitation of the DDP was a political decision that sought to reduce the accountability of the executive branch. Normally, when the Ombudsman's term in office expires, he/she must be replaced through a two-thirds majority in both chambers of congress (this is a greater threshold than for Supreme Court judges, who need a two-thirds majority only in the Senate). According to Juan Pablo Jorge, the reason that congress failed to appoint a new Ombundsman was

> because of politics…Within congress, we depend on political games in order to name an Ombudsman, yet because of a lack of interest on the part of the executive and legislative branches to name an Ombudsman, it happens that we have been [for several] years without an assigned Ombudsman.[56]

In short, despite the potential of the *Defensor del Pueblo* to oversee the executive branch, the capacity of this institution has been severely weakened because of inaction by congress to name a leader.

The Central Bank

The central bank in Argentina has suffered from extreme institutional weakness. It has lacked independence and has not fulfilled its role as a veto player. The main criterion through which we can assess the capture of the Central Bank by the executive branch is the degree of turnover among its top leadership. There has been significant turnover among Argentine central bank presidents, and their tenures have often been cut short through political interference. Argentina between 1990 and 2018 had 16 central bank presidents, with the average tenure being under two years (in contrast, since 1990, the USA has had only four Federal Reserve Chairs). Executive intervention in central bank governance is widespread. Notably, former central bank president Juan Carlos Fábrega resigned under pressure from President Cristina Kirchner; Cristina Kirchner also outright fired long-time central bank president Martín Redrado (who had served from 2004 to 2010) after a dispute in which he refused to use $6.5 billion dollars of reserve money to pay down the country's debt. Central Bank autonomy continued to suffer even under Macri who pushed out the central bank president Alejandro Vanoli (who was seen as an ally of the Kirchner administration).

In short, I have attempted to describe the weakness of five institutions of horizontal accountability in Argentina, namely congress, the judiciary, the *Auditoría General de la Nación*, the Central Bank, and the Public Defender's Office. The weakness of these institutions created a political opportunity that allowed presidents to abuse power. In an interview, ex-governor Barrios Arrechea of the province of Misiones claimed that "[Argentina's constitution] allows for a president, not a hyper-president, which is a consequence of the poor institutional quality...Institutions are fragile...[and] I think I am going to die without seeing authentic democracy."[57] For a more in-depth discussion of institutional weakness in Argentina, see Levitsky and Murillo 2005.

Part II: Chile—A Case of Institutional Strength

In this part, I will examine institutional strength throughout Chile. I begin with a general analysis of institutional strength, after which I will describe in particular detail several institutions: congress, the judiciary (both the Supreme Court and Constitutional Tribunal), the *Contraloría*, the *Consejo para la Transparencia*, the Central Bank, and the *Ministerio Público*. Collectively, these institutions present the primary roadblocks for Chilean presidents who desire to concentrate power. As will become evident, unlike in the case of Argentina where institutions of horizontal accountability were weak, in Chile, these institutions exhibited significant strength.

Institutional Strength in Chile in General

As in the case of Argentina, the CPI provides a reliable indicator of the degree of rule of law in a country and the strength of state institutions. In Table 3.2, I have compiled the CPI scores and rankings of Chile since 1995.

As can be seen in this table, Chile has consistently been a leader in terms of clean government and institutional strength not only in comparison

Table 3.2 Illustrating Chile's strong institutional capacity through its high rankings on the Corruption Perceptions Index[a]

Year	Score	Ranking
1995	7.94	14/41
1996	6.80	21/54
1997	6.05	23/52
1998	6.80	20/85
1999	6.90	19/99
2000	7.40	18/90
2001	7.50	18/91
2002	7.50	17/102
2003	7.40	20/133
2004	7.40	20/146
2005	7.30	21/159
2006	7.30	20/163
2007	7.00	22/180
2008	6.90	23/180
2009	6.70	25/180
2010	7.20	21/178
2011	7.20	22/183
2012	72	20/198
2013	71	22/198
2014	73	21/198
2015	70	23/198
2016	66	24/198
2017	67	26/198
2018	67	27/198
2019	67	26/198

[a] I would like to thank Elizabeth Sanchez Flores for helping me compile this data

to Latin American countries but also relative to the rest of the world. Chileans are significantly more likely than other citizens in the region to believe that their state institutions are clean and follow the law, especially in comparison to Argentina. Institutions such as the police force earn particularly high praise.

Institutions of horizontal accountability in Chile that enforce the law on presidents are exceptionally powerful, and as Rodrigo Egaña (the National Director of the Civil Service) described in an interview:

In the institutional structure of Chile, there are various institutions with veto power: the Constitutional Tribunal for constitutional matters, the *Contraloría* which controls the legality [of decrees] and spending, the Council of Transparency in relation to access to information, the judicial branch which is completely autonomous from the executive, and the central bank which has complete autonomy in matters related to monetary policy.[58]

Congress

Unlike in Argentina, in Chile, congress possesses substantially more institutional strength. In this section, I will describe the Chilean legislature as a highly professionalized body with significantly greater technical capacity and resources than its Argentine counterpart.

Whereas reelection rates are low in Argentina, in Chile, legislators enjoy a high reelection rate and have substantially longer average tenures in office. They are significantly more professionalized and have strong incentives to perform well. In an interview, Valeria Palanza claimed that:

> On so many counts, the Chilean legislature does better...Your average legislator in Chile is more educated than in the rest of Latin America...their salaries are better...We arrive at the conclusion that it is a more professionalized legislature...They're reelected more and spend more time in their role as legislators. They know what they're doing [and] know how to legislate; they know what a law looks like as opposed to the guy who just arrived in congress and he's trying to figure out what he's doing.[59]

Federal Deputy Mario Venegas echoes this assessment and emphasizes the enormous advantage in having a highly professionalized congress. He claims that:

> You need preparation to be able to talk to and reach an agreement with the executive branch. This congress has a high percentage of professionals such as lawyers, engineers, or economists, doctors, professors...Because of their knowledge, they are capable of talking with a high degree of confidence about these topics.[60]

In terms of financial resources, Chilean legislators are not only among the best paid in Latin America but also have significant funds at their disposal to hire experts and conduct research.

The technical capacity of the congress is also reflected in the level of understanding that individual legislators seek to develop on the bills they vote for. As I mentioned earlier, in Argentina, there is a vertical culture where individual legislators are incentivized to follow the orders of party leaders, leading to little motivation to even research the bills they will vote for. In contrast, in Chile, the relationship between legislators and party leaders is significantly more horizontal in nature, and legislators vote for a law based on its merits rather than on the desires of top-level party leaders. Instead of merely following orders from party leaders, Chilean legislators each develop specialties in the areas of the committees to which they are assigned, and, in turn, legislators ask one another for guidance.[61] The result is that technical knowledge is dispersed throughout the whole chamber as opposed to being only among a handful of party leaders. Deputy Venegas described as follows the process through which legislators get informed on the bills they pass:

> Because committees are so diverse, it is impossible for a deputy to manage all of the topics. We have 2–3 committees in which we specialize. When it comes time to vote, the greatest influence is our colleagues, the deputies who are members of those committees.[62]

For example, a deputy who needs to vote on a bill focused on agriculture yet who is not specialist in the topic will ask for the advice of a colleague sitting on the relevant committee. Whereas for Chilean legislators their greatest influence in voting for bills is their own colleagues (as described by Venegas), for Argentine legislators, it is party leaders.

The Chilean legislature's respect for established norms, as well as the respect of legislators for the institution they work for, is evident in the desire of the body to prioritize a coherent, well-made law over the speed of passage. Whereas in Argentina the legislature oftentimes would pass laws that were poorly designed (e.g., the Convertibility Plan which eventually led to an economic crisis), in Chile, the legislature generally tries to ensure that these laws are high quality. In an interview with Federal Deputy Claudio Arriagada, when asked why time limits on urgencies were often not respected, he described that "these time limits are not respected because in the passage process, parliament has to represent the popular will which manifests itself through a technical analysis of the legislation." He describes how legislation is often subject to intense scrutiny, including providing an opportunity to all groups that would be affected by the legislation to come forward.[63] He also describes that the strength of congress has a lot to do with tradition and culture, claiming that "tradition in Chile is very powerful, and has governed presidential-congressional relations since 1833."[64]

Carey summarizes the overall strength of the Chilean Congress when he writes that "prior to 1973, the Chilean Congress was long regarded as the most powerful legislature in Latin America...Upon the return to democracy in 1990...Chile's Congress is reestablishing itself as an unusually professionalized and technically competent legislature."[65]

The Judiciary (Including the Constitutional Tribunal and Supreme Court)

In this section, I will discuss the strength of the judiciary in Chile. As I will show, the judiciary in Chile (a) has maintained significant independence throughout the past 30 years and has avoided the court-packing schemes that have plagued Argentina and (b) has established prestige through a historical legacy of challenging certain aspects of the military dictatorship under Pinochet.

The mechanism for nominating judges to the two Chilean high courts encourages more independence from the executive branch than the nomination procedures in Argentina. In Argentina, the president can select anyone for membership to the Supreme Court; in Chile, while the president still can make a nomination, that nominee must be chosen from a shortlist of five candidates prepared by the Supreme Court itself, which, according to Article 75 of the Constitution, must include the senior justice of the court of appeals. This nominee must afterward be ratified by the Senate with a two-thirds majority. The Supreme Court has 21 justices, who serve until mandatory retirement at the age of 75.

The Constitutional Tribunal contains ten members who are appointed for nine-year terms through multiple tracks. Three of these members are appointed by the Supreme Court from among its own members (the Court's appointment process is relatively independent as noted above), the president is able to select three members, the Senate by a two-thirds majority selects two of the members, and the Chamber of Deputies is able to vote on two members who then need Senate approval.[66] What is particularly noteworthy is that the membership is not monopolized by any one particular actor within the government, with four different entities having a say in who is able to serve. Nevertheless, it is important to note that before constitutional reforms in 2005, the appointment process of the Constitutional Tribunal was *even more independent* from any elected bodies. Based on the 1980 constitution, the Constitutional Tribunal had only seven members, of which three were selected by the Supreme Court, one was selected by the president, the Senate nominated one member, and the *Consejo de Seguridad Nacional* (National Security Council) selected two members. Under the previous scheme, only two of seven members would be selected by any democratically elected body, whereas after the reforms, this has increased to seven out of ten. Despite the increased politicization of the body after 2005, as noted above, the Constitutional Tribunal is still independent of any particular branch of government. Carroll and Tiede argue that:

> From an institutional perspective, the appointment mechanisms should allow the [Constitutional] Tribunal independence from the influences of any *one* political actor. Because the Tribunal's composition comes from multiple appointers representing different political interests (using separate actors and super majorities), it is difficult to exert political control, despite the extended period of control by the same political coalition...Thus the makeup is likely to produce a membership with diverse preferences reflecting compromises among various political forces...In sum, while the Tribunal's selection

mechanism could be thought of as politicizing the body—bringing it more in line with what we would expect from a court with direct legislative powers—the multiplicity of interests involved across and within appointments can preserve institutional independence without a technocratic or apolitical construction.[67]

Throughout the past two decades, the Constitutional Tribunal has also become more diverse ideologically, and as former Constitutional Tribunal President Carlos Carmona explained in an interview:

> Starting in 2005 the Tribunal pluralized and people came in who were not of a conservative tendency. You need to have positions on both sides, and what is new today is that you have a progressive wing of the Tribunal which before 2005 did not exist.[68]

The increasing ideological diversity within the Constitutional Tribunal certainly enhances its prestige and reputation in society as an independent arbiter of the constitutionality of laws.

Turning our attention to the other High Court, Chilean Supreme Court judges enjoy the highest average tenure of any Latin American high court judges, at over 16 years.[69] This figure is comparable to the average tenure of US Supreme Court judges, who serve for 16 years on average.[70] In Argentina, this figure in contrast is only about five years (despite judges also having "life tenure" to the age of 75).[71] The high average tenure for Chilean Supreme Court judges increases the independence of the high court, which, in turn, endows it with the institutional strength to be able to challenge presidential initiatives.

One historical episode which under some analyses may serve as a "critical juncture" for the independence of the Supreme Court is Salvador Allende's conflict with the body. Allende tried to pack the Supreme Court by proposing an age limit of 65 years on the then-judges. Paul Sigmund, in comparing this to Roosevelt's court-packing scheme, writes that "the retirement proposals, like those of the Roosevelt court-packing plan of 1937, were aimed at opening the court to new Allende appointments."[72] Ultimately, this attempt to pack the courts failed, and the fact that the Supreme Court survived this attack further helped to cement its perception as an institution that is independent and that cannot be tampered with.

Even though some question the independence of the Court during the Pinochet period, it is important to note that he did not take any steps to pack the court in his favor. Graver notes that:

> Chile had a tradition of independent courts before the coup in 1973, and the Junta in no way interfered with the independence of the courts...The history of democratic practice and respect for legality was longer and stronger in Chile than in Argentina and Brazil.[73]

Interestingly, in the first decree passed by the Junta, the military agreed to respect the independence of the judiciary. Couso et al. write that:

> In this context, it was quite remarkable that the military left the judiciary untouched...the DL [Decreto Ley] that ushered in the new regime stated that the new authorities would recognize the autonomy of the judicial branch. DL No 1 stated 'The Military Junta will guarantee the full efficacy of the faculties of the Judicial Power and will respect the Constitution and the laws of the republic as far as circumstances allow.'[74]

Pereira also confirms that the military in Chile respected the role of courts to a greater extent than the Argentine military. In comparing the degree to which Argentina, Chile, and Brazil attempted to "legalize repression,"[75] whereas the Argentine military regime often used extrajudicial killings or detention against critics, the Chilean military made a greater use of legal channels (although not as much as the Brazilian military regime).

It is important to note that although the Supreme Court during the Pinochet period enjoyed a certain degree of independence from the junta (it can even be argued that the Supreme Court under Pinochet was more independent than the Supreme Court under Menem), it did not choose to go against the government in several critical areas, most notably human rights. Helmke, for example, claims that the Chilean Supreme Court failed to take any action against the military with regards to human rights abuses. Hilbink also argues that "for seventeen years of dictatorship (and beyond), Chilean courts not only failed to defend human rights, but they legitimated, sometimes passively, sometimes actively, the laws and practices of the military regime."[76] *It is important however not to conflate a lack of action against human rights abuses with a "capture" of the judiciary by the Pinochet regime.* In other words, a judiciary can be independent yet still not promote human rights. Although this may sound counterintuitive, courts can be independent yet refuse to challenge the government on certain issues, as long as these courts refuse to challenge the government from their own initiative as opposed to because they are captured by the executive branch (through methods like court-packing). Hilbink herself concludes that "formal judicial independence, even when achieved and respected, is not enough to produce a judicial defense of rights."[77]

In other words, Hilbink argues that although judges may be independent from other leaders in power, this does not mean that judges will necessarily assert themselves against certain policies of those leaders. In the case of Chile, she claims that:

> After the 1973 military coup even judges personally at odds with the laws and practices of the military regime were professionally unwilling or unable to defend liberal democratic principles and practices.

Publicly challenging the validity of the regime's laws and policies in the name of liberal-democratic values and principles was viewed as unprofessional 'political' behavior, which threatened the integrity of the judiciary and the rule of law.[78]

Hilbink argues that while the Chilean judiciary is one of the oldest and most stable in Latin America, judges were often discouraged from independent thinking and were pushed to be conservative in their rulings. Judges were encouraged to be "apolitical," where this was understood as respecting the will of the executive branch. In discussing how the judiciary desired to be "apolitical" and avoid conflict with the executive branch, Hilbink claims the following:

> Although the judiciary was, by the mid-twentieth century, staffed largely by members of the emergent middle class and boasted high levels of independence and professionalism, judges were largely unwilling or unable to take stands in defense of liberal and democratic principles...[79]

The Chilean Supreme Court also ultimately survived Aylwin's attempt at a court-packing scheme (which was described in detail in Chapter 2). The independence of the Supreme Court since democratization has also trickled down to the lower courts. Although the Chilean Supreme Court does not have the power to set precedent in the same way as the US Supreme Court, the Supreme Court has the power to both advance as well as sanction lower-level judges. Judges who consistently defy Supreme Court doctrine will not be able to advance in their careers.[80] In the Chilean judicial system, one would begin as a lower-level trial judge (often with a low salary) and work his/her way up. Nevertheless, career advancement requires getting along with one's superiors, who are controlled by higher courts, and ultimately, the Supreme Court. The result was that "this bureaucratic structure produced strong incentives for judges to comply with the opinions and attitudes of the courts above"[81] and ensured that the independence of the Supreme Court would trickle down to lower levels as well. In other words, because of the strong top-down structure of control, the independence of the Supreme Court effectively also translates into the independence of the lower courts. This is in contrast to Argentina under the administrations of Néstor and Cristina Kirchner, where despite some independence at the Supreme Court level, the lower courts were politicized. In an interview with a former member of the Chilean Supreme Court, he described the high degree of competence within the judicial system when he claimed that:

> What differentiates us from other countries in Latin America and the United States is that entry into the judicial career is completely

non-political. Here, people who want to pursue a judicial career start from a young age. They enter the judicial academy after a very difficult admissions process.[82]

He also described more generally that within the judicial system, there are low levels of corruption and said that "within the years that I was in the contentious-administrative section, nobody tried to influence me... This is very normal."[83] He mentioned that although the Constitutional Tribunal has a certain degree of politicization (similar to the US Supreme Court), the Supreme Court is completely apolitical. He also claimed that throughout his time on the court, he did not know the political ideology of the majority of his Supreme Court colleagues.[84]

What further strengthens the ability of the judiciary to check the power of the executive branch is that the Supreme Court and Constitutional Tribunal are separate from each other in Chile. In an interview with Juan Jose Romero Guzmán, a Minister on the Constitutional Tribunal, he mentioned that splitting the high-level judiciary into these two separate organs helps prevent the capture of the judiciary by the president.[85]

Contraloría General

In addition to the judiciary, another institution of horizontal accountability that has established a strong historical legacy and reputation for independence is the *Contraloría General* (Comptroller General). As I mentioned in Chapter 2, the *Contraloría* has the power to review executive decrees and accept or reject their legality.

To ensure the independence and autonomy of the *Contraloría*, the mechanism for choosing the leader, the *Contralor General*, is similar to the mechanism for choosing Supreme Court judges. The president nominates a person, after which a two-thirds majority is necessary in the Senate; he/she then serves for eight years. Until recently, comptrollers were chosen from inside the *Contraloría*, but the last two were from the exterior (although they are from outside the *Contraloría*, these two recent comptrollers are nevertheless specialists in administrative law). Once chosen, the president has no authority to fire the *Contralor General*, and the only way to remove him/her is through an impeachment process in congress (*acusación constitucional*). The last time that that this occurred was in 1949.[86] The current *Contralor General*, Jorge Bermúdez, was approved unanimously in congress, and as he described in an interview, "this gives me a lot of power and independence."[87] Although the *Contralor* regularly meets with legislators and testifies in congress, it is critical to note that unlike the Argentine *Auditoría* which depends on congress, the *Contraloría* has complete independence. For example, although congress can request that the *Contraloría* investigate a certain matter, it is not obliged to conduct those investigations.

All lower-level employees report to the *Contralor*; this mid-to-lower-level bureaucracy also has its own admissions system over which the Chilean president has no control. Bermúdez notes that "the process [for selecting employees] is meritocratic and it is a highly respected career."[88] Overall, the *Contraloría* has approximately 2,000 employees in 15 offices, one in Santiago and 14 in other parts of the country. Another way in which the *Contraloría* is insulated from political pressure is that if either the executive or legislative branch desires to make changes to it, this change would have to fall into the realm of a *ley orgánica* that requires a 4/7 majority in congress. Cordero notes that since democratization, the *Contraloría* has been modified only once in 2002, and that although there were other proposals, they never saw the light of day.[89]

There are few mechanisms through which the Chilean president can exert political pressure on the *Contraloría* given its constitutional autonomy, and overall, Cordero claims that political pressures on the *Contraloría* "are either low or inexistent."[90] Jorge Bermúdez claimed in an interview that during the period that he was in office, he did not face pressure to drop investigations. He claimed that "I would not tolerate any pressure, and the *Contraloría* is an autonomous organ."[91]

The only way for the executive branch to be able to *in theory* exert control over the *Contraloría* is to reduce or eliminate its budget (recall that the president has exclusive initiative over the budget, and congress cannot propose any new expenditure). Nevertheless, this situation has never happened, with Cordero describing such a move as "impossible."[92] Indeed, if the *Contraloría* were to reject a presidential decree and in anger the president cut off the funding of the body, the president would incur a great political cost and risk retaliation by other institutions of checks and balances such as congress (including possible impeachment).

One of the main reasons for the strength of the *Contraloría* is its institutional reputation since its founding in 1927. The *Contraloría* was founded based on the advice of Princeton University Professor and Economist Edwin Walter Kemmerer who like other "money doctors" of his time sought to promote institutions throughout the world that would create economic stability. As foreign investment was pouring into Latin America, Kemmerer wanted to ensure that this money was not stolen,[93] and initially, the *Contraloría* was conceived as an organ that would help to control and account for the budget; it would later expand its mandate to also directly supervise the executive branch. During the period when the *Contraloría* was founded, Carlos Ibáñez was in power. Although Ibáñez is credited with founding many of Chile's institutions and setting the country on the path to being a modern state, he was nevertheless a dictator. Paradoxically, even though his regime was autocratic, rather than weakening the *Contraloría*, Ibáñez actually *strengthened* the body. There is speculation that due to the fact that he was a dictator, he knew first-hand the dangers of absolute power, and for this reason sought to promote checks and balances. During the first decade and a half of its existence, even though the *Contraloría* was supposed to restrain the president, in practice, it was very deferential to the executive branch, angering the Chilean Congress. Ultimately, in 1943, with the passage of a new constitution, a bargain was struck where the Chilean legislature granted the president more formal powers, yet at the same time strengthened the *Contraloría* even further. After the passage of the 1943 constitution, the legislature no longer tolerated comptrollers who were deferential to the executive and expected them to aggressively check presidential power. In what would be a critical juncture that would set the tone for the functioning of the *Contraloría*, congress in 1945 impeached the Comptroller Agustín Vigorena Rivera because of the perception that he was too deferential to the president. His successor, Humberto Mewes, along with future comptrollers, would be significantly more diligent in acting as a check on the president.[94] It is interesting to note that while during this critical junction in Chile presidents were becoming more and more constrained, in Argentina at roughly the same time, Perón was destroying institutions of horizontal accountability.

In short, in this section, I have attempted to illustrate the strength of the *Contraloría*, which was instrumental to keeping the power of Chilean presidents in check. Unlike its Argentine counterpart, the *Auditoria General de la Nación*, the Chilean *Contraloría General* has shown remarkable independence from the executive and has not been packed with political allies of the president.

Ministerio Público[95]

Another critical institution that is responsible for upholding the rule of law in Chile is the *Ministerio Público* (to be abbreviated as MP and also known as the *Fiscalía*). The MP can be considered the Chilean equivalent of the US Department of Justice and is responsible for prosecuting crimes.

One of the most significant impediments to presidential accountability in many countries throughout the world is that if the executive branch does commit wrongdoing and abuses power, it is also the executive branch that controls the authorities responsible for prosecuting these crimes. For example, in the USA, the Attorney General and other top officials within the Department of Justice are nominated by the president. In theory, the president is able to fire any unfriendly Attorney General, thus minimizing the ability to hold the president accountable.

In Chile, what has strengthened the MP is that it is completely outside of the control of the president. Unlike the US Department of Justice, the MP is constitutionally autonomous (in a manner similar to the *Contraloría*) and does not respond to the president. The appointment process of the *Fiscal Nacional* (the head of the MP who can be considered the equivalent of the US Attorney General) is also very independent. Although the president nominates the head of the MP, he can only do this from a shortlist of five individuals (referred to as a *quina*) compiled by the Supreme Court. These five individuals are selected based on a nationwide search undertaken by the Court. After nominating one of these five individuals, the candidate must be ratified by a two-thirds vote in the Senate. After selecting a *Fiscal Nacional*, he/she has sole control over the MP and is free from executive or legislative interference for the duration of his/her eight-year term. Below the national-level MP are the regional *fiscalías*, whose leaders are appointed in a process that is similarly independent of the executive branch. For each region, the respective court of appeals selects three candidates, and ultimately, the *Fiscal Nacional* chooses one of the three names.

The reason that the *Fiscalía* is so important for preserving checks and balances is that it serves as a deterrent for presidents who desire to abuse power. The MP in Chile has shown no aversion to investigating presidents, and various administrations faced probes by the body. The most recent high-profile corruption scandal which was broadly investigated by the MP was the *Caval* scandal in which former President Michelle Bachelet's son was accused of improperly obtaining a $10 million loan using his mother's influence; Michelle Bachelet's daughter-in-law Natalia Compagnon was also charged in this probe. Overall, this scandal was one of the factors that contributed to Michelle Bachelet's decline in popularity, and she was powerless to prevent the investigation from going forward (unlike in other countries where she would have been able to fire the prosecutors in charge).

Consejo para la Transparencia[96]

One of the most important organs of the state that acts as an institution of horizontal accountability of sorts is the *Consejo para la Transparencia* (to be abbreviated CT) or "Council for Transparency." The CT is an autonomous organ of the state, and its role is to ensure that other state organs are complying with transparency laws in place. The executive branch is one of the primary organs where the CT tries to ensure compliance with transparency laws, along with other institutions such as state universities, public corporations, and municipal governments.

The way through which the CT enforces transparency laws is as follows: any citizen may petition a state organization for information which legally should be made public (according to laws comparable to the Freedom of Information Act in the USA). Although by law the organization has 20 days to release the information, sometimes that organization may refuse to hand it over, and in those cases, the citizen may petition the CT to force its release (as opposed to going through the judiciary). The CT would assess the complaint and could then order the respective organization to release the information if the CT deems that it should be publicly available, after which the CT has the option to impose fines. Note that while the CT has certain functions that resemble the judiciary, it is not formally a court of law. Although a state organ may appeal an unfavorable decision in the courts, the judiciary in practice rarely goes against the CT. In a testament to the high strength and prestige of the CT, since the institution's inception in 2008, it has been extremely rare for a public organization to refuse to follow an order issued by the CT.

The CT is critically important as an institution of horizontal accountability since it promotes transparency at the level of the executive branch and makes it harder for a presidential administration to abuse its powers. One example of a case where the CT checked an abuse of power from the executive involved the construction of a bridge after the 2010 earthquake. An auction was held to determine which firm would receive a government contract, and the firm which lost the bid asked that information about the auction be made public. The Defense Ministry initially refused to release the information, citing that the money for this project came from a copper fund with ties to the military. Nevertheless, the CT determined that because the bridge was a civilian rather than a military construction, the information should be made public. Ultimately, it was revealed that the contract was not given to the cheapest firm, resulting in significant embarrassment for the Defense Minister who ultimately resigned.

The CT is able to check a president's power because of the independence of its governing board from the executive branch. The CT is made up of a board of four counselors, who are nominated by the president yet must be approved by a two-thirds majority in the Senate. Given the high voting threshold that must be achieved, these are always very qualified individuals with political backing from all major sectors of society. In practice, two of the four counselors come from the left of the political spectrum, and the other two come from the right. The term for a counselor is six years. The president of the CT rotates among these four individuals, and the main prerogative that a president possesses is the ability to break a tie vote.

Central Bank

In contrast to the Argentine Central Bank, the Chilean Central Bank has long been a bastion of independence that has provided restraints against the executive. Presidents in Chile have not been able to "pack" the bank with loyalists, and the bank has not bowed down to pressures from the executive branch. From 1990 to 2018, Chile had only seven central bank presidents (in contrast to the 16 in Argentina).

The independence of the Chilean Central Bank also came across in an interview with Nicolás de la Cuesta, the Manager of Human Resources at the Bank. In a wide-ranging interview, he discussed how the appointment process of both the leadership and lower-level employees of the organization is apolitical. The leadership is composed of the President, the Vice President, and three counselors, who are chosen by the president but must be approved by the Senate. In a manner similar to Constitutional Tribunal appointments, in practice, there is an informal norm where the candidates alternate between the left and the right of the political spectrum. De la Cuesta notes that all of these individuals are extremely qualified for the position. Similarly, all of the lower-level staff is chosen in a meritocratic way, completely free of political influence. De la Cuesta notes that "the Central Bank is one of the institutions with the most PhDs in Chile. We have specialists in the economic and financial realms."[97] The average tenure for employees at the Central Bank is 11 years. The autonomy of the Central Bank from the presidential administration is summarized by De la Cuesta, who argues that:

> [The president] has absolutely no influence, neither the president nor political parties [in the selection of Bank employees]...We have total independence, and this makes it so that the evaluation of economic information has nothing to do with what the government in power wants.[98]

When asked whether over the past 25 years there were any attempts to politicize the Central Bank, he replied "not that I know of."[99]

In short, in this part, I have attempted to show how, in Chile, institutions of horizontal accountability have been strong. I have centered the discussion on four primary characteristics of institutional strength, namely independence from the executive branch, institutional prestige, technical capacity, and respect for established rules/norms.

Part III: Generalizing the Theory Through a Large-N Analysis

In this part, I will provide some statistical evidence to support my first independent variable (institutional strength). While this analysis by no means fully confirms the mechanisms behind this variable, it does suggest that it may be generalizable beyond Argentina and Chile. While significantly more quantitative analysis is necessary in future research, this brief examination provides a strong starting point.

As I mentioned in Chapter 1, I will primarily make use of two datasets: a dataset of all presidential and semi-presidential systems in the world, and the dataset of all 20 presidential democracies in the Western Hemisphere.

The Link Between Institutional Strength (Measured Through the Corruption Perceptions Index) and Presidential Power (Measured Through Data from V-Dem)

Using the CPI as an indicator of institutional strength, in this part, I will attempt to illustrate the relationship between the strength of state institutions and legislative and judicial constraints on the executive. While the CPI is not a perfect measurement of institutional strength, countries with strong institutions generally receive better scores on this index than countries with weaker institutions (as I describe in the Appendix, I have also used other indicators for institutional strength besides the CPI).

The scatterplot in Figure 3.2 compares the 2012 CPI scores and 2012 Legislative Constraints on the Executive scores in my sample of 20 presidential democracies in the Western Hemisphere. Each scatterplot contains both the p-value and R-squared value for the data. Note that when reading the figures, higher CPI scores imply cleaner governments with *less* corruption, and higher legislative/judicial constraints indicate *less* hyperpresidentialism.

The scatterplots in Figure 3.3 illustrate the relationship between 2012 CPI scores and three measurements that are part of the 2012 Judicial Constraints on the Executive Index in my sample of 20 presidential democracies in the Western Hemisphere. The measurements of judicial

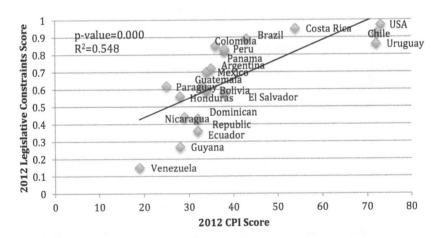

Figure 3.2 Relationship between Corruption and Legislative Constraints on the Executive in presidential democracies in the Western Hemisphere in 2012.

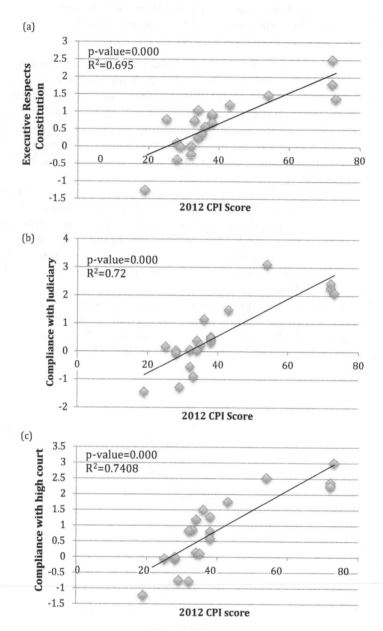

Figure 3.3 Relationship between corruption and three sub-measurements on the Judicial Constraints on the Executive index in presidential democracies in the Western Hemisphere in 2012. (a) Relationship between CPI and "Executive Respects Constitution" (v2exrescon). (b) Relationship between CPI and "Compliance with judiciary" (v2jucomp). (c) Relationship between CPI and "Compliance with high court" (v2juhccomp).

constraints that were used included "Executive respects constitution" (v2exrescon), "Compliance with judiciary" (v2jucomp), and "Compliance with high court" (v2juhccomp). The reason that I used these three values as opposed to the broader label of "Judicial Constraints on the Executive" (v2x_jucon) was because "Judicial Constraints on the Executive" is an aggregate measurement of five values that in addition to these three aforementioned variables, also included "high court independence" and "lower court independence."[100] Including these two variables would have produced suboptimal results given that in the CPI, there are several variables which similarly measure high court independence and lower court independence. Therefore, I have isolated the "Judicial Constraints on the Executive" index to merely include the three variables which are not fully captured in the CPI.

In this group of 20 presidential democracies in the Western Hemisphere, in addition to comparing CPI scores in 2012 to Legislative and Judicial Constraints scores in 2012, I also performed an analysis where I compared the scores in every country for every year between 1990 and 2012. On the scatterplot in Figure 3.4, each point represents country-year dyads for this period (e.g., Argentina 1990, Brazil 2001).[101]

In the previous figures in this part, I included data from only presidential democracies in the Western Hemisphere. In the scatterplot in Figure 3.5, I have included results comparing CPI scores and legislative constraints on the executive from my other dataset with *all presidential countries throughout the world in 2012* (as I mentioned earlier, semi-presidential systems are also included in this dataset). For context, note that for Figure 3.5,

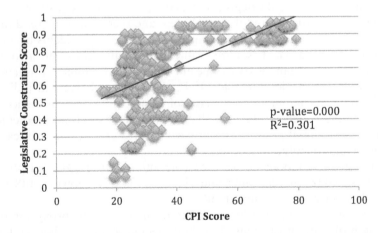

Figure 3.4 Relationship between Corruption and Legislative Constraints on the Executive in the 20 presidential democracies in the Western Hemisphere, 1990–2012.

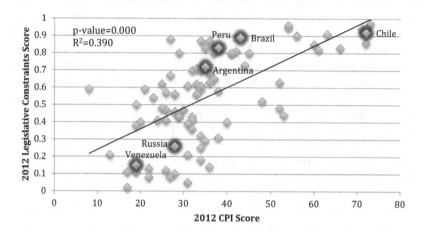

Figure 3.5 Relationship between Corruption and Legislative Constraints on the Executive in all presidential systems in the world in 2012.

I have highlighted where six cases are situated. In the introduction, I mentioned that my analysis would be mainly limited to studying the impact of my three independent variables on democratic systems. In expanding the analysis to all presidential systems throughout the world (democratic and nondemocratic), the large-N analysis suggests that my first independent variable may also be useful in analyzing differences in presidential power in authoritarian systems.

All of the figures illustrate that the relationship between the strength of state institutions and the degree of presidential power is very strong. The points wrap neatly around the trend lines, and there is a clear trend that as the CPI score increases (implying less corruption), presidents become more constrained. The R-squared values in the scatterplots were also significantly higher than the 0.07 value in Figure 1.1 of Chapter 1 (this figure compared constitutional presidential powers to legislative and judicial constraints as computed by Varieties of Democracy). The difference in these R-squared values indicates that strong state institutions predict informal presidential power in a significantly greater percentage of cases than formal constitutional powers.

This strong relationship between corruption and presidential power has persisted throughout time, and Figures 3.6 and 3.7 showing 2018 and 2019 data illustrate the same trend:

Until now, I have only used scores from the CPI to proxy for the strength of state institutions. This book recognizes that using the CPI may be controversial, and therefore, I have decided to also use several alternative measures of institutional strength to see if the correlation still stands. In the Appendix, I have included an analysis involving other

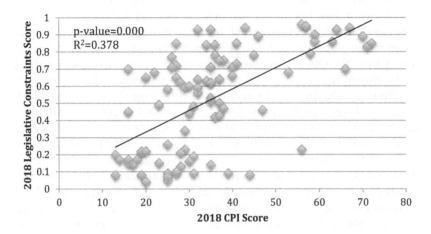

Figure 3.6 Relationship between Corruption and Legislative Constraints on the Executive in all presidential systems in the world in 2018.[a]

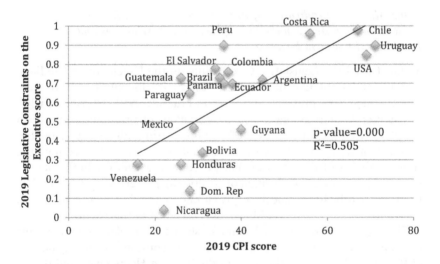

Figure 3.7 Relationship between Corruption and Legislative Constraints on the Executive in presidential democracies in the Western Hemisphere in 2019.

measures of rule of law, including Freedom House's Functioning of Government index, the World Bank's Rule of Law index and Control of Corruption index, The Rule of Law scores from the World Justice Project, as well as several indicators from the Quality of Government Institute

a I would like to thank Christy Lorenz for compiling the data for this scatterplot.

(QoG). These QoG measures include (a) an expert survey from the Quality of Government Institute on the percentage of $1,000 destined to reach the poor that would actually reach the poor (as opposed to being wasted/stolen while going through the government bureaucracy), (b) an expert survey from the Quality of Government Institute on the degree to which public employees are perceived to strive to be efficient, (c) an expert survey from the Quality of Government Institute on the degree to which public employees are perceived to strive to help other citizens, and (d) an expert survey from the Quality of Government Institute on the degree to which public employees are perceived to strive to follow rules. In all of these alternative measurements of institutional strength, there was a strong positive correlation between institutional strength and legislative constraints on the executive. As the scatterplots in the Appendix show, all results were statistically significant at the 5% level. In all scatterplots, there was also a clear upward trajectory (with better scores on these rule of law indicators translating into more constraints on the executive), with the points wrapping neatly around the trend line.

Using Alternative Indicators of Presidential Power to Measure the Relationship Between the Strength of State Institutions and Presidential Power in Practice

So far, I used the Legislative Constraints on the Executive and Judicial Constraints on the Executive indices (and their subcomponents) to measure the degree of presidential power in practice. As I described earlier in Chapter 1, there is one other measurement of presidential power in the literature that is partially useful in illustrating informal presidential power, namely Polity IV's xconst, "Executive Constraints." Despite the shortcomings of this indicator that I described earlier (including its use of several measures of formal/constitutional power), it is nevertheless useful as a robustness check in providing some additional evidence to substantiate the correlation I have just described in this section.

The scatterplots in Figures 3.8 and 3.9 show the correlation between rule of law as measured by the CPI and Polity IV's xconst in both (a) my dataset of the 20 presidential democracies in the Western Hemisphere and (b) my dataset of all presidential and semi-presidential systems in the world in 2012.

In addition to xconst, another indicator of presidential power that can serve as a useful robustness check derives from the work of Lucas González.[102] For 11 countries in Latin America, from the years 1980 to 2010, based on the coding of various country experts, he calculated the number of "attributes of delegative democracies." I compared the values in 2010 with the 2010 corruption scores (note in Figure 3.10 that the greater the number of attributes of delegative democracy, the more hyperpresidential a country is).

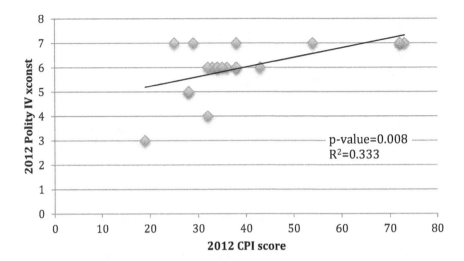

Figure 3.8 Exploring the relationship between the strength of state institutions and presidential power in the 20 presidential democracies in the Western Hemisphere (as measured through the Polity IV "xconst" index).

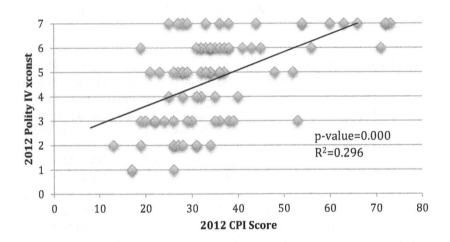

Figure 3.9 Exploring the relationship between the strength of state institutions in all presidential systems throughout the world (as measured through the Polity IV "xconst" index).

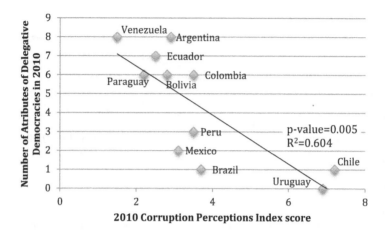

Figure 3.10 Comparing a country's score on the Corruption Perceptions Index with its number of attributes of delegative democracies.

The scatterplot in Figure 3.10 illustrates a similar trend as for Legislative Constraints on the Executive, and as the level of corruption decreases, a country becomes less hyperpresidential (with fewer and fewer attributes of delegative democracies).

Addressing the Problem of Endogeneity in My First Independent Variable

One of the problems that critics may rightfully identify is the problem of endogeneity. Critics might point out that one of the flaws with my analysis is that the direction of causality between institutional strength (as measured by corruption), and legislative and judicial constraints (as measured by expert surveys) could go the other way around. Their logic would be that rather than weak state institutions causing hyperpresidentialism to emerge, it is in fact a strong president that will destroy these state institutions and weaken the rule of law. Indeed, as the old saying goes, "power corrupts, and absolute power corrupts absolutely."

While I believe that there is certainly some truth to this critique and agree that the direction of causality also to a certain extent goes the other way around, my theory is in no way invalidated. In response to concerns over endogeneity, I would like to offer several arguments.

First, regarding the use of the CPI as an indicator of the strength of state institutions, it is based on an aggregation of various surveys regarding the extent of corruption in a country. Critics may argue that it is very easy for a group of experts to immediately suppose that corruption has increased after a president has concentrated power (since presumably when checks and balances diminish, this increases the opportunities and ease with which illicit activities can occur). Nevertheless, the key flaw in this argument is that many of the measurements in the CPI do not relate directly to high-level corruption at the level of the president and his/her ministers.

To summarize the methodology of the CPI, the 2012 CPI aggregated 13 data sources.[103] While it is true that some of these sources measure high-level corruption including among those in the executive branch, many of the measurements analyze corruption throughout the low- to mid-tiers of the public sector. For example, the Bertelsmann Foundation has a question which asks "to what extent are public officeholders prevented from abusing their position for private interests?" The Economist Intelligence Unit also asks the questions: "is there a professional civil service or are large numbers of officials directly appointed by the government?," "is there an independent body auditing the management of public finances?," and "is there a tradition of a payment of bribes to secure contracts and gain favors?" Similarly, the Freedom House Nations in Transit indicator has a question asking "does the government advertise jobs and contracts?" Given that the CPI has many measurements of lower-level corruption, it is therefore implausible that the sudden rise to power of a "superpresident" would necessarily lead to poorer scores on the CPI.

Also, if the high correlation that I discovered between corruption and presidential power was mainly due to a strengthening in executive power leading to poorer scores on the CPI (as opposed to poorer scores on the CPI leading to a strengthening in executive power as I argue in the book), we should expect that whenever there is a transition toward a representative democracy from authoritarian rule, corruption levels should significantly decrease. Following the logic of this alternative explanation, the increased checks and balances on a president after democratization should lead to a sharp decline in corruption. Nevertheless, many cases fail to corroborate this assertion. Although unfortunately the CPI does not go back before 1995 and thus cannot capture the moment of the Third Wave that would have allowed us to see the impact of democracy on corruption in Latin America and Eastern Europe, several more recent transitions serve as useful case studies. For example, Tunisia which transitioned to a vibrant democracy after the Arab Spring, despite seeing a surge in legislative and judicial constraints on the executive, actually witnessed a *decrease* on the CPI in the same time period. In 2008, its score was 4.4, whereas in 2015, the score was 38 (roughly equivalent to a 3.8 on the old scale which would imply that corruption increased). In Latin America, another illustrative case is Peru. In 1998, while the country was under the rule of Alberto Fujimori, the corruption score was a 4.5. Nevertheless, once Fujimori left power and a significantly more representative system took hold after 2000, the country's CPI score significantly slipped, and between 2004 and 2011, it hovered around 3.5. Therefore, if the driving force behind the strong correlation that I discovered between corruption and presidential power was that presidential power influenced corruption (rather than working in the direction I have proposed in this book), we should expect democratization to lead to less corruption, a phenomenon that so far has failed to materialize in a meaningful and consistent way.

The problem of endogeneity is further diminished through my use of other measurements of the strength of state institutions, particularly the ones from the Quality of Government dataset. As shown in the Appendix, all of the QoG indicators measure rule of law at the bottom level of the bureaucracy (as opposed to at high levels of government), and even if a strongman leader came to power who was perceived to be corrupt, it is unclear how this would affect the expert survey results for (a) the percentage of $1,000 that goes through the government bureaucracy and actually reaches its intended recipients, (b) the degree to which public employees strive to be efficient, (c) the degree to which public employees strive to help other citizens, and (d) the degree to which public employees strive to follow rules. In the Appendix, I show how higher values obtained on these indicators (which indicate stronger state institutions and rule of law) are correlated with higher legislative constraints on the executive. Given that it is difficult for a president to directly change the effectiveness and respect for the law among the general government bureaucracy, it is likely that the main direction of causality is that rule of law leads to more constraints on the president.

Another piece of evidence supporting the direction of causality advocated in this book is that rather than comparing CPI scores in 2012 with legislative and judicial constraints in 2012, I will instead compare 2012

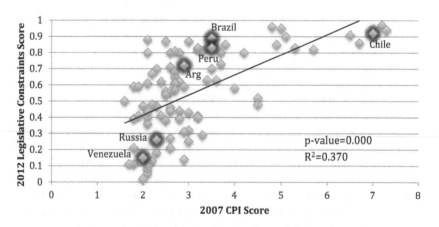

Figure 3.11 Relationship between 2007 CPI Scores and 2012 Legislative Constraints on the Executive in all presidential systems in the world.

legislative constraints scores with corruption scores from earlier, in 2007. The scatterplot in Figure 3.11 illustrates this relationship for all presidential systems throughout the world.

As the scatterplot shows, the relationship between the 2007 CPI scores and 2012 Legislative and Judicial Constraints is strong. The fact that I use CPI scores from 2007 and Legislative and Judicial Constraints from 2012 directly addresses the problem of endogeneity, since in this case my measurement of institutional strength *predates* the degree of presidential power. One can no longer argue that it is in fact presidential power that is causing a decrease in the degree of rule of law/institutional strength; rather, the weak rule of law in 2007 laid the foundations for the concentration of executive power which would occur later.

Finally, the most significant way in which I addressed the problem of endogeneity was through my case analysis of Argentina and Chile in this chapter. During my in-depth analysis of both countries, I showed how institutional weakness in Argentina directly led to weak legislative and judicial constraints on the executive; in the case of Chile, I showed how strong rule of law and strong institutions resulted in effective checks on presidential power.

Chapter Summary

In this chapter, for Argentina and Chile, I examined the primary institutions of horizontal accountability and contrasted the weakness of the institutions in Argentina to the strength of the institutions in Chile. I examined institutional strength through the lens of four criteria: the prestige of these institutions in society, the technical capacity of these institutions, the degree of independence from the executive branch, and the degree to which these institutions respect established rules/norms.

In Argentina, I examined congress, the judiciary, the *Auditoría General de la Nación* (AGN), the *Defensor del Pueblo*, and the Central Bank. Congress has been a remarkably feckless institution that has shown little ability to seriously challenge presidential initiatives; the Supreme Court has often been ineffective and subservient to the president following numerous rounds of court-packing; the *Auditoría* has been heavily politicized and has shown little ability to seriously investigate the executive branch; the Central Bank has also been politicized and has thus shown little willingness to challenge the president; finally, the Public Defender's Office has been completely decapitated through the failure to nominate a leader.

In Chile, I examined congress, the judiciary (both the Supreme Court and Constitutional Tribunal), the *Contraloría General*, the *Ministerio Público*, the *Consejo para la Transparencia*, and the Central Bank. Unlike in Argentina, in Chile, these institutions demonstrated significant strength.

Finally, I included a large-N analysis where I attempted to generalize the relationship between institutional strength and presidential power to all presidential systems in the world. The findings in this analysis suggest a very strong correlation between these two variables, and that these findings are applicable beyond simply Argentina and Chile.

Notes

1 Morgenstern and Manzetti 2003; p.153.
2 Gallo and Alston 2008; p.153.
3 Larkins 1998; p.427.
4 Kapiszewski 2012; p.77.
5 Rubio and Goretti 1998; p.37.
6 Chavez 2004b; p.456.
7 Helmke 2005; p.86.
8 Chavez 2004a; p.34.
9 Larkins 1998; p.431.
10 Chavez 2004b; p.458.
11 Chavez 2004b; p.458.
12 Larkins 1998; p.431.
13 Author's interview with Germán Garavano (Justice Minister of Argentina).
14 Author's interview with Germán Garavano (Justice Minister of Argentina).
15 *The Economist* December 18, 2012.
16 *The Economist* August 10, 2006.
17 Author's interview with Germán Garavano (Justice Minister of Argentina).
18 Author's interview with Raúl Madueño (Ex-Federal judge).
19 Author's interview with Esteban Lozina (Lawyer, ex-provincial deputy of the province of Misiones (FPV), former president of the Chamber of Deputies of Misiones).
20 Author's interview with Ricardo Biazzi (Minister of Education of Argentina for two days in December 2001 under President Puerta (PJ), Professor of Constitutional Law).
21 Author's interview with Germán Bordón (Lawyer and UCR Deputy in the Misiones Provincial Legislature, *Cámara de Representantes*).
22 Author's interview with Luis Jacobo (Former Minister of Education of the Province of Misiones (2011–2015) and the current representative of the province before the Federal Investment Council).
23 Author's interview with Abal Medina (Senator and Former Chief of Cabinet of Ministers for President Cristina Kirchner).
24 Author's interview with Ángel Rozas (Senator and ex-governor of Chaco, UCR).
25 Jones et al. 2002; p.658.
26 Author's interview with Matteo Goretti (Political scientist who coauthored a piece on decrees with Delia Ferreira Rubio).
27 Author's interview with Martín Maquieyra (Federal Deputy, PRO).
28 Author's interview with Orlando Gallo (Ex. Federal Judge in Mercedes Province during the military period, ex-Federal Deputy 1991–1995).
29 Isuani and San Martino 2005; p.51.
30 Author's interview with a source familiar with the passage process.
31 Manzetti 1999; p.72.
32 Berbecel 2012.
33 Author's interview with Orlando Gallo (Ex. Federal Judge in Mercedes Province during the military period, ex-Federal Deputy 1991–1995).
34 Author's interview with Julio Cobos (Ex-Vice President of Argentina, UCR senator from Mendoza).
35 Author's interview with Alicia Soraire (Federal Deputy, FPV).

36 Author's interview with Germán Garavano (Justice Minister of Argentina).
37 Author's interview with Oscar Lamberto (Director of the *Auditoría General*).
38 Author's interview with Oscar Lamberto (Director of the *Auditoría General*).
39 Rose-Ackerman 2011; p.309.
40 Rose-Ackerman 2011; p.310.
41 Author's interview with Raúl Madueño (ex-Federal Judge).
42 Author's interview with Raúl Allende (Head of the Press Department, *Auditoría General*).
43 Author's interview with Patricia Giménez (Federal Deputy, UCR).
44 Author's interview with Luciana Díaz Frers (Employee of the *Auditoría General*).
45 Author's interview with Raúl Allende (Head of the Press Department, *Auditoría General*).
46 Author's interview with Oscar Lamberto (Director of the *Auditoría General*).
47 Author's interview with Martín Maquieyra (Federal Deputy, PRO).
48 Author's interview with Alicia Soraire (Federal Deputy, FPV).
49 Author's interview with Abal Medina (Senator and Former Chief of Cabinet of Ministers for President Cristina Kirchner).
50 Author's interview with Germán Garavano (Justice Minister of Argentina).
51 Constitution of Argentina Article 86.
52 Author's interview with Juan Pablo Jorge (Employee at the *Defensor del Pueblo*).
53 Author's interview with Juan Pablo Jorge (Employee at the *Defensor del Pueblo*).
54 Rose-Ackerman 2011; p.314. Note that her article was written before a caretaker administration with little power was installed (since congress failed to appoint a new Ombudsman). This comment can be interpreted in terms of the power that the Ombudsman had in the past.
55 Rose-Ackerman 2011; p.313.
56 Author's interview with Juan Pablo Jorge (Employee at the *Defensor del Pueblo*).
57 Author's interview with Ricardo Barrios Arrechea (Ex-Governor of the Province of Misiones, 1983–1987, and Federal Deputy during the 1990s).
58 Author's interview with Rodrigo Egaña (National Director of the Civil Service).
59 Author's interview with Valeria Palanza (Professor specializing in presidential decrees in Latin America).
60 Author's interview with Mario Venegas (National Deputy, Christian Democrat).
61 Author's interview with Sebastián Soto (Head of the Juridical Legislative Division during the previous Piñera Government).
62 Author's interview with Mario Venegas (National Deputy, Christian Democrat).
63 Author's interview with Claudio Arriagada (National Deputy, Christian Democrat).
64 Author's interview with Ángel Fernández (Professor and Director of the Public Law Department at the Pontificia Universidad Católica de Chile).
65 Carey 2002; p.253.
66 Carroll et al. 2011; p.862.
67 Carroll et al. 2011; pp.863–864.
68 Author's interview with Carlos Carmona (Minister on the Constitutional Tribunal of Chile).
69 Stein and Tommasi 2005; figure 4.6 p.87.
70 Supreme Court of the United States.
71 Stein and Tommasi 2005; figure 4.6 p.87.

72 Sigmund 1977; p.180.
73 Graver 2015; p.245.
74 Couso et al. 2011; p.34.
75 Pereira 2005; p.5.
76 Hilbink 2007; p.224.
77 Hilbink 2007; p.7.
78 Hilbink 2007; p.7.
79 Hilbink 2007; p.42.
80 Author's interview with Carlos Carmona (Minister on the Constitutional Tribunal of Chile).
81 Graver 2015; p 246.
82 Author's interview with a former member of the Chilean Supreme Court.
83 Author's interview with a former member of the Chilean Supreme Court.
84 Author's interview with a former member of the Chilean Supreme Court.
85 Author's interview with Juan José Romero Guzmán (Minister on the Constitutional Tribunal).
86 Author's interview with Luis Cordero (Lawyer and expert on the *Contraloría*).
87 Author's interview with Jorge Bermúdez (Head of the *Contraloría* in Chile).
88 Author's interview with Jorge Bermúdez (Head of the *Contraloría* in Chile).
89 Author's interview with Luis Cordero (Lawyer and expert on the *Contraloría*).
90 Author's interview with Luis Cordero (Lawyer and expert on the *Contraloría*).
91 Author's interview with Jorge Bermúdez (Head of the *Contraloría* in Chile).
92 Author's interview with Luis Cordero (Lawyer and expert on the *Contraloría*).
93 Author's interview with Pablo Ruiz-Tagle (Specialist in Constitutional Law).
94 Author's interview with Alicia De La Cruz (Specialist on the Chilean *Contraloría*).
95 Based on the author's interview with Antonio Arancibia (Employee at the *Fiscalía Nacional*, Director of the Unit of International Cooperation).
96 Based on the author's interview with Christian Anker (Employee at the *Consejo para la Transparencia*).
97 Author's interview with Nicolás de la Cuesta (Manager of Human Resources, Central Bank of Chile).
98 Author's interview with Nicolás de la Cuesta (Manager of Human Resources, Central Bank of Chile).
99 Author's interview with Nicolás de la Cuesta (Manager of Human Resources, Central Bank of Chile).
100 See the V-Dem Codebook for more details.
101 Note that until and including 2011, CPI scores were calculated on a 0–10 scale, whereas, afterward, there was a switch to a 0–100 scale. Therefore, to have a common standard of measurement, all scores up to and including 2011 have been multiplied by 10.
102 González 2014.
103 (1) African Development Bank Governance Ratings 2011, (2) Bertelsmann Foundation Sustainable Governance Indicators 2011, (3) Bertelsmann Foundation Transformation Index 2012, (4) Economist Intelligence Unit Country Risk Ratings, (5) Freedom House Nations in Transit 2012, (6) Global Insight Country Risk Ratings, (7) IMD World Competitiveness Yearbook 2012, (8) Political and Economic Risk Consultancy Asian Intelligence 2012, (9) Political Risk Services International Country Risk Guide, (10) Transparency International Bribe Payers Survey 2011, (11) World Bank—Country Policy and Institutional Assessment 2011, (12) World Economic Forum Executive Opinion Survey (EOS) 2012, and (13) World Justice Project Rule of Law Index 2012 (Source Corruption Perceptions Index 2012: Full Source Description).

Bibliography

Berbecel, Dan. The Politics of Policy Stability: Explaining the Levels of Volatility in Economic Policymaking in Argentina and Brazil Between 1990 and 2010. Senior thesis. Harvard College, 2012.

Carey, John. "Parties, Coalitions, and the Chilean Congress in the 1990s." *Legislative Politics in Latin America.* Eds. Scott Morgenstern and Benito Nacif. Cambridge: Cambridge University Press, 2002, pp. 222–253.

Carroll, Royce, and Lydia Tiede. "Judicial Behavior on the Chilean Constitutional Tribunal." *Journal of Empirical Legal Studies.* Vol 8, Iss 4 (December 2011), pp. 856–877.

Chavez, Rebecca Bill. *The Rule of Law in Nascent Democracies: Judicial Politics in Argentina.* Stanford: Stanford University Press, 2004a.

Chavez, Rebecca Bill. "The Evolution of Judicial Autonomy in Argentina: Establishing the Rule of Law in an Ultrapresidential System." *Journal of Latin American Studies.* Vol 36, Iss 3 (August 2004b), pp. 451–478.

Couso, Javier, Domingo Lovera Parmo, Matías Guiloff, and Alberto Coddou. *Constitutional Law in Chile.* Alphen aan den Rijn: Kluwer Law International, 2011.

Gallo, Andres, and Lee Alston. "Argentina's Abandonment of the Rule of Law and Its Aftermath." *Journal of Law and Policy.* Vol 26 (2008), pp. 153–182.

González, Lucas. "Unpacking Delegative Democracy: Digging Into the Empirical Content of a Rich Theoretical Concept." *Reflections on Uneven Democracies: The Legacy of Guillermo O'Donnell.* Baltimore: Johns Hopkins University Press, 2014.

Graver, Hans Petter. *Judges Against Justice: On Judges When the Rule of Law is Under Attack.* New York: Springer, 2015.

Helmke, Gretchen. *Courts Under Constraints: Judges, Generals, and Presidents in Argentina.* Cambridge: Cambridge University Press, 2005.

Hilbink, Lisa. *Judges Beyond Politics in Democracy and Dictatorship: Lessons from Chile.* Cambridge: Cambridge University Press, 2007.

Isuani, Ernesto Aldo, and Jorge Antonio San Martino. "El nuevo sistema previsional Argentino. ¿Punto final a una larga crisis?" *Boletin Informativo Techint.* Vol 282 (1995), pp. 43–67.

Jones, Mark, Sebastian Saiegh, Pablo Spiller, and Mariano Tommasi. "Amateur Legislators—Professional Politicians: The Consequences of Party-Centered Electoral Rules in a Federal System." *American Journal of Political Science.* Vol 46, Iss 3 (July 2002), pp. 656–669.

Kapiszewski, Diana. *High Courts and Economic Governance in Argentina and Brazil.* Cambridge: Cambridge University Press, 2012.

Larkins, Christopher. "The Judiciary and Delegative Democracy in Argentina." *Comparative Politics.* Vol 30, Iss 4 (July 1998), pp. 423–442.

Levitsky, Steven, and Maria Victoria Murillo. *The Politics of Institutional Weakness: Argentine Democracy.* University Park: Pennsylvania State University Press, 2005.

Manzetti, Luigi. *Privatization South American Style.* Oxford: Oxford University Press, 1999.

Morgenstern, Scott, and Luigi Manzetti. "Legislative Oversight: Interests and Institutions in the United States and Argentina." *Democratic Accountability in*

Latin America. Eds. Scott Mainwaring and Christopher Welna. Oxford: Oxford University Press, 2003, pp. 132–169.

Pereira, Anthony. *Political Injustice: Authoritarianism and the Rule of Law in Brazil, Chile, and Argentina*. Pittsburgh: University of Pittsburgh Press, 2005.

Rose-Ackerman, Susan. "Hyper-Presidentialism: Separation of Powers Without Checks and Balances in Argentina and the Philippines." Faculty Scholarship Series. Paper 4155. 2011. http://digitalcommons.law.yale.edu/fss_papers/4155

Rubio, Delia, and Matteo Goretti. "When the President Governs Alone: The Decretazo in Argentina, 1989–93." *Executive Decree Authority*. Eds. John Carey and Matthew Shugart. Cambridge: University of Cambridge, 1998, pp. 33–61.

Sigmund, Paul. *The Overthrow of Allende and the Politics of Chile, 1964–1976*. Pittsburgh: University of Pittsburgh Press, 1977.

Stein, Ernesto, and Mariano Tommasi. *The Politics of Policies: Economic and Social Progress in Latin America*. Washington, DC: Inter-American Development Bank, 2005.

4 The Impact of the Size of the President's Party in Congress on Presidential Power

A critical factor that has influenced presidential power in Argentina and Chile is the degree to which presidents possessed a working majority in congress. In Part I of this chapter, I will describe how Argentine presidents were often able to concentrate power through their majorities or near-majorities in congress. I will show how it was likely for Peronist presidents to have unified government (or be just shy of unified government). Part II shows how Chile differed from Argentina in the ease of forming a working majority in congress; I will describe how a lack of a party majority checked the ability of presidents to concentrate power. In Part III of this chapter, I will attempt to further reinforce the importance of majoritarianism by briefly describing the case of Mexico. Finally, in Part IV, I discuss three institutional mechanisms that reduce presidential power by lowering the ability of presidents to form a working majority in congress.

In theory, the legislature can check executive overreach to the extent that the constitution permits. However, whether the president's party wields a majority in the assembly shapes the degree to which legislators employ these powers. In other words, whereas constitutionally the legislature is able to contain hyperpresidentialism, formal rules are no guarantee that congress will actually exercise its oversight prerogatives. If the president's party holds a majority in the legislature, it is possible that no one will move to check executive overreach.

There are two theoretical reasons why a presidential majority in congress would lead to hyperpresidentialism. First, legislative majorities increase the likelihood that presidents can pass their proposals quickly. This can include presidential appointments requiring congressional confirmation (a congressional majority may be more willing to allow a president to pack institutions with political allies) as well as bills proposed in congress (a president will have an easier time obtaining support for a bill when they have majorities in congress, and in extreme cases, the legislature may simply rubber-stamp the law). Second, having a working majority in congress ensures that presidential abuses of power will be more tolerated and less harshly punished. For example, if a president abuses

DOI: 10.4324/9781003142904-4

decree power, as Menem did, it is less likely that a congress filled with allies will challenge these abuses of power than a congress controlled by the opposition.

Part I: Argentina—A Case of Strong Majoritarianism

In this part, I will discuss the case of Argentina, where for a significant part of the post-1990 period, Peronist presidents benefitted from de facto unified government (I will describe below in more detail what I mean by "de facto" unified government). Presidents could often rely on both the Chamber of Deputies and the Senate to pass their proposals. I will go into detail about how this majority strengthened presidential power under Peronists; I will also describe how non-Peronist presidents who did not have majorities in congress were significantly weakened. I will attribute the greater ability of Peronist presidents to gain majorities in congress to the high degree of malapportionment in the electoral system, which benefits the Peronists at the expense of other parties. I will also describe how party cohesion has been a factor that further strengthened a president's control over his/her working majority in congress.

Clarifying How Argentine Presidents Had De Facto Majorities for Many Years in the Post-1990 Period

Before continuing, it is important to clarify the extent to which Peronist presidents possessed majorities in congress. Technically, Peronist presidents only benefitted from unified government for 10 years out of the 22 years under Menem and the Kirchners (where unified government is defined as the president's party possessing 50% or more of the seats in each chamber of congress). Menem under this definition only possessed unified government between 1995 and 1997; the Kirchners under this definition enjoyed unified government for eight years, between 2003–2009 and 2013–2015. Although Peronist presidents always benefitted from Peronist control of 50% or more seats in the Senate since democratization, it was a different story in the Chamber of Deputies. As Table 4.1 shows, between 1989 and 1991, Menem's PJ party held only 47.2% of the seats in the Chamber of Deputies; between 1991 and 1993, it only held 45.1% of seats; between 1993 and 1995, it held 49.4% of seats; and between 1997 and 1999, it held 46.3% of seats.

Although in all but ten years the Peronists were technically just short of a majority in the Chamber of Deputies, *in practice*, Peronist presidents enjoyed de facto majorities in congress for a significantly longer period of time. The reason for this is that Peronist presidents enjoyed the almost certain support of smaller parties, including various

Table 4.1 Illustrating control of the three branches of government in Argentina from 1983 to 2015

	1983-84	1984-1985	1985-1986	1986-1987	1987-1988	1988-1989	1989-1990	1990-1991
President	Alfonsin (UCR)						Menem (PJ)	
Chamber of Deputies (%)	50.8 UCR		50.8 UCR		44.9 UCR (the PJ received 38.6%)		47.2 PJ	
Chamber president	Pugliese (UCR) December 1983-April 1989, Moreau (UCR) April 1989-July 1989						Pierri (PJ)	
Senate (%)	45.7 PJ				45.7 PJ		54 PJ	

	1991-92	1992-1993	1993-1994	1994-1995	1995-1996	1996-1997	1997-1998	1998-1999
President	Menem							
Chamber of Deputies (%)	45.1 PJ		49.4 PJ		51.0 PJ		46.3 PJ	
Chamber president	Pierri (PJ)							
Senate (%)	54 PJ	62.5 PJ			55.7 PJ			55.7 PJ

	1999-00	2000-2001	2002-2003		2003-2004	2004-2005	2005-2006	2006-2007
President	De La Rúa (UCR)	Duhalde			Kirchner, Néstor			
Chamber of Deputies (%)	31.9 UCR, 14.4 Frepaso, 38.5 PJ		47.1 PJ		54.9 PJ		50.1 FPV	
Chamber president	Pascual (UCR)		Camaño (PJ)				Balestrini (FPV-PJ)	
Senate (%)	55.7 PJ, 30.0 UCR		57.1 PJ, 32.9 UCR		57.8 PJ 28.2 UCR		59.7 FPV	

	2007-08	2008-2009	2009-2010	2010-2011	2011-2012	2012-2013	2013-2014	2014-2015
President	Kirchner, Cristina							
Chamber of Deputies (%)	59.5 FPV		40.9% FPV, 8.2% Dissident Peronists		44.3 FPV, 8.9% Dissident Peronists		51.4, FPV, 13.2 Dissident Peronists	
Chamber president	Fellner (FPV-PJ)				Domínguez (FPV-PJ)			
Senate (%)	61.1 FPV		50.0 FPV, 34.7 UCR		50.0 FPV, 23.6 UCR		54.2 FPV	

regional parties. Some of these parties included the UCeDe, the PRS (Salta province), Acción Chaqueña (Chaco province), MPF (Tierra del Fuego province), and MPN (Neuquén province); at times, Menem could also count on the support of the Fuerza Republicana (Tucumán), the Partido Demócrata Progresista, the Partido Bloquista (San Juan province), and MODIN. Many of these smaller parties behaved in a very opportunistic manner and were vulnerable to cooptation from the executive branch. *Because the PJ was very few seats short of a majority, Menem could effectively guarantee that he would get over the 50% threshold through support from these smaller parties.* Unlike in Chile, where I will describe how presidents had to make meaningful tradeoffs to satisfy coalition partners, in Argentina, Menem could reach the 50% mark without having to make serious concessions on bills. In other words, because the PJ party was so unified and because it was only a few seats short of a majority, although technically Menem required some support beyond the PJ, in practice, this support was easily achievable. The de facto control of the Chamber of Deputies by the Peronists is also reflected in the fact that *for the entire period that Menem and the Kirchners were in office,* the position of President of the Chamber of Deputies was held by a Peronist (this is the rough equivalent to the position of Speaker of the House in the USA).

Menem's de facto majority in congress throughout his administration was also recognized by numerous media outlets in that period (despite his party being slightly under the 50% threshold in some years). For example, although the PJ received 47.2% of the seats in the Chamber of Deputies in the 1989 election, *The New York Times* reported that "Mr. Menem...rode to easy victory in the elections Sunday and led his party to control of the lower house of Congress."[1] Similarly, Morgenstern and Manzetti argue that:

> President Carlos Menem could count for most of his two terms in office (1989–95 and 1995–99) with both a working majority in Congress and a docile Supreme Court, which in turn allowed him to undercut most checks and balances.[2]

They also describe a "working Peronist majority in congress supported by small parties."[3] Finally, Jones et al. also describe in their piece that starting in July 1989, "the PJ assumed de facto control of the Chamber of Deputies."[4]

Background Information on Majoritarianism in Argentina

The institutional structure in Argentina has increased the likelihood that Peronists would win both the presidency and majorities (or near-majorities) in the legislature. As described earlier, between 1983 and 2019, all presidents with the exceptions of Fernando De La Rúa, Raúl Alfonsín, and Mauricio Macri enjoyed long periods in which their party de facto controlled both chambers of congress. Hyperpresidentialism was more common in these periods than it was when the president's party did not control the legislature. As Germán Garavano, the former Justice Minister, stated, "[not having a majority] makes certain things difficult, but guarantees that there will be no accumulation of power as with the Peronist administrations who always had parliamentary majorities."[5]

In the case of Argentina, majoritarianism strengthened hyperpresidentialism in two distinct ways. First, during the Menem years, control of both chambers of congress helped to ensure that many of his decrees were never overturned. For example, between 1989 and 1994 during Menem's first term in office, less than 1% of presidential decrees were successfully overturned by congress.[6]

Second, during the Kirchner years, and particularly during the presidency of Cristina Kirchner, her working majority in the legislature allowed many projects to pass with few amendments. Deputy Javier David (who is a Peronist) claimed that "the laws that she [Cristina Kirchner] sent to congress would enter and exit within a 48 hour time span. Sometimes not even a comma was changed...."[7] While the reference to 48 hours was obviously meant more figuratively than literally, it illustrates the speed with which laws passed under Cristina Kirchner.

The situation was different for Alfonsín and De La Rúa, who were forced to negotiate more as a result of the lack of majorities they possessed in congress. After he came to office in December 2015, Macri was also forced to govern without a majority in either chamber. Macri was in an especially weak position because his party (*Propuesta Republicana*, PRO) had merely 21% of the seats in the Chamber of Deputies and 13% of the seats in the Senate. Even though Macri's *Cambiemos* coalition had a plurality (though not a majority) of seats in the Chamber of Deputies, Macri had to negotiate any proposals with the Radicals, the *Coalición Cívica*, and several smaller parties within the coalition. Having more coalition partners meant more veto players who could decide to opt out of supporting a legislative proposal the president introduced. As a result, Macri had less capacity to concentrate power than his recent predecessors.

One example of an incident where Macri had to compromise because of an intracoalitional revolt was when he tried to name two judges by decree to the Supreme Court. Because of opposition from the Radical Party, Macri was forced to go back and get Senate approval. Similarly, ex-Deputy Orlando Gallo who served from 1991 to 1995 claimed in reference to the Macri government that "this is the first time in my life that I have seen the congress functioning. Why? Because nobody has a majority."[8]

For Macri, one of the consequences of not having a majority was that many of his legislative projects were modified in congress. Senator Abal Medina claimed in an interview that "the laws that came out [under Macri] were profoundly altered. Laws would come out very different than when they came in."[9]

Malapportionment as a Factor That Increases the Likelihood for Hyperpresidentialism Among Peronist Presidents

Because of changes in electoral design that malapportioned the legislature, the Peronist party has been at a significant advantage in the fight for control over congress. Given that Peronists have dominated the presidency since 1990, the ease with which Peronist presidents could build majorities (or near-majorities) in congress has had significant implications for hyperpresidentialism.

Peronist politicians, notably Perón himself, were able to expand the number of provinces where the party's voters dominated, and within the current structure, it is very difficult for a non-Peronist president to achieve unified government. Several new provinces were created during Perón's first term between 1946 and 1952 as well as one province during Menem's term in 1990.[10] Collectively, these subnational jurisdictions represent 9 out of the 23 provinces in Argentina (39%). Table 4.2 demonstrates just how small these nine provinces are in terms of the rest of the country, yet how large an influence they have in politics (especially in the Senate).

Note that under the Argentine electoral law, the party that wins the Senate race in a province gets two of three seats, and the next party is entitled to one seat. Overall, the mechanism whereby each province irrespective of population receives three seats in the Senate and receives a minimum of five seats in the Chamber of Deputies has led to the engineering of one of the most gerrymandered congresses in the world and has created a playing field deeply unfair to non-Peronist parties.

Radical voters were thus increasingly underrepresented in the legislature. Snyder and Samuels noted in 2004 that provinces where just 31% of the population resided controlled 44% of the seats in the Chamber of Deputies.[11]

The fact that congress is skewed toward Peronists is important because since democratization, out of 37 years, 25 were under Peronist presidents.

Table 4.2 Illustrating the disproportionate influence that newly created provinces under Peronist administrations have in the Chamber of Deputies and Senate

Province	Year that the province was created	Population (2010)	# Deputies (minimum 5 per province)	# Senators (the winning party gets two of three seats, and the losing party gets one seat)
Chaco	1951	1,055,259 (2.57%)	7 (2.72%)	3 (4.17%)
Chubut	1955	509,108 (1.24%)	5 (1.95%)	3 (4.17%)
Formosa	1955	530,162 (1.29%)	5 (1.95%)	3 (4.17%)
La Pampa	1951	318,951 (0.78%)	5 (1.95%)	3 (4.17%)
Misiones	1953	1101593 (2.69%)	7 (2.72%)	3 (4.17%)
Neuquén	1955	551,266 (1.34%)	5 (1.95%)	3 (4.17%)
Rio Negro	1955	638,645 (1.56%)	5 (1.95%)	3 (4.17%)
Santa Cruz	1956	273,964 (0.67%)	5 (1.95%)	3 (4.17%)
Tierra del Fuego	1990	127,205 (0.31%)	5 (1.95%)	3 (4.17%)
Total for "new" provinces	–	5,106,153 (12.5% of total population)	49 (19.0% of total seats)	27 (37.5% of total seats)
Total for Argentina	–	Approximately 41 million	257	72

Since 1990, the situation is even more lopsided, with merely six total years under non-Peronist administrations.

The Province of Buenos Aires (which includes the area surrounding the Autonomous City of Buenos Aires) has roughly 38% of the country's population, yet merely 27.2% of the seats in the Chamber of Deputies and 4% of the seats in the Senate. To put this level of malapportionment in perspective, in the USA (which also suffers from a malapportionment problem), the most populous state, California, has roughly 12% of the country's population. It, however, also has approximately 12% of the representatives in the US House (unlike the 11-point difference observed in the case of the Province of Buenos Aires) and 2% of the seats in the Senate.

Because of malapportionment that favors Peronist parties, it is structurally easy for Peronist presidents to achieve majorities in both chambers of congress, especially the Senate; at the same time, it is difficult for any non-Peronist president to achieve unified government. Although there were brief periods of time when non-Peronist parties managed to gain small majorities in the Chamber of Deputies, ever since the return of democracy, Peronists have always controlled the Senate. As illustrated in Table 4.2, even though the "new" provinces together only hold 12.5% of the country's population, they control 37.5% of the total Senate seats. Since these provinces tend to vote for Peronist presidents, it is structurally nearly impossible for non-Peronist parties to gain control of the Senate.

The gerrymandering in the Argentine federal system has ensured that Peronists not only have an advantage in congress but also at the subnational level in terms of governorships. Whereas the PJ for a long time held de facto unified government in the post-democratization period, what is even more impressive is the degree to which the PJ held a majority of governorships each year (as shown in Table 4.3). In some years, these majorities were enormous, including 77.3% of governorships from 1987 to 1991.

The Effects of Peronist Majorities on Congress and the Judiciary as Veto Players

This structure whereby Peronist presidents have an easy time obtaining majorities or near-majorities in the Chamber of Deputies and Senate (especially the Senate), and control of most governorships, has given them enormous power to be able to push through projects they desired with relative ease. Peronist presidents have rarely faced serious opposition in congress to their major initiatives, and this has contributed to the hyperpresidentialism witnessed in Argentina for most of the post-1990 period.

Table 4.3 Percentages of governorships help by each party, 1983–2007[a]

Political party	1983–1987	1987–1991	1991–1995	1995–1999	1999–2003	2003–2007
Partido Justicialista	54.6	77.3	60.9	58.3	58.3	66.7
Unión Cívica Radical	31.8	9.1	17.4	25.0	29.2	25.0
Provincial-parties	13.6	13.6	21.7	16.7	8.3	4.2
Others					4.2	4.2
Total number of governorships	22	22	23	24	24	24

[a] This table is recreated from Jones 2008; p.47.

The de facto majorities that Argentine presidents had in congress, and particularly the Senate, also made it significantly easier for presidents to pass Necessity and Urgency Decrees. If a president issues a decree, in order to repeal it, *both* chambers of congress must acquiesce. In other words, the president requires a working majority in only one of the chambers in order to ensure that his/her decrees are not repealed. In practice, what this has meant was that presidents from the Peronist party were essentially free to enact whatever decrees they wanted given the traditional Peronist dominance in the Senate. As I mentioned earlier, in the 1989–1994 period under Menem, less than 1% of the decrees that he issued were fully repealed. Because Senate Peronists could block the repeal of any decree, presidents could "bully" the legislature and motivate congressional action through the threat to pass a reform by decree. Had the president not possessed a majority in any of the chambers of congress, the legislature could have credibly threatened to repeal a decree and thus prevented the abuse of NUDs. As Mustapic describes, "one of the reasons that Menem was able to use his [NUD] powers so frequently was that the opposition did not have majority control of either house of the Congress."[12] Although there is technically a bicameral commission in congress whose role it is to review NUDs, this commission was traditionally stacked with party loyalists.

The tendency toward majoritarianism of Peronist administrations in both the Senate and Chamber of Deputies has also affected the Supreme Court. The process for nominating Supreme Court judges bears many similarities to that of the USA, with the president nominating a judge who must be approved with a vote in the Senate. Nevertheless, because of the high number of seats that Peronists typically obtained in the Senate, achieving the required number of votes to approve a Supreme Court judge did not prove to be a problem. Therefore, because of the gerrymandering that has allowed Peronist presidents to control the Senate (and often the Chamber of Deputies), this control has spilled over to the Supreme Court, in which all Peronist presidents since democratization enjoyed comfortable "working majorities" (recall that the most extreme example of this was Menem's court). As I mentioned earlier, using his majority in congress, President Néstor Kirchner was also able to reform the Council of Magistrates in a way that also gave him control over lower-court appointments. According to Justice Minister Garavano, "through an accumulation of power in parliament, [the majority] minimized the power of institutions of horizontal accountability, including the judiciary."[13] Similarly, Deputy Maquieyra claimed that "when you have a large majority in congress, you start to control all of the powers, including the judiciary. The system contains checks and balances, but it is a problem when you have too many majority governments."[14] Similarly, the vast majorities that Argentine Peronist presidents enjoyed in congress allowed them to stack other critical institutions of horizontal accountability such as the *Auditoría General.*

In Argentina, the large working majorities of Peronist presidents also led to hyperpresidentialism because, according to ex-deputy Miguel Iturrieta, they made it significantly easier to invoke special sessions of congress. He claimed that:

> When you have an absolute majority, it becomes easier to call special sessions...If the president asks for a special session, it is very easy to convoke, and we surpassed the 129 deputies necessary for the quorum. We could hold a session even if nobody from the opposition showed up, and this is very bad.[15]

As I noted in Chapter 2, special sessions allow legislators to skip the committee process and go directly to a floor vote.

Several interviewees argued that in contrast to many Peronist presidents, Macri could not govern in as hyperpresidential a manner since he lacked unified government. Deputy Patricia Giménez noted that "with Cristina Kirchner there were no restrictions because the FPV had a majority...and laws of very poor quality came out...[President Macri] does not have a majority, and there has to be a greater dialogue."[16] Similarly, Deputy Barletta noted that the lack of a majority "obliges the legislators and the president to have a permanent sense of debate, consensus, and compromise, thus ensuring that projects are discussed, analyzed, improved and modified."[17] Former Vice President Julio Cobos who served under Cristina Kirchner described that during her administration, "there were no problems in passing laws because of her majorities, and it is said that congress functioned merely as a rubber-stamp."[18]

In short, as I have attempted to demonstrate in this section, one of the principal reasons for the emergence of hyperpresidentialism in Argentina is the extreme majoritarianism that has existed in the political system, with Peronist presidents having de facto unified government during most of the years since democratization. Peronist presidents who benefitted from these majorities (which were in large part due to gerrymandering in the electoral system) were able to concentrate power, with congress not only approving their initiatives but also allowing them to pack institutions such as the courts.

Party Cohesiveness in Argentina as a Factor That Strengthens Hyperpresidentialism

What further solidifies the majoritarianism in the Argentine political system is the extremely high level of discipline among parties, especially Peronist factions. In a political system like that of the USA, having a party majority does not guarantee that legislators will vote for the president's proposals. Cases such as John McCain's famous "thumbs-down" that sank the repeal effort of the Affordable Care Act are common in countries such as the USA, and it is often the case that certain legislators may rebel. *Generally, low party discipline reduces presidential power since the president cannot rely on his/her working majority to as great an extent.* Unlike in the USA, in Argentina, party discipline is extremely high, contributing to hyperpresidentialism. High party discipline strengthens a president's working majority in congress and makes it less likely that legislators will defect. Party discipline is so high in Argentina that many legislators will support a law backed by their party even if it hurts their province. Senator Ángel Rozas when asked whether he would vote in favor of a law supported by his party that would harm his province described that, "I would vote against it, but not everyone does this. Here, party discipline is prioritized more than the interest of the province."[19]

I will attribute the high party discipline to the immense control that party leaders have over legislators (when a party controls the executive branch, the president becomes the top party leader). Legislators are often at the mercy of party leaders who are instrumental in both securing deputies and senators a place on electoral lists as well as securing them employment in government following their tenures in congress. Such a system creates incentives for legislators to follow the party line, which often means supporting the president if he/she is from their party. It is theoretically possible that party bosses disagree with the president; however, in practice, Peronist presidents have strong control over the key officials in their faction (Peronism generally has a strong vertical culture which discourages dissent and debate).

Argentina uses a closed-list proportional representation system in which candidates are rank-ordered, and the number of candidates selected from a list depends on the percentage of the vote that the party won (the mean district magnitude is five). Because the party leaders are largely responsible for the lists (including the rank-ordering), aspiring legislators have a large incentive to be loyal to party leaders, especially the president. Rogers writes that "Argentina's party lists in the Chamber of Deputies and the Senate are determined by local party chiefs, most often the governor. To gain reelection, therefore, legislators need to stay in the good graces of their local boss."[20]

Néstor Migueliz in an interview claimed that "the closed-list system oftentimes causes a legislator to owe their political career to the executive branch. This goes against the separation of powers."[21]

As suggested by Jones,[22] in Argentina, one of the primary reasons why legislators will almost always vote with their party is due to career prospects. Virtually all deputies and senators in Argentina desire to either obtain reelection, or if this does not materialize, to pursue a career in politics outside of congress (e.g., within the government bureaucracy and politics at the provincial level). Jones writes that feuding with party leaders is likely to result in a legislator having a "difficult time achieving either reelection or pursuing a career elsewhere in politics due to the lack of an alternative viable political party to join."[23] Professor and ex-minister Ricardo Biazzi in an interview even more dramatically claimed that if a legislator goes against the party leadership, "the punishment is severe...You are sent to the desert and it is your last term in office."[24] Orlando Gallo also claimed that "if a person were to vote against their party leadership, they become dead to their party."[25] The power of party leaders over legislators is particularly strong considering that the reelection rate in the Chamber of Deputies is only approximately 20%.[26]

There are several reasons for this low reelection rate. First, governors do not like to choose the same person multiple times to serve in the legislature, out of fear that providing them multiple terms will strengthen their position in congress and in the long run threaten the governor's own supremacy.[27] Another major reason for the extremely low reelection rate in congress is because, culturally, reelection of legislators is not well viewed. Unlike in countries such as the USA where serving for 20–30 years is seen in a good light, in Argentina, career politicians are not viewed favorably. From a practical standpoint, unlike in other countries such as Chile where legislators are encouraged to return regularly to their province and maintain close contact with their respective electorates, in Argentina (which is more Buenos Aires-centric) upon being elected, they disappear from the local political scene in their home province, making it difficult to run a reelection campaign against an incumbent who is already there.[28]

Rather than being a serious career job, the position of lawmaker in Argentina is often a temporary stepping stone to another position in the public sector (where one depends upon party leaders for advancement).

Many legislators eventually take up positions in the administration of their provinces, and according to Mustapic:

> They [legislators] have the opportunity for careers in other areas. The career that they can follow in the provinces is more interesting than that in congress. Congress is merely a stepping stone, and a person's political life develops more in the provinces.[29]

Without a good working relationship with party leaders, a legislator will have a difficult time advancing in his/her political career.

In short, presidents in Argentina will be able to rely on support from disciplined political parties (especially Peronist presidents), and this high level of party discipline will perpetuate hyperpresidentialism.

The Futility of Primaries to Reduce the Power of Party Leaders

Some may argue that the control of governors and party leaders such as the president over party lists has weakened because of the recently implemented primary system in Argentina. In theory, primaries would significantly weaken the strength of party leaders and would greatly undermine the system that has permitted executives to wield such strong control over legislators. Independently elected legislators who are chosen not because a governor or president placed them on the list but because of their appeal to primary voters would theoretically have stronger incentives to deviate from the party line, causing more party indiscipline. However, as I will show, primaries in Argentina so far have not substantially weakened party leaders.

The Law of Democratization of Political Representation, Transparency and Electoral Equity (Law 26571) was passed in December 2009 and is more colloquially known as the "Ley de PASO," with PASO standing for *primarias abiertas simultáneas y obligatorias*, or "open, simultaneous and mandatory primaries." Although the spirit of the law was to democratize political parties, the law has not achieved its goal. As a New York Times article describes:

> The introduction of primaries in 2009 was also designed to promote democracy at the party level, by allowing voters to select the candidates rather than leave those decisions to backroom deals by political operatives...[However], with a few exceptions, voters won't really be selecting who will be running in October.[30]

The article goes on to say that in the primaries, most parties would only be presenting one list of candidates (chosen by party leaders).

In practice, the way that the system works is that several months before the general election, primaries are held. Unlike in the USA where primaries generate a strong competitive intraparty dynamic, in Argentina, most candidates run unopposed. A notable exception was the *Cambiemos* coalition, in which Mauricio Macri ran against Elisa Carrió and Ernesto Sanz for the presidency. The presence of competitive primaries in *Cambiemos* is not surprising given the strong tradition of competition and horizontal structure in the UCR (one of the key members of the coalition). In contrast, there is very little competition within the Peronist party. The diagram in Table 4.4 illustrates the results of the primaries at the presidential level in 2015, with all parties/coalitions except *Cambiemos*, UNA, and the *Alianza Frente de Izquierda* having only one list.

The situation was even more ludicrous in 2011, when *all* parties ran a single list at the presidential level.

In practice, primaries in Argentina, rather than accomplishing their legal goal of preselecting the candidates for the general election, serve two purposes: first, they serve as a preview of the results to come in the general election. Given that there is usually only one candidate per party

Table 4.4 Results of the Argentine presidential primary held on August 9, 2015[a]

	FORMULAS - AGRUPACIONES POLITICAS	VOTOS	% POSITIVOS	% VALIDOS
131	ALIANZA FRENTE PARA LA VICTORIA	8.720.573	38,67%	36,69%
	SCIOLI, DANIEL OSVALDO - ZANNINI, CARLOS ALBERTO	8.720.573	100%	
135	ALIANZA CAMBIEMOS	6.791.278	30,12%	28,57%
	MACRI, MAURICIO - MICHETTI, MARTA GABRIELA	5.523.413	81,33%	
	SANZ, ERNESTO RICARDO - LLACH, LUCAS	753.825	11,10%	
	CARRIO, ELISA MARIA AVELINA - FLORES, HECTOR ANTONIO	514.040	7,57%	
138	ALIANZA UNIDOS POR UNA NUEVA ALTERNATIVA (UNA)	4.639.405	20,57%	19,52%
	MASSA, SERGIO TOMAS - RUBERTO SAENZ, GUSTAVO ADOLFO	3.230.887	69,64%	
	DE LA SOTA, JOSE MANUEL - RUCCI, CLAUDIA MONICA	1.408.518	30,36%	
132	ALIANZA PROGRESISTAS	781.472	3,47%	3,29%
	STOLBIZER, MARGARITA ROSA - OLAVIAGA, MIGUEL ANGEL	781.472	100%	
137	ALIANZA FRENTE DE IZQUIERDA Y DE LOS TRABAJADORES	732.851	3,25%	3,08%
	DEL CAÑO, NICOLAS - BREGMAN, MYRIAM TERESA	375.874	51,29%	
	ALTAMIRA, JORGE - GIORDANO, JUAN CARLOS	356.977	48,71%	
133	ALIANZA COMPROMISO FEDERAL	472.341	2,09%	1,99%
	RODRIGUEZ SAA, ADOLFO - NEGRE DE ALONSO, LILIANA TERESITA	472.341	100%	
136	ALIANZA FRENTE POPULAR	106.324	0,47%	0,45%
	DE GENNARO, VICTOR NORBERTO - CODONI, EVANGELINA SOLEDAD	106.324	100%	
13	MOVIMIENTO AL SOCIALISMO	103.742	0,46%	0,44%
	CASTAÑEIRA, MANUELA JIMENA - AYALA, JORGE LUIS	103.742	100%	
134	MST - NUEVA IZQUIERDA	95.780	0,42%	0,40%
	BODART, HUGO ALEJANDRO - RIPOLL, VILMA ANA	95.780	100%	
81	PARTIDO POPULAR	67.798	0,30%	0,29%
	YATTAH, MAURICIO JORGE - MORETTA, MARIA BELEN	67.798	100%	
57	MOVIMIENTO DE ACCION VECINAL	39.512	0,18%	0,17%
	ALBARRACIN, RAUL HUMBERTO - DIB, GASTON	39.512	100%	
	VOTOS POSITIVOS	22.551.076	93,88%	
	VOTOS EN BLANCO	1.216.634	5,06%	
	VOTOS ANULADOS	254.106	1,06%	
	TOTAL DE VOTANTES	24.021.816		

[a] Table taken from Elecciones Argentinas: Dirección Nacional Electoral.

list, many have described these primaries as a massive "official" pre-election poll. As the *Washington Post* reports about the 2015 primaries:

> The Aug. 9 primaries weren't like U.S. primaries. Everyone already knew the names of the nominees for the country's three leading national alliances of political parties. Rather, the Argentine primaries matter because they are the best way to know the level of popular support for the leading presidential candidates.[31]

The article goes on to note that opinion surveys are generally distrusted in Argentina, and that these primaries (which are mandatory for voters between the ages of 18 and 69) provide an accurate picture of public opinion.

The second, and perhaps only significant effect that primary elections do indeed have on Argentine elections is that they eliminate small parties through a minimum threshold. If a party or presidential candidate fails to gather 1.5% of the total vote, they are disqualified and cannot participate in the general election. This measure meant to disqualify smaller parties was intentionally placed by the Kirchners, as they perceived that smaller parties siphoned votes away from them to a greater extent than from opposition parties. The way that Argentine presidential elections work is that a candidate can win in the first round if they obtain at least 40% of the total votes, with a minimum difference of 10 percentage points from the second-place candidate. Fearing that she would not win in the first round and be forced into a second round of voting, Cristina Kirchner tried to minimize the vote-splitting effect of third parties by attempting to eliminate them from the election, increasing her chances of achieving the requisite 40%. Originally, Cristina Kirchner had sought a minimum 3% threshold, but backed down after intense opposition not only from civil society but also from some of her allies in congress.[32] Ultimately, Cristina Kirchner easily won the first round of the 2011 elections with 54% of the vote.

Specifically with regard to legislative primaries (at the level of deputy and senator), although in theory a candidate can compete in the primary who is not favored by party leaders, in practice, it is very difficult for him/her to win.

In the 2015 primary for deputies and senators, as was the case at the presidential level, voters most of the time could only choose from one list for each party. The *Frente Para la Victoria* in almost all of the provinces ran only one list, and like at the presidential level, there was slightly more competition at the level of the *Cambiemos* alliance. Zelaznik confirms that:

> Primaries at the level of deputies are significantly more frequent in Radicalism than in Peronism. In the *Frente Para la Victoria*, they are not inexistent, but infrequent. In the majority of the provinces, in the primaries there is only one list.[33]

Table 4.5 contains the results for the primary in the City of Buenos Aires.

In short, primary elections have done little to erode the traditional system where legislators are tightly controlled by party leaders. Primaries have failed to provide incentives to legislators to deviate from the party platform, and based on their current structure, it is unlikely that they will encourage the types of rebellious legislators who would weaken the president's working majority and thus presidential power.

Summary of Part I

In short, throughout Part I of this chapter, I have attempted to describe the second major reason why hyperpresidentialism has occurred in Argentina, namely the strong tendencies toward majoritarianism under Peronist presidents, who often benefitted from de facto unified government. I have discussed how the malapportionment in the electoral

Table 4.5 Results in the 2015 legislative primaries (for federal *diputados*) in the City of Buenos Aires[a]

AGRUPACIONES POLITICAS - LISTAS		VOTOS	% POSITIVOS	% VALIDOS
503	ALIANZA CAMBIEMOS	871.549	47,93%	46,67%
	E - EL PODER DE LA UNION	63.635	7,30%	
	F - REPUBLICA DE LIBRES E IGUALES	69.829	8,01%	
	G - EL CAMINO DEL CAMBIO	738.085	84,69%	
502	ALIANZA FRENTE PARA LA VICTORIA	411.285	22,62%	22,02%
	A - CELESTE Y BLANCA K NESTOR KIRCHNER	411.285	100%	
505	ALIANZA UNIDOS POR UNA NUEVA ALTERNATIVA	226.900	12,48%	12,15%
	A - FRENTE RENOVADOR +A15	226.900	100%	
504	ALIANZA PROGRESISTAS	119.558	6,57%	6,40%
	A - CREO	72.325	60,49%	
	MS - IGUALDAD Y DECENCIA	47.233	39,51%	
506	ALIANZA FRENTE DE IZQUIERDA Y DE LOS TRABAJADORES	76.187	4,19%	4,08%
	1A - RENOVAR Y FORTALECER EL FRENTE	32.470	42,62%	
	2U - UNIDAD	43.717	57,38%	
187	AUTODETERMINACION Y LIBERTAD	53.073	2,92%	2,84%
	A - CAMINAMOS PREGUNTANDO	53.073	100%	
501	ALIANZA COMPROMISO FEDERAL	18.975	1,04%	1,02%
	1A	18.975	100%	
72	INSTRUMENTO ELECTORAL POR LA UNIDAD POPULAR	14.007	0,77%	0,75%
	A - PROTAGONISMO Y PARTICIPACION	14.007	100%	
38	MOVIMIENTO SOCIALISTA DE LOS TRABAJADORES	9.366	0,52%	0,50%
	A - UNIDAD	9.366	100%	
13	MOVIMIENTO AL SOCIALISMO	8.026	0,44%	0,43%
	SoB	8.026	100%	
76	DE LA CULTURA LA EDUCACION Y EL TRABAJO	5.277	0,29%	0,28%
	A - POR TU SALARIO	5.277	100%	
327	BANDERA VECINAL	2.845	0,16%	0,15%
	A - LEALTAD	2.845	100%	
333	FUERZA ORGANIZADA RENOVADORA DEMOCRATICA	1.357	0,07%	0,07%
	A - DIGNIDAD	1.357	100%	

[a] Table taken from Elecciones Argentinas: Dirección Nacional Electoral.

system has made it likely for Peronist presidents to gain control of both chambers of congress. Without a legislative majority, the president must negotiate with the opposition, and it should therefore not come as a surprise that the weakest Argentine presidents since democratization have been Alfonsín, De La Rúa, and Macri (none of whom benefitted from unified government). I have shown not only how Peronist presidents had party majorities (or near-majorities) but also how they could rely on the full support of these legislators given the high levels of party cohesion in Argentina.

Part II: Chile—A Case of Weak Majoritarianism

In the discussion on Argentina, I noted how one of the reasons for the development of hyperpresidentialism was that the president was able to build strong working majorities in congress. In this part, I will describe how majoritarianism was not as strong in Chile, and how Chilean presidents had a harder time achieving a working majority in congress. Chilean presidents (a) lacked a *party* majority, (b) were further weakened due to the open-list electoral system which lowered party/coalition discipline, and (c) were impeded by the "hard-wiring" of many laws which required supermajorities to change.

At a first glance, it may appear that Chile has had unified government for an even greater percentage of the time than Argentina, with unified government appearing to occur throughout all years except 2010–2014 and except recently since March of 2018 (after the start of the second Piñera administration). While in Argentina Peronist presidents often enjoyed working majorities, in Chile leftist *Concertación* and *Nueva Mayoría* presidents *always* had a coalitional majority in both chambers of congress. Although on the surface Chilean *Concertación* presidents appear to have enjoyed unified government, it is deceptive to see the Chilean party system in terms of two "parties," since the *Nueva Mayoría* and *Alianza* were actually coalitions of parties. Chilean presidents as mentioned above never actually possessed party majorities. Note that the *Nueva Mayoría* and *Concertación* both refer to the coalition of left-wing parties in Chile (the name *Concertación* was used until 2013, when it changed to *Nueva Mayoría*). In 2017, in the context of the presidential election, the *Nueva Mayoría* suffered a split, with the Christian Democratic party fielding its own candidate separately from the rest of the coalition. Similarly, the *Alianza* and *Chile Vamos* both refer to the coalition of right-wing parties (the name *Alianza* was used until 2015, and since 2015, *Chile Vamos* has been in use).

Chilean Coalitions as Heterogeneous and the Lack of a Party Majority by Presidents

Chilean coalitions cannot be seen as parties since they are extremely heterogeneous, with the parties in the coalitions sometimes having completely different stances on certain issues. For example, within the *Nueva Mayoría*, the far-left Communist Party had a platform entirely different from the centrist Christian Democrats. In fact, the differences between parties were so great that Professor David Altman claimed that "it's possible that a Christian Democrat feels closer to someone in the *Renovación Nacional* on certain issues than with a Communist."[34] Francisca Moya also claims that "[the *Concertación*] is a coalition where there are several different sectors represented across a broad political spectrum."[35] Even within parties themselves, there are divisions, and, for example, journalist and TV presenter Fernando Paulsen describes that "the Christian Democrats are divided into 3–4 fronts, and also the Socialist Party."[36] Similarly, in the rightist *Chile Vamos* coalition, the *Renovación Nacional* has far more moderate positions than the UDI party. The differences between these parties have led to significant friction, and Deputy Felipe De Mussy argued that:

> In the rightist coalition, the UDI and RN have historically clashed several times. On average, over the past 27 years since democratization, the UDI and RN have been divided at times and have not been united in voting. The two do not act like they were the same party.[37]

Lucas Sierra similarly claimed that there has been significant infighting among the RN and UDI.[38] When asked whether coalitions functioned like parties, journalist Fernando Paulson replied that "no, not in any shape or form. They are literally associations with common goals, but nothing more."[39]

If we were to look at election results in terms of parties rather than coalitions, the purported "majority" of Bachelet in congress vanishes completely. Tables 4.6a and 4.6b provide the results of the 2013 elections in the Senate and Chamber of Deputies.

If we break the alliances apart into separate parties, the former president's party had only a small fraction of the senators and deputies in

Table 4.6a 2013 Senate Election Results by coalition and party[a]

Party/Coalition	Total seats	% of seats
Nueva Mayoría Coalition	*21*	*55.3*
Socialist Party	7	18.4
Party for Democracy	6	15.8
Christian Democratic Party	6	15.8
Independent	2	5.2
Alianza Coalition	*16*	*42.1*
Independent Democratic Union	8	21.1
National Renewal	8	21.1
Independents not affiliated with a coalition	1	2.6

[a] Source: El Mercurio

Table 4.6b 2013 Chamber of Deputies Election Results by coalition and party

Party/Coalition	Total seats	% of seats
Nueva Mayoría Coalition	*67*	*55.8*
Christian Democratic Party	21	17.5
Socialist Party	16	13.3
Party for Democracy	15	12.5
Communist Party	6	5.0
Social Democrat Radical Party	6	5.0
Other/Independent	3	2.5
Alianza Coalition	*49*	*40.8*
Independent Democratic Union	29	24.2
National Renewal	19	15.8
Independent	1	0.8
Other parties and independents not affiliated with a coalition	4	3.3

congress. With Bachelet's Socialist Party holding only 13.3% of the Chamber of Deputies and 18.4% of the Senate, the situation in Chile rather than resembling the two-party democracy in the USA, in fact more closely resembled the party system in Brazil (with multiparty presidentialism where presidents are forced to build coalitions). The president is often reluctant to try to concentrate power for fear of alienating his/her coalition partners, and Siavelis argues that "presidents who dominate the legislative process would be accused of not respecting coalitional arrangements. Executives walked a fine line, and the full use of presidential authority would signal a deviation from this line."[40]

Within the Chilean coalitional dynamics, the main tool that the president wields to "control" his/her coalition is the ability to provide parties with ministerial positions. Michelle Bachelet after being reelected doled out ministries as follows: six were given to the Party for Democracy, five were given to the Christian Democrats, one was given to the Communist Party, two were given to the Radical Party, three were given to the Socialist Party, one was given to the Christian Left, and five were given to independents.[41] In other words, of the 23 ministries, only 3 positions were given to Bachelet's Socialist Party. As Olivares makes clear, if a party were to vote against the coalition, the ministries of this party would be in jeopardy.[42] Cabinet positions provide significant benefits for a party, since having a cabinet position allows that party to present projects directly to congress.[43]

Although this mechanism of control over congress through cabinet posts is significant, it does not guarantee the president that his/her coalitional majority will vote with them. This mechanism of control pales when compared to the degree of control that Peronist presidents in Argentina have over members from their party.

The fragmented party system in Chile that prevents hyperpresidentialism by denying the president a majority is neatly summarized by Fuentes, who when asked why congress has been such a strong check on the president, replied that

> I think it has to do with multipartism, where you have a president who is the head of a coalition where votes are divided, and where the executive is obliged to constantly negotiate with parties. This in my opinion gives congress the most leverage relative to the president, who requires votes to get legislation approved.[44]

The Hard-Wiring of Provisions Through Constitutional Norms and Organic Laws

Another factor that has weakened the effect of Chilean presidents' working majorities is the fact that many aspects of Chilean lawmaking require an elevated majority (more than 50% of the vote in congress) to be modified, thus minimizing the advantage of a simple majority. In this section, I will show how many aspects of Chilean lawmaking are codified either in the constitution, in organic laws, or in *leyes de quórum calificado* (laws of elevated quorums).

The constitution regulates several economic aspects of society. First, like the US constitution, the right of private property is enshrined in Article 24, which states that no citizen can be deprived of his/her property without "indemnification for patrimonial harm effectively caused." The constitution also guarantees an independent Central Bank in Article 108 and curtails the activities of unions. Other areas covered by the constitution include nationality and citizenry (including the right to vote), powers given to the president, powers given to congress, the autonomy of the *Contraloría*, etc.

The Chilean constitution before the 2005 amendment also directly protected high-level military officials from removal by elected civilian authorities and thus ensured the continued influence of the military in political life. Siavelis writes in a 2000 book prior to the constitutional reform that:

> But beyond ensuring the tenure of serving officials, the designers of the 1980 constitution also created a series of institutional mechanisms in an effort to establish a permanent tutelary political role for the armed forces. Foremost among these mechanisms is the constitutional proscription against the removal of high-level officials by civilian authorities. The currently serving commanders of the army, air force, navy, and national police cannot be removed by the president; neither could Aylwin remove members of the governing junta that continued to serve during his tenure. Though the president is

charged with naming commanders in chief, they must be chosen from among the five most senior officers in each of the services and are to be vested with a four-year term, during which they cannot be removed.[45]

In particular, the National Security Council had significant authority in the immediate post-democratization period; this body could self-convene even without the president's approval and had the right to name two of the seven members of the Constitutional Tribunal. Only the Commander in Chief, not the president, could hire, fire, and promote members of the armed forces. The armed forces also benefitted from positions of "appointed senators" until the 2005 constitutional reform. These unelected senators would prove pivotal to blocking any attempts to alter the framework of the constitution. Hollifield and Jillison summarize that in Chile, "the constitution made sure that military powers remained enhanced even if the military no longer controlled the executive."[46]

Changing the constitution is extremely difficult and requires either a three-fifths majority or a two-thirds majority in the legislature, depending on which part of the constitution one desires to change (Chapters 1, 3, 8, 9, 12, and 15 require a two-thirds majority, whereas the other chapters can be changed with support from three-fifths of the legislature). The provisions that require a two-thirds majority to change are those that involve the attributions of the president, armed forces, Constitutional Tribunal, and National Security Council.[47] Similarly, as Article 66 dictates, all laws made by congress that directly interpret constitutional precepts (*leyes interpretativas*) require a three-fifths majority. Regarding the power of the military which was also hard-wired in the constitution, Siavelis in his 2000 piece was pessimistic about the possibility for significant change, writing that:

> Given that a constitutional amendment would be necessary to transform the status of the armed forces, it is unlikely, at least in the near future, that there will be any significant erosion in the constitutional power of the armed forces.[48]

The only way in which right-wing parties were pushed to change the constitution was in the context of late 2004, when Pinochet was disgraced after a scandal in which it was revealed that the former dictator had hidden in foreign banks at least $8 million.[49] Ultimately, the most notable changes to the constitution included the elimination of appointed senators, the diminution of power of the National Security Council, and providing the president the ability to fire military commanders. Even after the 2005 constitutional reforms, some scholars still complained about the power that the military retained. Scholar Felipe Portales claimed that "the [political] right still retains veto power," and scholar Carlos Huneeus also complained that "this Constitution is Pinochet's, and it still has a lot of features that haven't been touched and don't belong in a democratic constitution."[50]

Another important tool that is provided by the constitution to hard-wire certain policies is the requirement of elevated quorums to pass laws in crucial areas. The *leyes de quorum calificado* require not just a simple majority of senators and deputies present in the chamber at that time to pass (*leyes de quorum simple*) but rather an absolute majority of all legislators. Laws covered by qualified quorums include social security, the establishment of profit-seeking state-owned enterprises that would compete with private corporations, etc.

Besides laws of qualified quorums, minorities in the legislature can also block certain changes enshrined in *leyes orgánicas* ("organic laws"). Organic laws require 4/7 approval in the legislature (57% of legislators), thus "hard-wiring" certain elements in the political system viewed as critical by the military. Several areas covered by organic laws include education, the public administration (laws concerning the civil service and the hiring of public employees), laws that create states of exception, laws that regulate courts, laws concerning the *Ministerio Público*, laws concerning the Constitutional Tribunal, etc.

Most notably, organic laws protected the armed forces and helped perpetuate the special role that they had during the immediate post-democratic period. As Siavelis noted in his 2000 book, "the military is further insulated from civilian authorities by the organic laws governing promotions, hiring, firing, training, internal affairs, and military justice. According to these laws, responsibility for each of these activities rests squarely with the individual military institutions."[51]

Given that organic laws require a four-sevenths majority to change, they can be considered extensions of the constitution (note that this threshold is also close to the two-thirds threshold required in the US congress to change the constitution). In an interview with Prof. Claudia Heiss, she notes that the size of the text of organic laws is actually greater than the size of the constitution. Prof. Heiss elaborated on how the Chilean constitution and organic laws prevent majority rule and proper democratic governance by describing that:

[The constitution] not only serves as an obstacle for the president, but for the whole democratic system, including congress. It prevents the majority from asserting its will, and prevents democracy from functioning normally...this system is designed to protect something imposed by the military, and it is difficult to enact constitutional reforms. There are also organic laws on all topics which form the nucleus of the project of the military. The military did not want governments to touch the central bank, the education system which they wanted to be private, as well as the organic law of the armed forces.

Everything that the military cared about was made an organic law...
This was a method so that nothing could be changed. You could not
approve a change without the right. The right had an antidemocratic
veto power. The constitution was in effect like a decree law made by
the military and imposed by force.[52]

The effects of these elevated voting majorities are also described by Francisca Moya when she claims that:

Chile has a composition in congress in which the executive has only
had a simply majority, not a total majority with respect to the elevated, supermajoritarian quorums...This makes it difficult to modify
organic laws and generates a very strong need to negotiate. There is
something in Chile called the democracy of consensus agreements...
Projects come out with votes from both the majority and the opposition...there is a need to negotiate with every legislator, every one.[53]

Moya also describes that the elevated quorums in Chile make it more
difficult to enact meaningful reforms.[54] Deputy Venegas similarly
claims that "we have many laws that require an elevated quorum. The
executive for practical reasons needs to negotiate to gain parliamentary
approval...[and] get the approval of both the government coalition and
the opposition."[55]

In short, in this section, I have attempted to show how even though on
paper it may seem like *Concertación* presidents since the return of democracy have possessed working majorities with their coalitions in the same
way as Peronist presidents did, the constitution was designed in such a
way as to minimize the advantage this majority would give the president
to implement change. The constitution and the legal system hard-wired
numerous provisions, which required supermajorities in congress to
change. Until 2005, these laws provided outsized influence to the military
in politics, and even with majority coalitions, *Concertación* presidents in
Chile were not as free to enact change as their counterparts in Argentina.

The Ability of Chilean Legislators to Rebel from the Party Platform

Whereas earlier I described how Argentine legislators are highly dependent on party leaders and thus are afraid to stray from the party platform,
in Chile by contrast, legislators have significantly greater independence.
Unlike in Argentina, it is very rare for legislators in Chile who desire to
run for reelection to be denied a position on a party list (Navia describes
this as the "holder's-keeper" right[56]). Chile also has an open-list system
where candidates from the same party are forced to compete against each
other. As a result of this increased competition, legislators in Chile are
often well-known in the communities they represent, and this greater

personal political capital gives legislators an additional source of leverage within their party/coalition. On the other hand, in Argentina, there is less incentive for legislators to become well-known among voters, since placement on a list is often at the discretion of top party officials; because the list is closed, there is no incentive for candidates from the same party to differentiate themselves. In Chile's open-list system, the fact that candidates within the same coalition compete against each other creates incentives for these politicians to go against the party/coalition platform to distinguish themselves, and as Christian Democratic Senator Patricio Walker (who in the past served as president of both the Chilean Chamber of Deputies and Senate) claimed in an interview, "here we vote for a person from an open list…in this sense, there are many incentives to be an outsider."[57] As I will describe in Part IV, open-list systems provide legislators greater incentives to stray from the party platform than closed-list systems such as the one in Argentina, and ultimately, the result is that open-list systems like those in Chile serve to constrain presidential power by making it more difficult for executives to create a cohesive working majority using their own party/coalition. According to Deputy Venegas, "[party indiscipline] happens here regularly. This indiscipline is a particular problem for the current government coalition [of Bachelet] which is made up of 7 parties with differences over several areas."[58] Fernando Paulsen similarly argues that "Bachelet has many projects that needed to be reformed because her own coalition was opposed, including the educational and tax reform."[59] Obando adds that "[presidents] cannot take for granted the votes of deputies from their coalition. They can intuitively count on their support, but this is not guaranteed."[60] Professor Carlos Huneeus, a specialist on Chilean politics and an expert on the presidency, when asked in an interview about how much control the president has over members from her party, tersely replied, "none."[61] The lack of control by President Bachelet over her coalition is neatly summarized by Senator Walker, who when asked whether Bachelet's coalition was an automatic majority replied that:

> No, there is no automatic majority. All presidents know that the parliament every day claims its role as a co-legislator. Thus, you do not have automatic support. The most significant reforms of Bachelet such as the tax law, education, and labor reform, underwent many modifications in the parliamentary passage process.[62]

Senator Walker also described that Bachelet had little control over her own Socialist Party, claiming that "at times, the [Socialist] party has not supported her." He gave examples of significant laws where the Socialist Party opposed Bachelet, including public sector readjustment (of salaries), and certain aspects of Bachelet's educational reform and labor reform.[63]

More generally, Chilean legislative politics is highly personalized, with parties being relatively weak at the regional, micro level and dependent

on the individual legislator. Because of the greater profile of Chilean legislators in their community and their greater political capital (compared
to their Argentine counterparts), it is less likely for party elites to try
to punish legislators who occasionally defect from the party platform.
Soto described the significant influence of individual legislators when
he claimed that legislators in Chile "have more liberty [than those in
Argentina]. Many of them can be compared to caudillos [in their local
communities]!"[64]

Reelection rates are overall significantly higher in Chile, and according to Bunker and Navia, in the Chamber of Deputies between 1989 and
2009, 82.3% of deputies who sought reelection were successful (three
out of four deputies seek reelection). The breakdown in the Chamber
of Deputies is roughly 38.5% junior (first-term) deputies and 61.5% senior deputies (recall that the reelection rate in the Argentine Chamber
of Deputies is only about 20%). Overall, the expected number of terms
per deputy is 2.4 terms.[65] Higher reelection rates incentivize legislators
to stray from the party platform, since a legislator with a good chance
of being reelected knows he/she will not be at the mercy of their party
boss for employment once their current term ends. The longer tenures
of legislators in Chile also incentivize them to invest in congress as an
institution, since they know that they will spend many years there rather
than just one term.

Given that individual legislators have significantly more clout in Chile
both because they are more experienced and because they are better
known among the general population, it is harder for the president to exert control over the legislators within his/her coalition. The main "stick"
that presidents and party leaders have to control the legislative behavior
of deputies and senators from their coalition is to threaten to kick them
out of that party/coalition. Nevertheless, this control is highly diminished in the context of a high degree of personalism at the local level,
since an individual legislator can credibly threaten to leave their party,
run as an independent, and win.

Additionally, party leaders have an incentive to place popular deputies
or senators on a list even if they may be "rebellious," for fear that not having him/her on the ticket will imperil the coalition's chances of winning.
In other words, coalitions perceive that as long as a candidate is popular
enough in their district to attract votes and win, it is better to have a "rebellious" legislator than a legislator from the opposing coalition. Senator
Walker describes that even if a legislator sometimes votes against the
party, "in the majority of cases, they still let him be the candidate...He
brings votes." He notes that the party system has "perverse incentives"
against party discipline, since candidates perceived as "outsiders" tend to
obtain more votes, and, in turn, parties who need their votes reward them
by keeping them on electoral lists. He further describes that punishments
for rebellious legislators happen only "exceptionally."[66] Statistically,

like in the USA, incumbents are likely to maintain their seats in the next election, providing a further incentive for party elites not to go against incumbents. Navia writes that "all *Concertación* deputies who seek re-election are almost automatically guaranteed to keep their districts."[67] As a result, even if a legislator occasionally dissents from the party platform, Deputy De Mussy argues that party leaders will "close their eyes" in order to ensure that the party wins that seat.[68]

In short, I have tried to show in this section how individual Chilean legislators have significantly more independent authority than their Argentine counterparts, and how this has increased their tendency to rebel from the party platform.

Effects of a Lack of a Party Majority on Presidential Power

Chilean presidents were prevented from being able to take advantage of many potential tools in their arsenal of presidential powers because of their lack of party majorities (and their limited control over even their own party/coalition). Earlier, I noted that powers such as exclusive initiative and urgencies are powerful in theory, yet in practice, they are not as strong as they appear. The reason for this is that, unlike in Argentina, Chilean presidents lack party majorities in congress. In an interview, Professor and specialist in Public Law Raúl Letelier described that "on paper, the president seems very powerful, but he would only be powerful if he also had a majority in congress. Since he lacks a majority in congress, these powers are minimized."[69]

Regarding the power of exclusive initiative, as numerous interviewees mentioned, although only the president can propose laws in areas such as social security, congress is free to reject these initiatives (and a fragmented congress makes it a real possibility that the initiative will be rejected). As a US parallel, the exclusive initiative of the American president to nominate Supreme Court judges did not prove very helpful to Obama in 2016, as congress was able to stall his appointment of Merrick Garland. Similarly, the Chilean congress has been able to resist many initiatives coming from the executive branch, and this has been facilitated by the fact that the president does not possess a party majority. Also, although presidents could in theory ram a budget through congress, presidents avoid doing this for fear of antagonizing legislators who they will need for other projects in the future. Siavelis writes that "formally, presidents have the capacity to simply implement their budget, but it makes little sense to do so given the consequences this would have for the long-term capacity of presidents to legislate."[70] He also states that:

> Given that neither postauthoritarian president [Aylwin or Frei] has been afforded the luxury of a majority in the Senate, after the budget, the president must continue to legislate and rely on at least a few

votes of the opposition or institutional senators in order to have a viable legislative program.[71]

Several concrete examples illustrate the significant issues former President Bachelet had from disunity within her party and coalition. In the case of the tax reform under Bachelet, the more moderate Christian Democrats rebelled and opposed many of the provisions. According to an article from Reuters:

> The reform has put considerable strain on her governing Nueva Mayoria bloc, which takes in communists to centrist Christian Democrats. Many senators in the latter have joined business leaders and the right-wing opposition in fighting against some aspects of the bill.[72]

The article also goes on to note that of the three parts of the bill most in dispute, two of them were passed in the Senate after "being watered down by Christian Democrats and other centrists."

Regarding labor reform, once again, the more conservative Christian Democrats resisted many of Bachelet's efforts to strengthen unions, and although a deal was eventually reached with the Christian Democrats, there were tense moments in which it seemed as though the Christian Democrats might even vote against their own coalition (specifically, four of the eight senators in the Christian Democratic bloc, Andres Zaldivar, Patricio Walker, Manuel Antonio Matta and Ignacio Walker threatened to vote against the reform[73]). At a meeting in which government ministers met with the eight sitting senators of the Christian Democratic party, one of the participants at the meeting claimed that "the government was told that the Christian Democrats do not play games."[74] Unions have traditionally been an area of great friction within the left-wing alliance, with the parties more to the left of the coalition desiring strong pro-union reforms, and the Christian Democrats desiring a more moderate approach.

Additionally, in the infamous case of the *Transantiago* financing where the capital's transit system did not receive an adequate sum of money to maintain operations, it is important to note that Bachelet's coalition held a narrow majority of seats in the Senate. However, she was betrayed by her own coalition, with two *Concertación* senators voting against the financing package.[75]

Finally, there were divisions within Bachelet's coalition on the recent legislation to approve abortion under certain circumstances (when the mother's life is at risk, when a fetus is unviable, and in case of rape). Whereas there was strong support for the law among almost all parties in the *Nueva Mayoría*, there were divisions within the Christian Democratic Party. Based on their personal ethical beliefs, some legislators from this party voted in favor, whereas some did not.

During Piñera's first term in office, coalitional infighting among the rightist *Alianza* contributed to the derailment of certain initiatives. According to Deputy De Mussy:

> I worked in the government of Piñera. In the government, there was bad coordination between the parties. This was the reality that occurred, and is reflected in legislative projects that either were not introduced, or that did get introduced but ultimately failed because of opposition from our own coalition.[76]

One of the examples he gave of a failed such project was the idea of reforming the ISAPRE health system. Although Piñera's Health Minister Jaime Mañalich desired to enact reform, the idea failed because of opposition from within Piñera's coalition.[77] Additionally, as mentioned in Chapter 2, opposition from the UDI party delayed Piñera's effort to pass a law allowing for civil unions for same-sex couples; the delay was so long that the law ended up being signed by Bachelet after Piñera's term ended.

In short, in this part, I have attempted to show how in Chile, presidents did not enjoy party majorities in congress (unlike in Argentina where Peronist presidents had de facto majorities for long periods of time). I have also shown how Chilean presidents often lack control over individual legislators from their party or coalition. Additionally, I described how numerous policies are "hard-wired" in Chile, where reforms would require a super-majority in congress. These elevated quorums have served to significantly reduce the ability of presidents to enact change through merely using a simple coalitional majority in congress. Fundamentally, the Chilean political system has many anti-majoritarian elements, and these have prevented the country from becoming hyperpresidential.

Part III: Reinforcing the Importance of Majoritarianism for Hyperpresidentialism Using the Case of Mexico

In Parts I and II, I described the importance of majoritarianism to the emergence of hyperpresidentialism using the cases of Argentina and Chile. Nevertheless, I found it important and highly relevant to mention the case of Mexico, in which unified versus divided government has played an important role in presidential power. Constitutionally, the Mexican president is one of the weakest in Latin America, and Table 4.7 shows the constitutional strength of the Mexican president in comparative perspective.

As this table illustrates, the Mexican president in theory has the fifth weakest legislative powers in Latin America. The Mexican president, for example, has little ability to issue decrees and, as per Article 49 of the constitution, can only do this either during an emergency or when

Table 4.7 The constitutional strength of the Mexican president in comparative perspective[a]

	Decree	Budget	Proactive Power (subtotal)	Veto	Partial veto	Exclusive Initiative	Reactive Power (subtotal)	Power to convoke plebiscite	Total legislative powers
Chile	0.33	0.73	0.50	0.85	0.85	0.67	0.77	1.00	0.68
Ecuador	0.33	0.73	0.50	1.00	0.69	0.33	0.62	1.00	0.62
Brazil	1.00	0.91	0.96	0.15	0.15	0.67	0.38	0.00	0.60
Colombia	0.67	0.64	0.66	0.31	0.31	0.67	0.46	1.00	0.57
Peru	0.67	0.73	0.70	0.15	0.15	0.33	0.23	1.00	0.49
Argentina	0.33	0.45	0.38	0.85	0.85	0.00	0.48	0.50	0.47
Panama	0.17	0.55	0.33	0.77	0.77	0.33	0.58	0.00	0.45
Uruguay	0.17	0.64	0.37	0.54	0.54	0.33	0.45	0.00	0.39
El Salvador	0.00	0.82	0.35	0.77	0.00	0.00	0.22	1.00	0.35
Guatemala	0.33	0.18	0.27	0.77	0.00	0.00	0.22	1.00	0.31
Venezuela	0.33	0.64	0.46	0.08	0.08	0.00	0.04	1.00	0.31
Dominican Republic	0.00	0.64	0.27	0.92	0.15	0.00	0.31	0.00	0.30
Honduras	0.33	0.36	0.34	0.77	0.00	0.00	0.22	0.00	0.28
Mexico	0.17	0.36	0.25	0.92	0.00	0.00	0.26	0.00	0.26
Costa Rica	0.00	0.64	0.27	0.77	0.00	0.00	0.22	0.00	0.25
Bolivia	0.00	0.27	0.12	0.85	0.00	0.33	0.38	0.00	0.24
Paraguay	0.00	0.64	0.27	0.23	0.23	0.00	0.13	0.00	0.20
Nicaragua	0.00	0.73	0.31	0.15	0.15	0.00	0.09	0.00	0.19

[a]This table is recreated from Payne 2007; p.96

congress has already delegated him/her decree power in a defined area.[78] The Mexican president also cannot seek reelection.

Despite the constraints on the Mexican president, prior to the late 1990s/early 2000s, the president was the main player in politics. In discussing the historical weakness of congress, Levy and Bruhn write that "its opinion mattered so little that interest groups in Mexico rarely bothered to lobby congressmen, preferring to establish direct contact with federal agencies, or, if possible, the president."[79] The excessive strength of the president originated with the fact that presidents had a majority in congress. For many decades, Mexico had been a one-party system in which the PRI (the Institutional Revolutionary Party) had full control of congress. Nevertheless, all presidents elected from 1928 until to 2000 were also from the PRI, and given that the president was also the head of the PRI, this provided the president with strong indirect control over congress. Levy et al. write that:

> The Mexican legislature's conversion into a presidential puppet resulted less from constitutional prerogatives than from the informal characteristics of the party system....It was the president's status as the de facto head of the PRI—with veto power over candidate selection –that most ensured the submissiveness of PRI legislators. Since the PRI in turn controlled the Congress, Congress rubber-stamped presidential initiatives with minimal debate."[80]

One of the factors which ensured that congress would rubber-stamp presidential initiatives was the fact that party discipline was extremely high. There were several reasons for the high levels of party discipline. First, legislative candidates were selected by party leaders (specifically the president) rather than through primaries; only candidates expected to be loyal to the party would be placed on lists, and once these legislators got into office, they would feel the need to "repay" party leaders to whom they owed their jobs. Second, legislators would continue to be dependent on party leaders in the PRI for employment even after leaving office, given that reelection in Mexico is prohibited.[81] It is important to note that the ban on reelection in Mexico also weakened the legislature vis-à-vis the president for the obvious reason that, in just one term, it is nearly impossible to develop significant legislative expertise. Party discipline within the PRI was historically so high that between 1997 and 2000, PRI deputies voted with their party (which was controlled by the president) 99% of the time.[82]

Changes in the 1990s

Although PRI presidents were able to rule hegemonically through control of their party in congress, this changed in the 1990s when the opposition started gaining strength. The first sign that the PRI was beginning to lose its dominant position was in 1988, when although the PRI maintained its majority in congress, it lost the two-thirds majority necessary to change the constitution. 1988 was also a year in which a PRI candidate was at serious risk of losing the presidential election, and although Carlos Salinas eventually emerged victorious, there were allegations of significant voter intimidation (through the placement of troops throughout Mexico City) and voter fraud. In fact, all ballots were eventually burned to destroy any evidence.

The year 1997 would be the first time when the PRI lost a majority in the lower house of congress, and in what was a prescient observation, Burki and Perry of the World Bank wrote in 1998 that "if future political developments in Mexico lead to more power-sharing with other political parties, then it is likely that Mexican presidential power will diminish due to the formal constitutional provisions."[83] Following the PRI's 1997 loss of the lower house, the next crucial moment that changed the Mexican political landscape was the 2000 election of president Vicente Fox of the PAN (National Action Party). This was the first time in nearly eight decades that a non-PRI president would lead the country, and ushered in an era of divided government. Since 2000, until only recently under AMLO, no president had a majority in congress.

Following the end of the era when PRI presidents controlled a PRI-dominated congress, the legislature came back to life. Suddenly, the constraints on presidential power which had previously only existed on paper began to affect the power of Mexican presidents in practice. Levy et al. write that:

> With the 2000 election, the situation became still more complex. Fox did not preside over a passive party bench, nor did he control a majority of the legislature. He could not simply assume, like PRI predecessors, that Congress would do whatever he wanted. Indeed, he could not even assume that fellow party members would follow his lead. On the other side of the aisle, freed of presidential interference in internal party matters, PRI legislators had incentives to take more independent stands, particularly when it came to potentially unpopular issues like taxes or the budget. PRI legislators may be reluctant to give up this discretion even if the party recaptures the presidency.[84]

In short, the loss of a majority in congress suddenly required presidents to seek broad support for their initiatives beyond their party. Although unified government had enabled Mexican presidents to govern in a hyperpresidential manner, following the end of PRI hegemony over the executive and legislative branches, divided government served to substantially decrease presidential power and embolden congress. Casar summarizes that "experience has shown that, deprived of the majorities and associated partisan powers imposed by the previous undemocratic electoral system, the president is not as powerful as he or she was thought to be."[85] Nacif further writes that "with the emergence of divided government, a lengthy period of presidential dominance over Mexican politics was brought to an end."[86]

Part IV: Three Institutional Mechanisms That Reduce Hyperpresidentialism

In this part, I would like to propose three simple institutional changes that will reduce the strength of a president's working majority in congress through the reduction of party discipline. These institutional changes could thus reduce the likelihood of hyperpresidentialism. As mentioned earlier, one of the primary reasons that Argentine presidents can rely so much on their working majorities in congress is because of the high degree of party cohesion. Therefore, any institutional mechanism that would reduce party discipline would also lower the strength of president's working majority in congress, since he/she would no longer be able to rely on the members of his/her party to as great an extent. I will begin this section by quantitatively illustrating the link between party discipline and presidential power in practice. I will then propose three simple institutional changes that should reduce party discipline, namely (1) adopt an open-list electoral system, (2) lower district magnitude, and (3) pass laws that encourage reelection among legislators.

Figures 4.1 and 4.2 illustrate the correlation between party discipline and legislative constraints on the executive (note that party discipline is

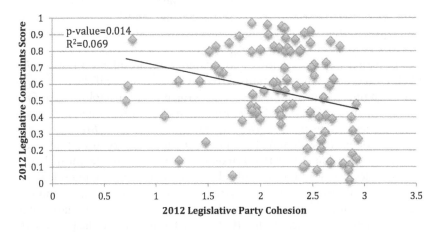

Figure 4.1 Illustrating the correlation between party cohesion and Legislative Constraints on the Executive in my sample of all presidential systems in the world in 2012.

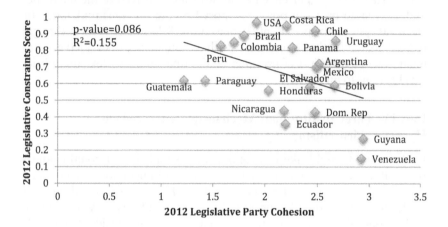

Figure 4.2 Illustrating the correlation between party cohesion and Legislative Constraints on the Executive in my sample of 20 presidential democracies in the Western Hemisphere in 2012.

measured through the indicator, "Legislative Party Cohesion" by Varieties of Democracy, v2pscohesv_osp, where higher values indicate more party discipline). As these two scatterplots show, as party cohesion increases, constraints on presidents tend to fall.

These scatterplots illustrate how party cohesion is significantly correlated with legislative constraints on the executive (Figures 4.1 and 4.2 show that the results are significant, respectively, at the 5% and 10% levels). Although it is true that in Figure 4.1, the R-squared value is low at only 0.069, these initial results still have value, and I would encourage more quantitative research using additional indicators of party cohesion across a large sample of countries.

Given that party cohesion is correlated with presidential power, the likelihood of hyperpresidentialism to develop is lessened if the party system is engineered in such a way as to reduce party discipline. *The first concrete way to achieve this is to move from a closed-list system such as the one in Argentina, to an open-list system such as in Chile or Brazil.* Switching to an open-list system will automatically lower party discipline given the intraparty competition that is likely to result from the electorate being able to select on a ballot not only the party, but also individual legislators.[87] In other words, open-list systems are a more "candidate-centered electoral formula"[88] and thus provide legislators incentives to gain votes based on personal appeal rather than a strict adherence to the party platform. In turn, *this reduced party discipline will be more likely to prevent hyperpresidentialism from emerging* (since legislators from the president's party have incentives to disobey party leaders such as the president).

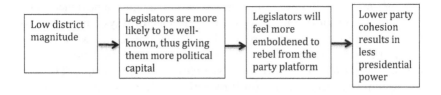

Figure 4.3 Illustrating the link between district magnitude and presidential power.

The second mechanism that can reduce party discipline and thus decrease presidential power is having a low district magnitude. As the district magnitude decreases, legislators are likely to be more well-known in a community simply because the fewer the number of politicians, the easier it is to keep track of them. It is likely that the electorate will be familiar with their representatives in a system like that of the USA (with a district magnitude of one), and until recently, in Chile under the binomial system (with a district magnitude of two). It is less likely, however, that legislators will be well-known in their community in countries with higher-N magnitudes such as Argentina. The greater familiarity of the electorate with their representatives in political systems with low district magnitudes is likely to increase the political capital of individual legislators, which strengthens their position vis-à-vis the president. This increased political capital makes them more likely to rebel, thus weakening party discipline and, consequently, the strength of the president's working majority in congress. This concept is illustrated in Figure 4.3.

Finally, third, I would like to suggest that countries where reelection rates in congress are higher would also tend to have less presidential power in practice. Legislators who serve for multiple terms are significantly more experienced than one-term legislators. Individuals who expect to serve for a long time also have stronger incentives to invest in congress as an institution. They will be more likely to ensure that rules, both formal and informal, are followed, and will respond forcefully to attacks on the legislative branch by the executive. They also will be significantly more likely to stand up to presidential abuses of power. One of the debates currently taking place in several democracies is whether to impose term limits on legislators. Based on the research in this book, such a move would significantly strengthen presidential power, since legislators would be much more inexperienced and institutional norms would weaken in congress as a whole. One of the reasons why the Argentine congress is so weak is that the reelection rate is low, whereas in the Chilean congress, most deputies and senators are reelected. Therefore, any legislation that would increase the tenures of members of congress is likely to constrain presidential power (e.g., passing a law guaranteeing that incumbents will have a spot on the party lists for the next election).

Therefore, in short, I have argued that the electoral system most likely to reduce presidential power by weakening the president's working majority in congress is an *open-list system with as low a district magnitude as possible, where legislators have an easy time obtaining reelection*. This was the system that was in place until recently in Chile, and it is my expectation that the new electoral mechanism that increases district magnitude will strengthen presidential power there in the long term. The three mechanisms that I described in this section all work to reduce presidential power by making the president's party less cohesive, and unlike many works in the literature which view party fragmentation in a negative light (see, for example, Ames 2001 and Mainwaring 1993), I suggest that party system fragmentation can actually be beneficial in reducing the likelihood of having a strongman leader. These three mechanisms can also be implemented overnight by simply changing the electoral system and the laws surrounding reelection (on the other hand, it is significantly harder for a country to strengthen institutions and prevent economic crises).

Chapter Summary

In short, in this chapter, I have argued that the reason that presidential power was stronger in Argentina than in Chile is because Argentine presidents have benefitted from stronger working majorities in congress than Chilean presidents. I have shown that Peronist presidents not only enjoyed party majorities or near-majorities but also that the Peronist party was extremely disciplined. On the other hand, no Chilean president since democratization had a party majority, and although coalitional majorities were common, there was significantly less voting discipline than in Argentina (and for many important initiatives, even if a president could obtain a simple majority, this is not sufficient to modify either the constitution or an organic law). One of the reasons for the difference in party discipline in Argentina versus Chile is the fact that the former utilizes a closed-list system, whereas the latter has an open-list system. Chile also has a lower district magnitude and higher reelection rates than Argentina, which further increased the strength of legislators vis-à-vis the executive.

Based on this chapter, I would like to suggest that in fledgling presidential democracies, fragmented party systems could be highly beneficial for preventing hyperpresidentialism from emerging, and ultimately, democratic backsliding. Whereas as I noted in the introduction there are various pieces in the literature which assume that fragmented party systems are dangerous for a democracy since they increase the likelihood for gridlock, such a party system can also prevent a president from using a working majority in congress to rubber-stamp his/her proposals.

In the next chapter, I will discuss the third factor that contributed to the differences in presidential power between Argentina and Chile, namely a recent history of economic crises.

Notes

1 *New York Times* May 16, 1989.
2 Morgenstern and Manzetti 2003; p.156.
3 Morgenstern and Manzetti 2003; p.158.
4 Jones et al. 2009; p.73.
5 Author's interview with Germán Garavano (Justice Minister of Argentina).
6 See Rubio and Goretti 1998; p.53 and Berbecel 2018; p.26.
7 Author's interview with Javier David (Federal Deputy (Salta), Partido Justicialista).
8 Author's interview with Orlando Gallo (Ex. Federal Judge in Mercedes Province during the military period, ex-Federal Deputy 1991–1995).
9 Author's interview with Juan Manuel Abal Medina (Senator and Former Chief of Cabinet of Ministers for President Cristina Kirchner).
10 Chaco (1951), Chubut (1955), Formosa (1955), La Pampa (1951), Misiones (1953), Neuquén (1955), Río Negro (1955), and Santa Cruz (note that although it became a province in 1956, the law that made it a province, Law 14408, was passed in June of 1955 when Perón was still in power). Notably, Tierra del Fuego also became a province much later under the Peronist administration of Carlos Menem.
11 Snyder and Samuels 2004; p.145.
12 Mustapic 2002; p.45.
13 Author's interview with Germán Garavano (Justice Minister of Argentina).
14 Author's interview with Martín Maquieyra (Federal Deputy, PRO).
15 Author's interview with Miguel Iturrieta (Ex-Deputy for Misiones 2005–2009, PJ-FPV bloc).
16 Author's interview with Patricia Giménez (Federal Deputy, UCR).
17 Author's interview with Mario Barletta (Federal Deputy (Santa Fe), ex-president of the UCR, 2011–2013).
18 Author's interview with Julio Cobos (Ex-Vice President of Argentina, UCR senator from Mendoza).
19 Author's interview with Ángel Rozas (Senator and ex-governor of Chaco, UCR).
20 Rogers 2016; p.134.
21 Author's interview with Néstor Migueliz (Director de Asistencia de Apoyo Parlamentario).
22 Jones 2002; p.158.
23 Jones 2002; p.159.
24 Author's interview with Ricardo Biazzi (Min of Education of Argentina for two days in December 2001 under President Puerta (PJ), Professor of Constitutional Law).
25 Author's interview with Orlando Gallo (Ex. Federal Judge in Mercedes Province during the military period, ex-Federal Deputy 1991–1995).
26 Jones 2002; p.164.
27 Author's interview with Martín Medina (Political Scientist, Professor of Public Law at Universidad Cuenca del Plata).
28 Author's interview with Federal Deputy Javier David (Federal Deputy (Salta), Partido Justicialista).

29 Author's interview with Ana María Mustapic (Professor who specializes in executive-legislative relations in Argentina).

30 *New York Times* August 8, 2013.

31 *Washington Post* (Mark Jones) August 20, 2015.

32 Jones 2011.

33 Author's interview with Javier Zelaznik.

34 Author's interview with David Altman. Note that the *Renovación Nacional* is the center-right party in the rightist *Chile Vamos* coalition.

35 Author's interview with Francisca Moya (Employee in the Ministry General Secretariat of the Presidency, which is responsible for the relation between the executive and legislative branches).

36 Author's interview with Fernando Paulsen (Journalist and TV presenter).

37 Author's interview with Felipe De Mussy (National Deputy, UDI).

38 Author's interview with Lucas Sierra (Vice president of the think tank, *Centro de Estudios Publicos*, CEP).

39 Author's interview with Fernando Paulsen (Journalist and TV presenter).

40 Siavelis 2002; p.107.

41 *Buenos Aires Herald* January 25, 2014.

42 Author's interview with Alejandro Olivares (Professor and Political Scientist).

43 Author's interview with Alejandro Olivares (Professor and Political Scientist).

44 Author's interview with Claudio Fuentes (Professor specializing in Chilean politics).

45 Siavelis 2000; pp.36–37.

46 Aguero 2000; p.91.

47 Siavelis 2000; p.41.

48 Siavelis 2000; p.37.

49 *New York Times* December 12, 2004.

50 *New York Times* December 12, 2004.

51 Siavelis 2000; p.37.

52 Author's interview with Claudia Heiss (Professor specializing in constitutional politics).

53 Author's interview with Francisca Moya (Employee in the Ministry General Secretariat of the Presidency).

54 Author's interview with Francisca Moya (Employee in the Ministry General Secretariat of the Presidency).

55 Author's interview with Mario Venegas (National Deputy, Christian Democrat).

56 Navia 2008; p.105.

57 Author's interview with Patricio Walker (National Senator (ex-president of the Chamber of Deputies, and ex-president of the Senate), Christian Democrat).

58 Author's interview with Mario Venegas (National Deputy, Christian Democrat).

59 Author's interview with Fernando Paulsen (Journalist and TV presenter).

60 Author's interview with Ivan Obando (Professor specializing in Public Law and Political Science).

61 Author's interview with Carlos Huneeus (Professor specializing in Chilean politics).

62 Author's interview with Patricio Walker (National Senator (ex-president of the Chamber of Deputies, and ex-president of the Senate), Christian Democrat).

63 Author's interview with Patricio Walker (National Senator (ex-president of the Chamber of Deputies, and ex-president of the Senate), Christian Democrat).

64 Author's interview with Sebastián Soto (Head of the Juridical Legislative Division during the Piñera Government).
65 Bunker and Navia 2015 Abstract.
66 Author's interview with Patricio Walker (National Senator (ex-president of the Chamber of Deputies, and ex-president of the Senate), Christian Democrat).
67 Navia 2008; pp.104–105.
68 Author's interview with Felipe De Mussy (National Deputy, UDI).
69 Author's interview with Raúl Letelier (Professor specializing in Public Law).
70 See Siavelis 2006; p.49.
71 Siavelis 2002; p.99.
72 *Reuters* March 11, 2016.
73 *El Mostrador* March 2, 2016.
74 *El Mostrador* March 2, 2016.
75 *La Nación* November 22, 2007.
76 Author's interview with Felipe De Mussy (National Deputy, UDI).
77 Author's interview with Felipe De Mussy (National Deputy, UDI).
78 Remington 2014; p.49.
79 Levy and Bruhn 2006; p.103.
80 Levy and Bruhn 2006; p.103.
81 Madrid 2003; p.90.
82 Domínguez 2015; p.256.
83 Burki et al. 1998; p.33.
84 Levy et al. 2006; p.104.
85 Casar 2013; p.108.
86 Nacif 2005; p.8.
87 The notion that open lists discourage party discipline is widely accepted in the literature. See, for example, Mainwaring and Pérez-Liñán 1997 and Carey 2007.
88 Shugart and Haggard 2001; p.86.

Bibliography

Aguero, Felipe. "Transition Pathways: Institutional Legacies, the Military, and Democracy in South America." *Pathways to Democracy: The Political economy of Democratic Transitions.* Eds. James Hollifield and Calvin Jillson. New York: Routledge, 2000, pp. 73–92.

Berbecel, Dan. "The Politics of Policy Stability: Explaining the Levels of Volatility in Economic Policymaking in Argentina and Brazil between 1990 and 2010." *Canadian Journal of Latin American and Caribbean Studies/Revue canadienne des études latino- américaines et caraïbes.* Vol 43, Iss 1 (2018), pp. 18–46.

Bunker, Kenneth, and Patricio Navia. "Incumbency Advantage and Tenure Length in the Chilean Chamber of Deputies, 1989–2009." *Revista de Ciencia Política.* Vol 35, No 2 (2015), pp. 251–272.

Burki, Shahid, and Guillermo Perry. *Beyond the Washington Consensus: Institutions Matter.* Washington, DC: The World Bank, 1998.

Carey, John. "Competing Principals, Political Institutions and Party Unity in Legislative Voting." *American Journal of Political Science.* Vol 51, Iss 1 (January 2007), pp. 92–107.

Casar, María Amparo. "Representation and Decision-Making in the Mexican Congress." *Representation and Effectiveness in Latin American Democracies:*

Congress, Judiciary and Civil Society. Eds. Moira MacKinnon and Ludovico Feoli. New York: Routledge, 2013, 91–110.

Domínguez, Jorge. "Mexico's 2012 Presidential Election: Conclusions." *Mexico's Evolving Democracy: A Comparative Study of the 2012 Elections.* Eds. Jorge Domínguez, Kenneth Greene, Chappell Lawson, and Alejandro Moreno. Baltimore: Johns Hopkins University Press, 2015, pp. 252–270.

Jones, Mark. "Explaining the High Level of Party Discipline in the Argentine Congress." *Legislative Politics in Latin America.* Eds. Scott Morgenstern and Benito Nacif. Cambridge: Cambridge University Press, 2002, pp. 147–184.

Jones, Mark. *The Recruitment and Selection of Legislative Candidates in Argentina.* University Park: The Pennsylvania State University, 2008.

Jones, Mark. Argentina 2011. 2011. http://www.americasquarterly.org/node/1898

Jones, Mark, Wonjae Hwang, and Juan Pablo Micozzi. "Government and Opposition in the Argentine Congress, 1989–2007." *Journal of Politics in Latin America.* Vol 1, Iss 1 (2009). pp. 67–96.

Levy, Daniel, and Kathleen Bruhn. *Mexico: The Struggle for Democratic Development.* Berkeley: University of California Press, 2006.

Madrid, Raúl. *Retiring the state: The politics of pension privatization in Latin America and beyond.* Stanford: Stanford University Press, 2003.

Mainwaring, Scott, and Aníbal Pérez-Liñán. "Party Discipline in the Brazilian Constitutional Congress". *Legislative Studies Quarterly.* Vol 22, Iss 4 (November 1997), pp. 453–483.

Morgenstern, Scott, and Luigi Manzetti. "Legislative Oversight: Interests and Institutions in the United States and Argentina." *Democratic Accountability in Latin America.* Eds. Scott Mainwaring and Christopher Welna. Oxford: Oxford University Press, 2003, pp. 132–169.

Mustapic, Ana María. "Oscillating Relations: President and Congress in Argentina." *Legislative Politics in Latin America.* Eds. Scott Morgenstern and Benito Nacif. Cambridge: Cambridge University Press, 2002, pp. 23–47.

Nacif, Benito. "Congress Proposes and the President Disposes: The New Relationship Between the Executive and Legislative Branches in Mexico." *Mexican Governance: From Single-Party Rule to Divided Government.* Eds. Armand Peschard-Sverdrup and Sara Rioff. Washington, DC: Center for Strategic and International Studies, 2005, pp. 1–26.

Navia, Patricio. "Legislative Candidate Selection in Chile." *Pathways to Power: Political Recruitment and Candidate Selection in Latin America.* Eds. Peter Siavelis and Scott Morgenstern. University Park: The Pennsylvania State University Press, 2008, pp. 92–118.

Payne, J. Mark. "Balancing Executive and Legislative Prerogatives: The Role of Constitutional and Party-Based Factors." *Democracies in Development: Politics and Reform in Latin American Countries.* Eds. J. Mark Payne, Daniel Zovatto, and Mercedes Mateo Díaz, Washington, DC: Inter-American Development Bank, 2007, pp. 81–116.

Remington, Thomas. *Presidential Decrees in Russia: A Comparative Perspective.* Cambridge: Cambridge University Press, 2014.

Rogers, Melissa Ziegler. *The Politics of Place and the Limits of Redistribution.* Routledge: New York, 2016.

Rubio, Delia, and Matteo Goretti. "When the President Governs Alone: The Decretazo in Argentina, 1989–93." *Executive Decree Authority.* Eds. John Carey and Matthew Shugart. Cambridge: University of Cambridge, 1998, pp. 33–61.

Shugart, Matthew, and Stephan Haggard. "Institutions and Public Policy in Presidential Systems." *Presidents, Parliaments and Policy.* Eds. Stephen Haggard and Mathew McCubbins. Cambridge: Cambridge University Press, 2001, pp. 64–104.

Siavelis, Peter. *The President and Congress in Postauthoritarian Chile: Institutional Constraints to Democratic Consolidation.* University Park: The Pennsylvania State University Press, 2000.

Siavelis, Peter. "Exaggerated Presidentialism and Moderate Presidents: Executive-Legislative Relations in Chile." *Legislative Politics in Latin America.* Eds. Scott Morgenstern and Benito Nacif. Cambridge: Cambridge University Press, 2002, pp. 79–113.

Siavelis, Peter. "Accommodating Informal Institutions and Chilean Democracy." *Informal Institutions and Democracy: Lessons from Latin America.* Eds. Gretchen Helmke and Steven Levitsky. Baltimore: The Johns Hopkins University Press, 2006, pp. 33–55.

Snyder, Richard, and David Samuels. "Legislative Malapportionment in Latin America: Historical and Comparative Perspectives." *Federalism and Democracy in Latin America.* Ed. Edward Gibson. Baltimore: The Johns Hopkins University Press, 2004, pp. 131–172.

5 The Impact of Economic Crises on Presidential Power

The third independent variable that contributes to the emergence of hyperpresidentialism is the presence of recent economic crises. By "economic crisis," I refer to a period of sharp economic decline during which living standards fall considerably. A mild recession would not qualify as an economic crisis under this definition.

In Part I of this chapter, I will begin with a theoretical discussion of why economic crises allow presidents to concentrate power. I will argue that during an economic crisis, congress and the judiciary will be more deferential to presidents. I will also discuss the role of blame attribution and claim that during an economic crisis, a president will only be able to concentrate power if he/she is not directly blamed for the crisis.

In Part I, I will also identify a specific type of economic crisis which is especially important in the development of hyperpresidentialism. While economic crises by themselves will help a president concentrate power, he/she is especially likely to have the opportunity to usurp power from congress and the judiciary under what I call a "bust-boom cycle." As I will describe, a "bust-boom cycle" occurs when the economy experiences a downturn under the previous president, followed by a strong recovery under the subsequent president; this subsequent president will be in an especially strong position to concentrate power.

In Parts II and III, I examine the respective cases of Argentina and Chile. In Argentina, two severe economic crises allowed Peronist administrations to concentrate power, whereas in Chile, the lack of economic crises helped to prevent hyperpresidentialism. I will also show how the Argentine case perfectly fits the description of a bust-boom cycle. Finally, in Part IV, I examine the question of whether economic crises help the president concentrate power because of bottom-up pressure from the population, or through a high-level process where institutions of horizontal accountability voluntarily give up power or have power usurped from them. In other words, during an economic crisis does the president concentrate power because of the desire from the citizenry for strong leadership, or is it because power shifts to the executive as a result of a high-level process (without the approval of the electorate)?

DOI: 10.4324/9781003142904-5

Part I: Theoretical Analysis of the Role of Economic Crises in Helping a President Concentrate Power

The idea that economic crises promote presidential power has been discussed in the literature, and Larkins for example writes that "emergencies demand a dynamic policy response from the president which circumvents the bureaucratic trappings of formal constitutionalism. Delegative democracy in Argentina originated in the economic crisis of the late 1980s..."[1] Anderson similarly argues that:

> crises usually result in greater concentrations of presidential power. In the United States, crises have increased central power in a highly decentralized context and have contributed to nation building. [In Argentina]...the advent of crisis...contributed to greater power concentration in a nation that needs such concentration to decrease.[2]

In an interview, Deputy Javier David similarly claimed that:

> It seems to me that when there is a situation of crisis...the Argentine people look to the president and ask the president to take certain measures. Congress has always shown solidarity, and every time that there was a political, social, or economic crisis, congress has been able to go beyond parties and support the president.[3]

The Willingness by Congress and the Judiciary to Delegate Power to Presidents in a Crisis

The primary mechanism by which an economic crisis increases presidential power is that congress is willing to delegate more powers to the president. Members of congress, including those from the opposition, generally consider that the executive branch is better equipped to handle the economic emergency than the legislature. This is due to several reasons, including that (a) congress suffers from the collective action problem and cannot make the rapid, swift decisions that are necessary, and (b) congress might not have the technical capacity to understand the best course of action to take during a crisis.

This sentiment was expressed in interviews conducted with two Argentine deputies from opposing sides of the aisle. One of the deputies, Martín Maquieyra, is from Macri's PRO party, whereas the other deputy, Alicia Soraire, is from Cristina Kirchner's FPV faction. Despite their political differences, both of these deputies agreed that during an economic crisis, presidential powers should be increased, even if the president was from an opposing party. When asked whether congress or the president is better equipped to handle an economic crisis, Maquieyra replied that:

the president, because due to the complexity of the country and the different political actors, it is difficult for a collegial body to come to an agreement on a certain economic solution. Additionally, people elected the president to do this.[4]

He was also open to giving such powers to a president who might be from the opposing party, as long as there was a "true crisis."[5] The other deputy, Alicia Soraire, when similarly asked if she would give emergency powers to a president from an opposing party argued that:

> if we had an economic crisis of course. I think that in moments of crisis we have to be united to move our country forward. We have to go above politics, and in these cases I would support the president.[6]

Like Maquieyra, she also mentioned that she believed that the president is better equipped than congress to handle a crisis.[7]

In times of economic crises, it is not just congress that allows presidents to concentrate power. As I will show in the case of Argentina after the 1989 crisis, the judiciary also plays a significant role in the emergence of hyperpresidentialism. During a crisis, of the three branches of government, the judiciary is the least equipped to handle the downturn. Courts cannot create laws to fight the economic crisis and usually lack the technical capacity to understand the complexities of the downturn. Given that the judiciary by itself can do very little to fight an economic crisis, courts will avoid trying to obstruct the other two branches of government. Given that the president is in the strongest position to fight a crisis, courts will be especially reluctant to try to block executive actions during this period.

The Effect of Blame Attribution on the Timeline of Strengthening Presidential Power

Above, I described how economic crises help presidents concentrate power through the deference by the legislative and judicial branch to the executive branch. Nevertheless, it is also critical to add that *presidents will only be able to concentrate power during a crisis if they are not directly blamed for it.* If a president is directly blamed for a crisis, he/she will likely be impeached, be pressured to resign, or will become a lame duck throughout the remainder of their term in office (and lose the next election or simply not run). In this case, it will be their successor who will be able to concentrate power. Therefore, although economic crises will generally result in a concentration of power in the executive branch, whether the current president benefits or the next president has to do with whether the population blames the current president for causing the slowdown. Figure 5.1 illustrates how blame attribution affects the timing of the concentration of power that occurs during a crisis.

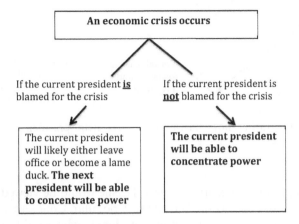

Figure 5.1 Understanding which president will be the beneficiary of increased executive authority during an economic crisis.

As I will describe in Part II, neither Alfonsín nor De La Rúa was able to concentrate power during the economic crises that happened toward the end of their administrations. The reason is that both leaders were blamed by the public for helping to cause the economic decline, and ultimately both of them left office early.

Note that while in this book I focus on economic crises in the context of democracies, in an authoritarian regime, an economic crisis can prompt democratization. In a democracy, if the population blames the leader in power for an economic crisis, as I mentioned above, that leader will likely become a lame duck president or lose power altogether (with the next leader having the potential to concentrate power). However, in the context of an authoritarian regime, this blame attribution could result in the discreditation of the regime and may trigger democratization. See Haggard and Kaufman 1995 for a detailed exploration of the link between economic crisis in authoritarian regimes and democratization.

How a Bust-Boom Cycle Creates Especially Favorable Circumstances for Presidents to Concentrate Power

Whereas economic crises by themselves may lead to hyperpresidentialism for the reasons I mentioned earlier, crises have an especially strong ability to help a president concentrate power *when they are followed by periods of solid growth*. In other words, *the combination of an economic "bust" followed by an economic "boom" is the most effective in helping a president concentrate power.*

If a country experiences a crisis under one president and a subsequent president is able to restore growth, this will give the latter president the

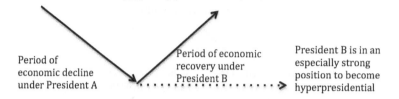

Figure 5.2 Illustrating how bust-boom cycles help presidents concentrate power.

political capital to concentrate power. He/she would be viewed by many as a "savior," and they would become very popular. Congress would have a difficult time opposing a popular president, who would be granted more leeway to pursue the policies he/she desires. During the "boom" period, the president will also likely have greater resources at their disposal (presumably tax revenues would increase during a period of sustained growth), which will allow them to essentially "buy" support throughout different segments of society.

In Figure 5.2, I illustrate how the bust-boom cycle functions. President A under this scenario is delegitimized because of his/her handling of the economy, and is likely to either leave office early or become a lame duck president. In the case of President B, hyperpresidentialism is more likely to develop because he/she will likely have benefitted from (a) the aforementioned demand for strong leadership, which, in many cases, caused congress to confer the executive substantially greater authority (the judiciary is also more restrained since it does not want to be seen as obstructionist during a time of crisis), (b) a strong sense of legitimacy stemming from the fact that voters associate his/her government with economic growth (especially when compared to the legacy of President A), and (c) the greater resources available to the president in order to distribute as patronage to coopt different groups in society.

Part II: Assessing the Role of Economic Crises in Promoting Hyperpresidentialism in Argentina

In this part, I will provide an overview of the Argentine economy since democracy took root. I will describe how the two crises in the late 1980s and early 2000s contributed to the emergence of hyperpresidentialism in the governments of Menem, and Néstor and Cristina Kirchner. I will then describe how both of these crises were followed by periods of rapid growth, which further contributed to the concentration of power under these presidents.

Overall Performance of the Economy since Democratization

The Argentine economy since democratization can be characterized as highly volatile, with sharp, pendulum-like swings between periods of rapid growth and periods of deep recession. The graph in Figure 5.3 illustrates GDP growth data for Argentina between 1982 and 2014. The economic declines in 1989 and 2001–2002 are especially notable.

GDP growth does not tell the full story of the Argentine economy, and inflation and unemployment data are also highly volatile. The historical unemployment rate is illustrated in Figure 5.4. The historical inflation rate is illustrated in Figure 5.5, with a very notable spike in 1989.

1989 Crisis

The first major economic crisis since democratization took place in the 1985–1989 period and culminated in hyperinflation in 1989. To explain this economic crisis, it is important to put it in context. During the end of the military period, the Argentine budget deficit exploded, reaching a value of 20% of GDP.[8] To finance this enormous deficit, the Argentine government resorted to printing money, and the result was a massive spike in inflation.

In response to the hyperinflation, the Alfonsín government in June 1985 launched the *Austral* plan (which was enacted through Necessity and Urgency Decree 1096/85) that sought to lower inflation through the demand side. This was considered a *heterodox* policy in that it sought

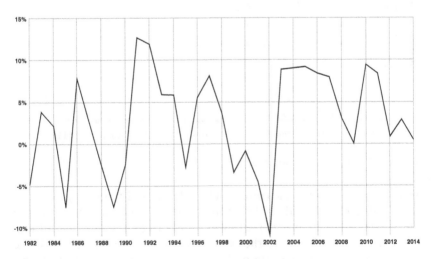

Figure 5.3 GDP growth rate for Argentina since 1983.[a]

a   World Bank. GDP Growth (Annual %). Percentage change of real GDP compared to previous year. Real GDP is adjusted for inflation.

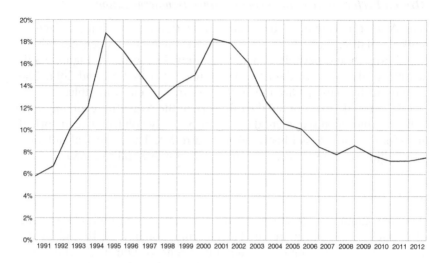

Figure 5.4 Unemployment data for Argentina (1991–2012).[a]

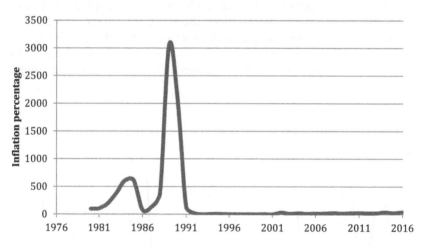

Figure 5.5 Inflation data for Argentina.[b]

to combine orthodox measures such as fiscal and monetary restraint (e.g., reducing the budget deficit and making a commitment to stop excessively printing money) with wage and price controls. In addition, the currency at the time, the *peso argentino*, was replaced with the *austral* at the exchange rate of 1,000 *pesos argentinos*: 1 *austral*. Initially, the program was successful; nevertheless, despite the reduction

a　World Bank.
b　World Bank DataBank. Inflation, GDP Deflator, (Annual %).

of inflation during the first year, subsequently, it went back up and peaked in 1989–1990.

The *Austral* plan failed for various reasons, including the inability of the government to enforce the wage freezes due to pressure from unions (e.g., during Alfonsín's time in office, there were a total of 13 general strikes). Mc-Guire summarizes the ultimate failure of the *Austral* plan when he writes that "by mid 1987, however, the *Austral* plan had unraveled because of union pressure for wage increases, business pressure for easier credit and higher prices, and the government's inability to make major spending cuts."[9]

The Emergence of Hyperpresidentialism After the Crisis of the Late 1980s

In the context of crisis of the late 1980s, Carlos Menem easily won the 1989 election with a margin of 47.5–37.1% in the popular vote (he won a majority of the vote in what would be the last Argentine presidential election to use the electoral college). Following the election, Alfonsín chose to resign early in order to let Menem deal with the economic meltdown. The two centerpieces of Menem's economic reform to combat the economic crisis involved (a) privatization of most state-owned enterprises (including power, oil, the post office, the railways, and water) and a partial privatization of the pension system, and (b) the Convertibility Plan. To briefly explain the Convertibility Plan, Argentina decided to take the radical step of pegging its currency to the US Dollar at a rate of 1:1. The government effectively tied its hands with respect to monetary policy, and rather than pursuing the decades-long habit of printing money to finance the deficit, the central bank could now only print as many pesos as it had dollars (after 1991, Argentina replaced the *austral* and readopted the *peso*). The Convertibility Plan was successful in quashing inflationary expectations, and during the 1990s, the inflation rate fell into the single digits. Foreign investment increased, and the country experienced what many deem to have been an economic miracle. Inflation and growth rates for Argentina during the 1990s are shown in Table 5.1.

Table 5.1 GDP growth rates and inflation in Argentina, 1990–1998

	1990	1991	1992	1993	1994	1995	1996	1997	1998
Inflation[a] (%)	2078	141	16.1	−3.6	2.8	3.2	−0.1	−0.5	−1.7
GDP growth[b] (%)	−2.5	9.1	7.9	8.2	5.8	−2.9	5.5	8.1	3.9

[a] World Bank DataBank. Inflation, GDP Deflator (annual %)
[b] World Bank. GDP Growth (annual %). Percentage change of real GDP compared to the previous year. Real GDP is adjusted for inflation

Domingo Cavallo, the Harvard-trained Minister of Economy, became an enormously popular figure, as well Menem.

Menem significantly expanded presidential power in this period. Eaton explains how the legislature delegated broad economic powers to Menem,[10] including the power to privatize numerous state-owned enterprises deemed to be in an "emergency" through a bill called the State Reform Law. Although the country at the time was going through a hyperinflationary episode, the law delegated too many powers to Menem, who would continue to use some of the decree rights conferred to him even after the crisis was over. Legislators in other words made no effort to assure that the president would only be able to use decree authority during true emergences, and several privatizations were done by decree based on a crisis-era law, *in a period of time when the crisis was over* (the hyperinflationary crisis had died down by the end of 1991, yet Menem continued to use crisis-era powers during his time in office). The State Reform Law, in addition to giving the president the power to privatize companies after the crisis ended, also arguably gave the president powers that were too broad. Shever notes that:

> The State Reform Law pronounced a "state of emergency" for all state-owned enterprises, declared many of them "subject to privatization," and authorized the president to put their management in the hands of corporate trustees who would prepare them for their transformation to private ownership...[this privatization process] has been called 'one of the broadest and most rapid in the Western Hemisphere,' if not the world.[11]

A second bill, the Economic Emergency Law, gave the president authority over tax incentives, fiscal subsidies, the power to issue a new foreign investment code, etc.[12] In describing why congress decided to voluntarily give up so much power, Eaton blames the nature of the economic emergency and writes that:

> While legislators had never delegated such extensive powers to the executive branch, neither had such a sudden and dramatic policy transformation been attempted in Argentina. ... In 1989 an effective response to the country's deep crisis required simultaneous policy change on a number of fronts. This crisis simply exceeded the legislature's capacity to act and helps explain why delegation was the most attractive solution for the governing party despite levels of party discipline that seemed to obviate the need to delegate. Delegation of emergency powers in 1989 enabled President Menem to demonstrate his reformist credentials across a range of policy areas at a time when both domestic and foreign investors needed assurance. ... Though Menem could wait to introduce his comprehensive tax reforms, the pressing nature of the economic crisis demanded immediate measures.[13]

In addition to the legislature, the judiciary also made several decisions during this crisis which increased executive authority. In Chapter 2, I noted that the Argentine Supreme Court made two particularly controversial decisions during Menem's tenure, namely legitimizing decree power through the *Peralta* decision and using the *per saltum* legal doctrine to rapidly intervene in favor of the executive in the privatization of *Aerolíneas Argentinas*.

Although as I mentioned in the previous chapter the Supreme Court was packed with members loyal to Menem, it is clear that a second factor that played a role in their support for strengthening presidential power was the economic crisis that was taking place at the time. In the case of *Aerolíneas Argentinas*, Larkins writes:

> Allusions in the [Court's] opinion to the benefits of the sale may indicate that the justices were more interested in the merits of privatization than in its constitutionality. More significantly, though, the language used to affirm the legality of the sale was strongly supportive of some of the underlying concepts of delegative democracy. Parting from the precedent set by the previous court in the retirees' case, the majority argued that the seriousness of the nation's economy justified the president's otherwise questionable policies, including the privatization of the airline.[14]

Similarly, in the *Peralta* decision, the poor state of the nation's economy also played a significant role in the Court's support for increasing presidential power. The Court's opinion claims that it is reasonable for the State to exercise power in a more "energetic"[15] manner during an economic crisis than in normal times; it also notably states that:

> In times of severe socio-economic upheaval, the greatest threat to judicial security is not the comparatively small one stemming from the non-application of the smallest of legal norms, but rather what would happen if they were respected with absolute rigidity; although they have been effective in periods of calm and normalcy [these legal norms] suffer from inefficiency in the face of a crisis.[16]

As this opinion makes clear, the Supreme Court essentially was willing to suspend the application of legal norms during periods of economic crises. In describing the *Peralta* decision, Morgenstern and Manzetti neatly summarize the role of economic crises in having the courts grant power to presidents when they write:

> The Court justified its decision by stating that situations of 'high social risk', required the application of 'swift measures whose efficacy were not conceivable through other means'. The ruling thus justified the executive's usurpation of legislative powers. It went still further, adding that although the Constitution established the division of

power among the three branches of government, this should not be interpreted in a way to allow the 'dismemberment of the State so that each of its parts acts in isolation to the detriment of national unity'. Ironically, this implies that under emergency situations (which the executive could define) not only the Congress, but also the Court should subordinate itself to the executive.[17]

2001 Crisis and How It Affected Presidential Power

Although the crisis of the late 1980s was very deleterious to the welfare of citizens, the worst economic crisis in modern Argentine history would come in the early 2000s. Initially, the aforementioned reforms of the 1990s boosted the economy, and Argentina was seen as a poster child for IMF policies and a model for other Latin American countries to emulate. Nevertheless, by the time that Menem left power and De La Rúa assumed the presidency in the late 1990s, several problems in this model emerged that would ultimately lead to a crisis. Convertibility, while taming inflation, also created an overvalued currency that led to a strong trade imbalance by hurting exports and encouraging imports. Industry suffered, and unemployment rose sharply. At the same time, deficits ballooned in large part because of the high costs associated with the privatization of the pension system. The country was also hurt by the East Asian crisis, which spread to Latin America. At this time, investors became worried about the ability of the country to service its debt, and many began pulling their money out of Argentina. One of the factors that served as a nail in the coffin for Argentina was the fact that the IMF ultimately refused to grant the country a bailout. Normally, facing such an economic crisis a country would have devalued the currency or printed money to provide monetary stimulus, but this was impossible given the constraints of the Convertibility Plan. Ultimately, depositors began withdrawing money rapidly from banks, and following the financial panic, banks were forced to freeze accounts.

During the economic crisis, the statistics are startling: the unemployment rate was close to 25%, the poverty rate rose to over 50%, and the country defaulted on approximately $100 billion in debt, the largest sovereign default in world history at the time. In 2001, the economy contracted by 4.4%, and in 2002, it fell a further 10.9%. There were riots in the streets, and numerous supermarkets were looted. A political crisis ensued, and after De La Rúa was airlifted in a helicopter from the presidential palace in December of 2001 (to escape the large protest outside), by January of 2002, the country had shifted between four presidents (Puerta, Sáa, Camaño, and finally, Duhalde).

During the economic crisis, the congress provided significant emergency powers to Duhalde (who emerged after a succession of presidents in a short time span). These emergency powers included the ability to devalue the peso.[18] The problem with these types of emergency powers was that although in theory they were meant to be temporary, in reality, they were extended so much by the Peronist congress that they took on a permanent form. Biazzi claimed in an interview that "because of an emergency situation, the congress gave significant powers to the executive. The problem was that these powers were extended in time."[19] He also claimed that stretching emergency powers beyond the crisis is not limited to the presidency, and that in the provinces, governors often acted similarly. For example, he described that the province of Misiones has been in a state of "crisis" for the past 20 years, and that every year when congress passes the budget, it chooses to leave economic emergency provisions intact.[20] Similarly, political scientist and law professor Martín Medina in discussing the effects of economic crises described to me that:

> once congress gives powers to presidents for use under exceptional circumstances, these powers never return to congress. The president will continue to use and abuse those powers, including once the crisis has ended, and including during periods of economic booms.[21]

At the federal level, the Kirchners ultimately benefitted from the economic emergency measures of the 2001–2002 crisis, and this helped them consolidate their grip on power. Rubio in an interview described this when she claimed that:

> What has happened was that emergency laws remained in place. These laws established that the executive could extend them for a certain period of time, and the executive extended them. When this period of time finished, congress made another law stretching the time limit. For example, during the 12 years of the Kirchner government, emergency laws from the 2001–2002 crisis were in effect which delegated many powers [to the president]. This was in spite of the fact that the country had gotten over the crisis and was experiencing "Chinese" growth rates.[22]

Indeed, as Rubio describes, it is strange that the Kirchners would continue to benefit from economic emergency measures given that Argentina was growing at significant rates. Table 5.2 shows the GDP growth rates between 2003 and 2015, the time that the Kirchners were in office.

Former vice president Julio Cobos describes the absurdity of how the Kirchners prolonged emergency powers despite the absence of a crisis when he states that Cristina Kirchner "took advantage [of emergency laws delegating power to her] to a maximum extent, because when you declare an economic emergency, it helps you get more power... This country is always under an economic emergency, even since exiting [the

Table 5.2 GDP growth rates in
Argentina, 2003–2015[a]

Year	GDP growth rate (%)
2003	8.8
2004	9.0
2005	9.2
2006	8.5
2007	9.0
2008	6.8
2009	0.9
2010	10.1
2011	8.9
2012	−1.0
2013	2.4
2014	−2.5
2015	2.7
Average	5.6

[a] World Bank. GDP growth (annual %). Percentage change of real GDP compared to the previous year. Real GDP is adjusted for inflation

crisis]."[23] Senator Ángel Rozas also claimed that in 2001, when congress decided to grant the Duhalde government emergency powers

> we were on the brink of a civil war and were looking for a way to get out of that difficult situation. They were exceptional laws that were supposed to be in place for a brief time period…They were supposed to be for 1,2,3 years, not 15 years.[24]

As well, Senator Abal Medina admitted in an interview that economic emergency laws meant to be for the short term "persist afterwards" and that this "is not justified."[25]

How Argentina Exhibited Characteristics of the "Bust-Boom Cycle"

Earlier in this chapter, I mentioned that presidents are especially likely to concentrate power when they benefit from a bust-boom cycle. In other words, a president is in a particularly advantageous position to become hyperpresidential if the economy is growing, *and* his/her predecessor ended their term during an economic crisis.

In the case of Menem, as mentioned earlier, throughout the 1990s, growth was restored to Argentina, and many not only in Argentina but also in the international community credited Menem with the recovery. While the 1989 economic crisis did help Menem concentrate power through the aforementioned crisis laws, he would not have been able to concentrate so much power had Argentina not grown as rapidly under his tenure.

Similarly, Peronist presidents Duhalde and the Kirchners came to power after the 2001 crisis, and during their tenures, the economy experienced a boom similar to the one in the initial years of the Menem administration. On average, during the Kirchners' tenures in office, the economy grew by 5.6% (see Table 5.2), especially during their early years in office when they were able to significantly consolidate power. As well, it is important to note that even apparent failures such as the near-zero growth rate in 2009 were perceived as successes given the global financial turmoil that year which saw other countries go into sharp recessions. In an article, Larkins writes that a

> characteristic common to many delegative democracies is the existence of some crisis which confers an aura of 'savior' upon the president. This crisis tends to justify the increased centralization of authority in the president's hands and further validates his efforts to surmount constitutional and horizontal controls.[26]

Following Larkins's logic, if the president is actually able to restore growth, then in the eyes of many citizens and legislators, he would truly be viewed as a "savior" and would be rewarded with even greater presidential power.

Another one of the primary reasons that power became more concentrated in the executive branch in Argentina following the economic boom of the 2000s is that the central government had significantly more resources at its disposal. Between 2001 and 2009, the tax revenue composed of import and export duties increased dramatically. This money that resulted in large part from the commodity boom provided a significant boost to Néstor and Cristina Kirchner, as they could more easily coopt the provinces through discretionary transfers. Mazzuca refers to the populism arising out of resource booms as "rentier populism" and writes that:

> Argentina, Bolivia, Ecuador, and especially Venezuela display a new and intensely plebiscitarian version of "superpresidentialism" in which the president dominates the entire decision-making process at the expense of the national legislature and receives nothing more than nominal scrutiny from other branches of government or nonpartisan oversight agencies...The roots of South American rentier populism lie far away across the oceans, in India and China. It was the rise of those two huge countries...as industrial superpowers and voracious consumers of raw material and proteins that launched the global commodities boom which has been rentier populism's jet fuel. Starting in 2002, surging prices for oil, minerals, and agricultural commodities not only reversed a decades-long trend of "deteriorating terms of trade" for South American countries, but also sparked

an extraordinary period of economic growth whose speed and consistency were like nothing the region had ever seen.[27]

A concentration of power under the Kirchners would have been more difficult if the economy had not grown so rapidly. It is no surprise therefore that Cristina Kirchner's power began to wane in recent years as the economy slowed, which ushered in the conditions that led to Macri winning the presidential election in December of 2015.

Examining the Administration of Mauricio Macri

Earlier in the book, I mentioned that Mauricio Macri was weak relative to Menem and the Kirchners (although he was notably still stronger than Chilean presidents). Given that there was an economic crisis in 2014 (the penultimate year of Cristina Kirchner's presidency and the year before the election), one may have expected Macri to be able to concentrate power. Although the economic crisis gave Macri the momentum to win the 2015 election, he was not able to use the economic crisis to concentrate power to the same extent as previous presidents for two reasons. First, the economic crisis in 2014 in Argentina was relatively mild compared to previous crises, and GDP growth "only" fell by 2.5%. Note that the economic crises that occurred during the presidencies of Alfonsín and De La Rúa were significantly more painful than the crisis in 2014, and the public in 2014 did not feel the economic pain to the same extent as in the past. Second, Macri did not benefit from a bust-boom cycle like either Menem or the Peronist administrations that followed De La Rúa. Whereas Menem, Duhalde, and the Kirchners were able to enjoy robust economic growth immediately after they took office (and thus cemented their popularity through their image as "saviors" who helped restore growth), Macri's term was marked by lackluster growth. Rather than bringing back the double-digit growth rates that characterized the beginnings of the aforementioned Peronist administrations, Macri's term included recessions in 2016, 2018, and 2019 as well as a currency crisis in 2018 (where the peso lost about half of its value relative to the dollar). It also included an embarrassing outreach to the IMF, which is greatly maligned in Argentine society, for a line of credit. While voters did not fully blame Macri for the economic troubles during his term (with many voters still pointing to Cristina Kirchner), Macri's economic reforms did not produce the kind of boom that would have helped elevate him to the status of "savior."

It is also important to mention that the recessions during the Macri administration, while painful, were not severe. In 2016, the economy declined by 2.1%, followed by a period of 2.8% growth in 2017, and then another decline of 2.6% in 2018. Given the absence of a deep recession, this did not provide Macri the opportunity to use economic emergency laws to concentrate power in a manner similar to previous presidents. In fact, Macri relinquished some of the emergency powers from which he had benefitted. Notably, since 2002, there had been an economic emergency law in place which allowed the president to bypass congress on a broad range of economic policies including the exchange rate and tariffs. Although initially the law had been meant for two years (to tackle the economic crisis that Argentina was facing in 2001/2002), it kept being extended by various administrations, most recently by Cristina Kirchner in 2015. Macri did not seek to renew the economic emergency measure, and in 2018, it expired.

In short, Macri has not been able to concentrate power to the same extent as previous presidents since (a) the "bust" during which he came to power was relatively mild by historical standards, and (b) during his time in office, there was neither a "boom" nor a very severe recession that would have generated a demand among the population for a powerful response.

Summarizing How Argentina Fits the Theoretical Model of Hyperpresidentialism and Economic Crisis

In short, Argentina provides an excellent example of how economic crises can promote hyperpresidentialism. Whereas Menem was able to concentrate power during the 1990s after the crisis of the late 1980s, Duhalde and the Kirchners were able to concentrate power after the 2001–2002 downturn. Both of these crises also follow the pattern of "bust-boom cycles." Although Alfonsín and De La Rúa left office early as the above two crises were unfolding, their successors enjoyed periods of strong economic growth and gained significant political capital during the "boom" periods.

Part III: Growth Patterns in Post-democratic Chile and the Non-emergence of Hyperpresidentialism

Unlike Argentina which experienced the aforementioned cycles of busts followed by booms that cemented hyperpresidentialism, since the return to democracy, the Chilean economy has been remarkably robust. What is conspicuously absent in the case of Chile from the late 1980s through 2019 is a full-blown economic crisis, and Figure 5.6 shows the GDP growth rate for Chile since 1989.

Since the period of democratization and until the COVID-19 pandemic, the Chilean GDP growth rate dipped slightly below zero on only two occasions, in 1999 as well as during the global financial crisis of 2009. Inflation, another problem which has plagued many countries in Latin America, has also been very tame in Chile. As indicated in Figure 5.7, inflation has never exceeded 30% since 1990 and has continuously

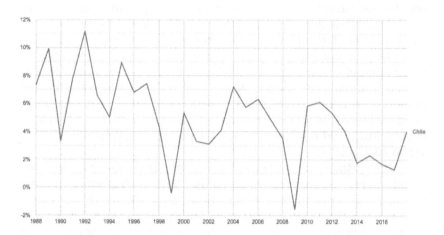

Figure 5.6 GDP growth rate for Chile since 1989.[a]

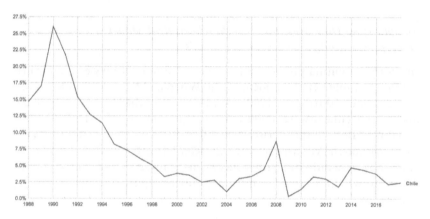

Figure 5.7 Inflation rate in Chile (1989–2016).[b]

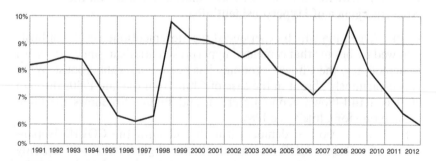

Figure 5.8 Unemployment rate in Chile.[c]

a   World Bank. GDP Growth (Annual %). Percentage change of real GDP compared to
     previous year. Real GDP is adjusted for inflation.
b   World Bank. Inflation (annual %)-consumer prices.
c   World Bank.

hovered in the 5% range. Most notably, there have never been any periods of hyperinflation since democratization.

Figure 5.8 illustrates how unemployment in Chile has also been remarkably stable historically, hovering around 8% per year.

Remembering How a Bust-Boom Cycle Contributed to Pinochet's Rise to Power

Although since democratization Chile has not had the economic crises that have allowed Argentine presidents to consolidate power, one historical case in Chile which would lend support to the theory advanced in this chapter is the period before and after the 1973 coup. Although the circumstances under which Pinochet took power as well as the authoritarian system through which he held power differ from the hyperpresidential regimes of Menem and the Kirchners, there is no doubt that the economic crisis under Allende helped create the climate that led to the 1973 coup. In 1973, the economy contracted nearly 5%, and inflation reached nearly 500%. While the 1973 crisis created fertile conditions for the coup, what helped Pinochet remain in office was the economic boom following the 1973 military takeover. Between 1976 and 1981, Chile was one of the fastest-growing economies in Latin America, and inflation plummeted. The fact that the previous democratic government ended amidst economic turmoil and the fact that Pinochet was able to make the economy grow again certainly helped lend Pinochet the legitimacy and public support needed to hold on to power.

Table 5.3 summarizes how economic factors helped shape presidential power in Argentina, Chile, and other countries.

I will briefly elaborate on the cases of Venezuela and Russia illustrated in the aforementioned table. The case of Venezuela represents a bust-boom cycle because when Chávez took office in 1999, Venezuela was facing an economic crisis that had started under the previous president, Rafael Caldera. Venezuela had in fact been in a general decline for two decades in the 1980s and 1990s, and both major parties AD and CO-PEI were discredited. During the 2000s, under the Chávez presidency, the economy surged due to the global increase in oil prices. Over time, Chávez strengthened more and more power, and this was partially because despite coming to power during an economic crisis, during his time in office living standards improved. It is important to note that the economic improvement had little to do with Chávez's policies, and a lot more to do with global commodity prices. Chávez was simply president at the right time, and the economy grew in spite of Chávez and not because of him. However, voters often give credit to a sitting president when the economy improves, and even though Chávez did not cause this growth, he was still seen as a savior in the eyes of many Venezuelans.

Table 5.3 Illustrating how bust-boom cycles correlate to hyperpresidentialism in several cases

	Bust period	**Boom period**	**Regime outcome**
Argentina	Late 1980s: Alfonsín	1990s: Menem	Hyperpresidentialism under Menem
Argentina	2001–2002: De La Rúa	Mid- to late 2000s: Duhalde and the Kirchners	Hyperpresidentialism under Néstor and Cristina Kirchner
Chile	No severe economic crises from 1990 to 2019	Steady growth during most of the post-1990 period	No Hyperpresidentialism
Venezuela	1999 under Caldera	Most of the 2000s: Chávez	Hyperpresidentialism under Chávez
Russia	Most of the 1990s under Yeltsin	Most of the 2000s under Putin	Hyperpresidentialism under Putin

The case of Russia also represents a classical bust-boom cycle. In the 1990s, the Russian economy was in shambles, and the country was experiencing political chaos. In 1998, the Russian economic crisis deepened, and the country defaulted on its debt. Throughout the 1990s, poverty increased substantially, life expectancy fell, and alcoholism skyrocketed. Although the situation in Russia was difficult during the 1990s, the economy improved almost immediately after Putin came to power in 1999. Throughout the 2000s, the Russian economy expanded rapidly due to the increase in global oil prices (just like in the case of Venezuela, oil is one of the top Russian exports). The bust-boom cycle in Russia gave Putin the aura of "savior" among some segments of the population, since although he came to power during a period of crisis, he was able to claim credit for improving the economy. Ultimately, this gave him the political capital necessary to strengthen the presidency, and if Putin had not gotten lucky with the increase in oil prices in the 2000s, it is uncertain whether he would have been able to concentrate power to this extent.

Part IV: Using a Survey to Understand Whether the First and Third Independent Variables in This Book Work Through a Bottom-Up or High-Level Process

Throughout this chapter along with Chapters 3 and 4, I have discussed the logic behind my three independent variables. However, a new question emerges regarding the mechanism through which they work. It is unclear whether my first and third independent variables work in a bottom-up manner where the electorate desires to confer greater power to the presidency or through a high-level mechanism in which the president directly usurps power from institutions of horizontal accountability without the electorate's permission. In other words, do institutional weakness and economic crises create a *desire among the population* for a strong leader, or does a leader gain strength in this environment in a high-level process where the president directly usurps power from institutions like congress without a direct mandate from the electorate?

To test the importance of popular opinion on the expansion of presidential power, I conducted an in-person survey as part of my fieldwork in Argentina during the summer of 2017. This was a national-level survey and was performed by a highly reputable firm between July 7, 2017 and July 22, 2017.[28] It is important to note that that this was an omnibus survey that the firm was conducting on a range of topics, and I was permitted to add on my questions. In terms of personnel, 60 individuals were sent to gather data, and there were eight regional supervisors.

Regarding the methodology behind the survey, it involved 1,003 participants throughout the country who were 16 years of age or older (they were interviewed at their residences across 26 localities). Note that only one person was surveyed in each individual residence; households were chosen based on a predetermined methodology, and the data gatherers had no individual discretion when selecting which residences to visit. There was also significant diversity in terms of age, region, population density, education levels, political affiliation, etc. In terms of political affiliation, participants were separated into six groups: the front led by Cristina Kirchner, *Cambiemos*, the group led by Sergio Massa, non-Kirchnerist Justicialism/Peronism, leftist parties, and other parties. In terms of population density, the respondents were divided into four types of communities: (1) a population over 1.5 million, (2) a population between 500,000 and 1.5 million, (3) a population between 10,000 and 500,000 people, and (4) a population below 10,000 people. The survey was conducted in 13 provinces: the city of Buenos Aires, the province of Buenos Aires, Catamarca, Córdoba, Corrientes, Chaco, Chubut, La Rioja, Mendoza, Salta, San Luis, Santa Fe, and Tucumán. Respondents were also divided into five age groups: 16–24, 25–34, 35–49, 50–64, and 65+ years (in selecting the ages of the sample of respondents, census data was taken into account). In terms of education, people were separated into three categories: primary education, secondary education, and tertiary education. The margin of error for the survey is ±4.2% (95% confidence interval).

During the survey, three questions were asked of the participants. The first two questions address my first independent variable, institutional strength, and the third question addresses my third independent variable, economic crises. The results are illustrated in Tables 5.4–5.6.

Table 5.4 Answers to the following survey question in Argentina (translated): If you had confidence that a president was committed to improving rule of law, fighting corruption, and making institutions more efficient, would you be in favor of an expansion in presidential powers?

	Percent of respondents (%)
Yes. I would be in favor of an expansion in presidential powers if I was confident that a president will try to improve the rule of law	35.6
No. I would not be in favor of an expansion in presidential power, even if I was confident that the president will try to improve the rule of law	63.1
Don't know/Didn't reply	1.3

Table 5.5 Answers to the following survey question in Argentina (translated): Would you support a candidate promising a heavy-handed style of governing if at the same time he promised to fight against corruption and improve inefficient state institutions?

	Percent of respondents (%)
I would **never** support a presidential candidate with a heavy-handed style, even if he promises to fight against corruption and improve inefficient state institutions	32.1
I would **possibly** support a presidential candidate with a heavy-handed style if he promises to fight against corruption and improve inefficient state institutions	30.4
I would **probably** support a presidential candidate with a heavy-handed style if he promises to fight against corruption and improve inefficient state institutions	25.0
I would **definitely** support a presidential candidate with a heavy-handed style if he promises to fight against corruption and improve inefficient state institutions	12.5
Don't know/Didn't reply	0

Table 5.6 Answers to the following survey question in Argentina (translated): During an economic crisis, do you think that Congress should give special powers to the president to deal with the crisis?

Yes. Congress should give special powers to the president to deal with the crisis	36.4%
No. Congress should not give special powers to the president to deal with the crisis	59.0%
Don't know/Didn't reply	4.6%

As the results from my survey show, in a country like Argentina which has experienced significant episodes of hyperpresidentialism, the population in fact does *not* want to give the president more power.

Given the lack of support among the population for strengthening presidential powers, even in the face of corruption/institutional weakness and economic crisis, one conclusion that can be drawn is that the process of the emergence of hyperpresidentialism is not a bottom-up process where the population deliberately confers greater power to a president, but rather a high-level process where institutions of horizontal accountability either voluntarily give up power to the executive branch or where the executive branch is able to usurp power from them (without the approval of the electorate). In simple terms, *hyperpresidentialism emerges as a result of a power grab, not a power grant.* In terms of my third independent variable, during an economic crisis, *members of congress* (who may fear they may not have the capacity to tackle the economic crisis with the same ability as the executive) will delegate more powers to the president. Notably, the population would not necessarily approve of this transfer of power from the legislative to the executive branch.

While this survey is very informative, it does contain two limitations that are important to mention. First, because the survey was conducted in 2017 after many years of hyperpresidentialism, it may reflect a temporary exhaustion by the population with strongman leaders. Had this survey been conducted in the late 1980s prior to the start of the Menem administration, it is possible that the results would have reflected more enthusiasm for concentrating power in a president. Second, this survey was not conducted during a year of economic crisis. While during a year of growth respondents argued that they would not support giving special powers to a president in a hypothetical downturn, this attitude might change if respondents were surveyed during the middle of an actual economic crisis. In other words, people may have one attitude during a time of plenty, yet this attitude may change during a time of adversity. Despite these two limitations, the survey data provided crucial insight on peoples' attitudes toward hyperpresidentialism, and future surveys could build on these findings and address the aforementioned limitations.

Chapter Summary

Throughout this chapter, I have attempted to describe how economic crises (or their absence) in Argentina and Chile contributed to the diverging outcomes of these countries in terms of hyperpresidentialism. Whereas Argentina had two severe economic crises from the late 1980s until 2019 (followed by periods of strong growth under different presidents), Chile in that period did not experience any sharp economic contractions. In this chapter, I also proposed that the *combination* of an economic crisis under one president followed by a period of strong recovery under a subsequent president is especially likely to lead to hyperpresidentialism under that subsequent president. This is a novel concept in the political science literature, and it is my hope that future works will analyze this unique combination.

In this chapter, I also more generally analyzed whether my first and third independent variables (institutional strength and the presence of recent economic crises) work through a bottom-up mechanism or high-level process. Based on the results of the 2017 survey I conducted in Argentina, the conclusion that I can draw is that they work through a high-level process. Populations rarely explicitly desire to grant significant powers to a president; rather, presidents obtain it from institutions of horizontal accountability like congress and the judiciary in a high-level game. While this study had the limitations I described earlier, I would encourage future work to further explain the role of the general population in power grabs by presidents.

One of the important limitations of this chapter is that I only look at economic crises. The logic by which economic crises increase the likelihood for hyperpresidentialism also applies to virtually any type of crisis that occurs in a society, including social crises, health crises, and security crises. For example, if a country was attacked either by another country or by a terrorist organization, it is likely that congress and the judiciary would be willing to delegate increased powers to the president. One fruitful line of future research would involve analyzing how these other different types of crises also impact presidential power in practice.

Notes

1 Larkins 1998; p.425.
2 Anderson 2016; p.32.
3 Author's interview with Javier David (Federal Deputy (Salta), Partido Justicialista).
4 Author's interview with Martín Maquieyra (Federal Deputy, PRO).
5 Author's interview with Martín Maquieyra (Federal Deputy, PRO).
6 Author's interview with Alicia Soraire (Federal Deputy, FPV).
7 Author's interview with Alicia Soraire (Federal Deputy, FPV).
8 Kiguel 1989; p.2.
9 McGuire 1997; p.186.
10 Laws 23,696 and 23,697.
11 Shever 2012; p.84.
12 Eaton 2002; p.161.
13 Eaton 2002; p.161.
14 Larkins 1998; p.433.
15 Supreme Court of Argentina *Peralta* Decision p.1518.
16 Supreme Court of Argentina *Peralta* Decision p.1518.
17 Morgenstern and Manzetti 2003; p.162.
18 *CNN.com* January 6, 2002.
19 Author's interview with Ricardo Biazzi (Minister of Education of Argentina for two days in December 2001 under President Puerta (PJ), Professor of Constitutional Law).

20 Author's interview with Ricardo Biazzi (Minister of Education of Argentina for two days in December 2001 under President Puerta (PJ), Professor of Constitutional Law).
21 Author's interview with Martín Medina (Political Scientist, Professor of Public Law at Universidad Cuenca del Plata).
22 Author's interview with Delia Ferreira Rubio (Lawyer and scholar with a deep knowledge of Necessity and Urgency Decrees).
23 Author's interview with Julio Cobos (Ex-Vice President of Argentina, UCR senator from Mendoza).
24 Author's interview with Ángel Rozas (Senator and ex-governor of Chaco, UCR).
25 Author's interview with Senator Abal Medina (Senator and Former Chief of Cabinet of Ministers for President Cristina Kirchner).
26 Larkins 1998; p.424.
27 Mazzuca 2013; pp.109–110.
28 VOICES! Research & Consultancy.

Bibliography

Ames, Barry. *The Deadlock of Democracy in Brazil.* Ann Arbor: University of Michigan Press, 2001.

Anderson, Leslie. *Democratization by Institutions: Argentina's Transition Years in Comparative Perspective.* Ann Arbor: University of Michigan Press, 2016.

Eaton, Kent. *Politicians and Economic Reform in New Democracies: Argentina and the Philippines in the 1990s.* University Park: The Pennsylvania State University, 2002.

Haggard, Stephan, and Robert Kaufman. *The Political Economy of Democratic Transitions.* Princeton: Princeton University Press, 1995.

Kiguel, Miguel. "Inflation in Argentina: Stop and Go Since the Austral Plan." World Bank Policy, Planning, and Research: Working Papers (Macroeconomic Adjustment and Growth). WPS 162. (March 1989).

Larkins, Christopher. "The Judiciary and Delegative Democracy in Argentina." *Comparative Politics.* Vol 30, Iss 4 (July 1998), pp. 423–442.

Mainwaring, Scott. "Presidentialism, Multipartism, and Democracy: The Difficult Combination." *Comparative Political Studies.* Vol 26, Iss 2 (1993), pp. 198–228.

Mazzuca, Sebastián. "Lessons from Latin America: The Rise of Rentier Populism." *Journal of Democracy.* Vol 24, Iss 2 (April 2013), pp. 108–122.

McGuire, James. *Peronism Without Peron: Unions, Parties, and Democracy in Argentina.* Stanford: Stanford University Press, 1997.

Morgenstern, Scott, and Luigi Manzetti. "Legislative Oversight: Interests and Institutions in the United States and Argentina." *Democratic Accountability in Latin America.* Eds. Scott Mainwaring and Christopher Welna. Oxford: Oxford University Press, 2003, pp. 132–169.

Shever, Elana. *Resources for Reform: Oil and Neoliberalism in Argentina.* Stanford: Stanford University Press, 2012.

Supreme Court of Argentina. Luis Arcenio Peralta y Otro v. Nacion Argentina (Supreme Court Decision Opinion). December 27, 1990, pp. 1513–1564.

6   Conclusion

Summary of Argument

In this book, I have attempted to provide an explanation for the degree of presidential power *in practice* among presidential systems throughout the world, with a focus on Latin American democracies. I began by describing how presidential powers in theory often do not correspond to presidential powers in practice. Whereas some countries have constitutionally strong presidents, in practice, these executives may be highly constrained. Similarly, whereas a large number of countries do place significant constitutional restraints on their presidents, in practice, they may rule almost unilaterally with few constraints by congress and the judiciary. Given the weakness of presidential power in theory in predicting informal presidential power, this book proposed that the following three conditions increase the likelihood that the president will be able to concentrate power *in practice*: (a) weak state institutions, (b) the possession by the president of a strong working majority in congress, and (c) a recent history of economic crises in a country, especially a "bust-boom" cycle where a president assumes power during an economic crisis and gets credit for restoring growth. The occurrence of these three variables together provides fertile ground for hyperpresidentialism to emerge.

In Chapter 1, the introduction, I began by discussing two theory-building cases, namely Argentina and Chile. I noted that these two countries provide an excellent most similar system design, since despite being similar on many variables, they critically differ in the extent to which the president has been able to concentrate power. Whereas Chilean presidents have been highly constrained by institutions of horizontal accountability such as congress, the judiciary, and the *Contraloría*, Argentine presidents for most of the post-democratization period have been able to concentrate significant power (especially during the period between 1990–1999 and 2002–2015 when Peronist presidents were in power). As I described in the book, these two cases are particularly fascinating since, on paper, the Chilean president is in fact significantly stronger than his Argentine counterpart.

In the analysis of the dependent variable in Chapter 2, I substantiated my assertion that presidential power in practice since democratization

DOI: 10.4324/9781003142904-6

has overall been stronger in Argentina than in Chile. I showed this by analyzing in-depth how whereas Argentine presidents were able to pass many of their projects either by decree or through a rubber-stamp congress, Chilean presidents were significantly restricted in their use of decrees and had to conduct serious negotiations with congress. Also, whereas Chilean presidents faced restrictions by the judiciary, Argentine presidents were significantly less constrained by courts.

In Chapter 3, I described how my first independent variable, the strength of state institutions, varied across my two cases. In this chapter, I analyzed various institutions of horizontal accountability in both countries, and whereas these institutions have been remarkably strong in Chile, they have been very weak in Argentina. While institutions such as the Chilean congress, judiciary, and *Contraloría* were able to keep presidential power in check, similar institutions in Argentina failed in their mandate. Such institutions in Argentina suffer from a mixture of severe partisanship, weak technical capacity which makes it difficult to conduct serious oversight of the president, a lack of prestige, or a lack of respect for established norms/procedures. I then generalized my argument through a large-N analysis of presidential systems throughout the world; as I showed, there was a strong correlation between corruption (as a measure of institutional strength) and presidential power.

In Chapter 4, I examined my second independent variable, the size of a president's party in congress (and the degree to which a president possessed a working majority). I showed that whereas Argentine Peronist presidents enjoyed substantial working majorities in the legislature in the post-democratization period, Chilean presidents never benefitted from unified government. Although Chilean presidents did often have *coalitional* majorities, these coalitions were very heterogeneous and cannot be considered to have the same effectiveness and discipline as the party majorities enjoyed by Argentine presidents.

In Chapter 5, I attempted to show how whereas Argentina suffered two severe economic crises from democratization until 2019 (which allowed presidents to concentrate power), the Chilean economy in the same period was crisis-free. Argentine presidents have also benefitted from the aforementioned "bust-boom" cycle. As I noted, if a president comes to power during a period of economic crisis and is able to restore growth, this will help that president gain the political capital necessary to concentrate power. For example, Carlos Menem came into office during a period of economic upheaval, yet was able to take credit for restoring the economy.

Main Contributions to the Literature

This piece is unique since it seeks to provide a general, systematic theory for explaining presidential power *in practice* as opposed to presidential power in theory. Although many studies have been done where presidential power was the dependent variable, they typically measure presidential power based on constitutional prerogatives/constraints. The findings in this book also have significant predictive capabilities; the theories presented can be used to predict based on current conditions whether presidents will be able to usurp power. This is one of the first pieces to systematically measure presidential power *in practice* as a dependent variable using expert survey data (from Varieties of Democracy). Similarly, this book is one the first pieces in the literature which quantitatively illustrates the weak correlation between presidential power in theory versus in practice (see Figures 1.1 and 1.2 in Chapter 1).

In terms of my first independent variable, this book has also found a direct link between institutional strength/rule of law and presidential power in practice. Whereas strong state institutions are widely accepted as being critical to promoting economic growth, I have shown that they are also critical in maintaining a strong system of checks and balances. Although improvements in rule of law are often correctly assumed to help a country's economy and to attract foreign investment, improvements in rule of law are also correlated with a decrease in presidential power. This book is also one of the first works in the literature (perhaps even the first) to identify a direct correlation between corruption and presidential power in practice. The relationship that more corruption is correlated with more presidential power is particularly notable, since from an intuitive standpoint, more corruption and thus greater institutional chaos conjures an image of a lack of control (rather than the greater presidential control that my two cases and the large-N analysis suggest).

In terms of my second independent variable, this piece builds on an emerging literature that suggests that having fragmented, undisciplined parties in the context of presidentialism could be an asset for a democracy (since it makes hyperpresidentialism less likely).

In their recent book on coalitional presidentialism, Chaisty, Cheeseman, and Power identify a trend whereby there is "increasing fragmentation of party systems."[1] They identify that in 1974, in competitively elected legislatures, the average number of parties was 2.94; however, by 2005, this average increased to 3.83.[2] They note that:

> The odds that executives will enjoy a majority of copartisans in the legislature have fallen dramatically. More than half of all directly elected presidents can now be classified as 'minority presidents'. And as we illustrate later in this chapter, most minority presidents try explicitly to overcome this status by constructing coalitions.[3]

In light of the global trend toward party fragmentation, my book offers important insight into the effect that this may have on presidential power.

Relatedly, this book also expands the political science literature by proposing institutional mechanisms that could decrease the likelihood of hyperpresidentialism by creating incentives for legislators to deviate from the party platform. Although strengthening state institutions and preventing economic crises is often difficult and takes many years of reforms, there are several simple institutional modifications that could make it significantly harder for a president to achieve a cohesive working majority in congress. Three specific mechanisms identified in this book involve (a) shifting from a closed-list electoral system to an open-list system, (b) decreasing district magnitude, and (c) passing laws that encourage the reelection of legislators (for example, laws that would guarantee incumbents a place on the electoral lists for the next election). As I noted in Chapter 4, all of these institutional features tend to decrease party cohesion. Given that under these mechanisms legislators from the president's party are more likely to defect from the party platform, the result is a reduction in the strength of the president's faction in congress and a decrease in presidential power.

Another major contribution that this book makes is that it clearly distinguishes between a coalitional presidential majority versus a party majority. This book illustrates how party majorities provide the president substantially more power than coalitional majorities. As I discussed in the case comparison between Argentina and Chile, the party majorities that Argentina Peronist presidents enjoyed in congress provided these presidents significantly more power than the coalitional majorities enjoyed by Chilean presidents. While Argentine presidents could count on the support of a unified party, Chilean presidents had to negotiate with the various members of their coalition. As Chaisty et al. note, coalitional presidentialism "is an increasingly common form of governance in emerging democracies,"[4] and given the global trend away from party majorities toward coalitional majorities, it is reasonable to expect that, as presidents have to negotiate with multiple parties, their power will decrease. A trend away from Menem and Kirchner-style party-driven working majorities in congress toward Chilean-style coalitional majorities may very well lead to less hyperpresidentialism around the world.

In terms of my third independent variable, although it is widely accepted in the political science literature that economic crises can lead to democratic backsliding and a decline in democratic norms, I have identified the unique combination of a "bust-boom cycle" which is especially conducive to an increase in presidential power. More future research is needed to study how "bust-boom" cycles operate.

One of the most surprising findings in this book relates to the role of the citizenry in the expansion of presidential powers. As I mentioned in Chapter 5, I conducted an in-person survey where I sought to determine whether the citizenry is more likely to desire an expansion in presidential powers in the context of either an economic crisis or institutional weakness. To my surprise, respondents across Argentina overwhelmingly indicated that they would not favor increasing presidential powers even if that candidate promised to fight corruption and strengthen state institutions.

Also, they indicated that even in an economic crisis, they would not support the congress giving special powers to the president. These results suggest that when presidents concentrate power, rather than this being because of bottom-up pressure from the population, this is the result of a high-level game in which congress and the courts give up power to the president (or have the power stolen from them). As I described in the book, when presidents concentrate power, rather than this being a power grant by the general population, this is a power grab by the president. This finding overall contradicts the popular perception that strongman presidents reflect dictatorial tendencies among the population.

For this book, I also conducted nearly 100 interviews with high-level figures in politics, the judiciary, the public administration, NGOs, and academia in Argentina and Chile. I also conducted a systematic analysis of the various institutions that constrain presidential power in both countries, and I show how together they influence the strength or weakness of the presidents in power.

On an even broader level, this book significantly increases our knowledge of how democracies function. By focusing on hyperpresidentialism and the conditions under which it occurs, I have significantly expanded our understanding of executive takeovers of democracy. By applying the framework described in this book, one can predict whether a president will be able to concentrate power or whether he/she will be restrained by institutions such as congress and the judiciary. This is a very important contribution to the literature, since the quality of democracy will be completely different in a country with a restrained president than in a country with a hyperpresident. In some cases, the concentration of power in a president may be one step along the path toward dictatorship. Although hyperpresidentialism does not necessarily imply that a country is authoritarian (and, for example, Argentina under Menem and the Kirchners was a full democracy despite the immense concentration of power in the executive branch), the concentration of power in the executive branch in some cases is part of a general process of democratic backsliding that eventually results in a dictatorship. For example, Hugo Chávez in Venezuela did not become a dictator overnight, yet the gradual path toward authoritarianism included a slow erosion of checks and balances (and this erosion of checks and balances would have been predictable based on the theory outlined in this book).

Democratic backsliding, in many cases, occurs slowly over many years, and as Levitsky and Ziblatt describe in their recent book, "the backsliding of democracy is often gradual, its effects unfolding slowly over time."[5] They elaborate in more detail when they write that:

> How do elected authoritarians shatter the democratic institutions that are supposed to constrain them? Some do it in one fell swoop. But more often the assault on democracy begins slowly. For many

citizens, it may, at first, be imperceptible. After all, elections continue to be held. Opposition politicians still sit in congress. Independent newspapers still circulate. The erosion of democracy takes place piecemeal, often in baby steps. Each individual step seems minor—none appears to truly threaten democracy.[6]

When a president concentrates power through the mechanisms outlined in this book, this may represent the gradual erosion of democracy that Levitsky and Ziblatt describe. Each additional power given to the president may represent part of the "baby steps" described by Levitsky and Ziblatt. While in Argentina the increased powers given to Menem and the Kirchners did not ultimately lead to a dictatorship, other countries may very well have continued the descent toward authoritarian systems (for example, the hyperpresidentialism that characterized Chávez in Venezuela has over time slowly devolved into the authoritarianism that characterizes the current Maduro regime). Therefore, by shedding light on the conditions under which presidents will be able to concentrate power, this book increases our understanding of the gradual process of democratic decline that characterizes some countries.

Alternative Explanations

While I am confident that the variables I presented in this book provide the most compelling explanation for the variation in presidential power, no theory in political science works in 100% of cases. As the scatterplots I have used throughout this book illustrate, not all points wrap perfectly around the trendline, and there are numerous outliers. I would like to thus acknowledge that there are certainly other factors at play and will focus on several alternative explanations. These alternative explanations include (a) an analysis of the political party of the president in power, (b) the role of individual leaders, (c) differences in the status of the military during the post-democratization period, and (d) the approval rating of presidents.

The Nature of the Political Party of the President in Power

The first alternative explanation for why some presidents abuse (or do not abuse) power relates to the values of their party. An argument can be made that presidents will concentrate power when they come from a party that emphasizes powerful leaders and lacks a strong commitment to democratic governance. Similarly, one can argue that when a party has a tradition of democratic governance and deliberation, presidents from that party will avoid hyperpresidentialism in favor of consulting institutions such as congress.

In the case of Argentina, one of the reasons that congress often failed to oppose the president is the top-down nature of the Peronist party that favors strong leaders (as I described in the book, for most of the post-democratization period, the Peronist party has dominated the presidency and congress). The affinity toward strong leaders partly relates to the founding culture of the Peronist party, as Juan Perón was a general in the Argentine army. In addition to the cultural affinity of Peronists for strong leaders rooted in the history of the party, the Peronist party (which is weakly institutionalized) also had few intraparty constraints to presidents desiring to abuse power. A classical example of how the Peronist party, because of a lack of institutionalization, failed to constrain Menem is described by Levitsky, who writes:

> ...the weakly routinized nature of the PJ organization left them [party officials] with few opportunities, and little incentive, to challenge Menem. The PJ's organizational structure enhanced Menem's strategic autonomy in three ways. First, in the absence of a stable bureaucracy with established career paths and secure tenure patterns, many non-Menemist party leaders bandwagoned to Menemism in an effort to reserve or advance their careers. Second, the weakness of the PJ's authority structures allowed Menem either to ignore the formal party leadership (as he did between 1989 and 1990) or to stack it with government officials (as he did between 1990 and 1999). Third, the absence of horizontal links undermined the capacity of internal critics to build intraparty coalitions. Secondary party leaders fell into a hub-and-spokes relationship with the executive branch, which left internal opposition coalitions vulnerable to cooptation.[7]

Menem's electoral victory in 1989 followed a highly personalistic campaign in which one of his campaign slogans was simply "follow me." The militaristic, personalistic nature of the Peronist party was described by Federal Deputy Luis Pastori, who claimed that:

> There is the conception of Peronism as a vertical party centered around Perón, where nobody second guesses what the leader decides. The leader makes a decision which is transferred from the top down, in a military-style way...[and] this is even more accentuated when this leader happens to be the president. On the other hand, the Radical party has a much more horizontal structure where everything is debated and discussed...The structure is more democratic.[8]

Similarly, Federal Deputy Mario Barletta argues that the Peronist party is "a military-populist party. Peronism was born with Perón who was a member of the military, and who had a military-style, vertical conception."[9] Ex-governor Ricardo Barrios Arrechea also described that Peronism in general had an "authoritarian fascist strain...[whereas] Radicalism is more democratic than Peronism."[10] Lawyer and ex-Federal

Table 6.1 Answers to the following survey question in Argentina (translated): If you had confidence that a president was committed to improving rule of law, fighting corruption, and making institutions more efficient, would you be in favor of an expansion in presidential powers?

	Cristina Kirchner's Peronist faction (%)	Peronist factions opposed to Cristina Kirchner (%)	Cambiemos voters (PRO, UCR, Coalición Cívica) (%)
Yes. I would be in favor of an expansion in presidential powers if I was confident that a president will try to improve the rule of law	38.3	46.6	30.6
No. I would not be in favor of an expansion in presidential power, even if I was confident that the president will try to improve the rule of law	60.4	53.4	68.4
Don't know/Didn't reply	1.3	0	1.0

Deputy Orlando Gallo also ominously stated that "in Peronism, orders are followed, not discussed."[11]

In order to test the hypothesis that Peronists have a greater cultural affinity toward strongman leadership than other political groups in society, I took the data from the aforementioned in-person survey that I undertook in Argentina in the summer of 2017. As Table 6.1 for one of the questions illustrates, when filtering the results based on the party affiliation of the respondents, Peronist voters seem to be more open to strongman leaders than those supporting the *Cambiemos* coalition.

Although most voters oppose expanding presidential power (as was discussed in Chapter 5), the results suggest that a higher percentage of Peronist voters are comfortable with hyperpresidentialism than voters from the other main political group, *Cambiemos*.

Based on the logic of this argument, it is not surprising that presidents Alfonsín and De La Rúa did not try to abuse power. Alfonsín and De La Rúa were from the Radical Civic Union which emphasizes democratic deliberation; on the other hand, given that Menem and the Kirchners came from the Peronist party, it is logical that they were less constrained.

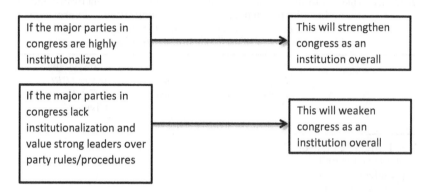

Figure 6.1 Illustrating how the institutionalization of individual parties relates to the overall institutional strength of congress.

This party-centered explanation certainly has significant merit and deserves further study. However, I would like to note that in a sense, this explanation is an extension of my first independent variable, institutional strength. In Chapter 3, I described how congress in Argentina exhibited significant weakness, whereas its counterpart in Chile exhibited significant strength. Fundamentally, the degree to which the main parties in congress are institutionalized—including the degree to which they value established rules/norms of deliberation as opposed to personalist rule by a president—is a component of what makes congress overall a strong or weak institution. This concept is illustrated in Figure 6.1.

The Role of Individual Leaders

The second alternative explanation which is certainly significant yet difficult to systematically analyze is the role of individual leaders. While I believe that the three structural factors I described are the most important in determining presidential power in practice, I acknowledge that the temperament and political acumen of presidents also play critical roles. For example, whereas certain presidents will try to push through their agenda at any cost, other presidents have significantly greater respect for the democratic process and for the role of institutions such as congress and the judiciary. Although institutional weakness, a majority in congress, and economic crises may create an opportunity for a president to concentrate power, I acknowledge that not all presidents may take advantage of these factors due to their varying degrees of respect for democratic institutions. As well, leaders have varying degrees of political expertise, and while some are very skillful at "playing politics" and using Machiavellian-like strategies to concentrate power, others are simply incompetent and do not have the expertise to exploit political opportunities.

In the Argentine case, part of the reason why President De La Rúa abused power to a lesser degree than other presidents certainly has to do with his personality. Ex-Federal Deputy Iturrieta described that "Menem exercised his presidency with significant charisma, yet his successor De La Rúa did not have the same attributes as Menem and this diminished the personalist presidency."[12] A Newsweek article also describes De La Rúa as "a gray, indecisive politician."[13]

Future research in political behavior would be especially valuable. While my book identifies opportunities to concentrate power, future research could determine why some presidents will take advantage of these opportunities better than others.

The Nature of the Military in the Post-democratization Period

A third alternative explanation for presidential power, particularly, in Latin American countries, has to do with the nature of the military in the post-democratization period. Several years ago in the early stages of research for this book, one of my initial hypotheses to explain the difference in presidential power in practice between Argentina and Chile was that the military remained significantly stronger in Chile after the democratic transition. Consequently, leftist Chilean presidents would exercise more restraint out of a fear of angering a powerful military (who had a conservative right-wing political stance). In other words, I initially hypothesized that whereas Chilean presidents felt restrained given the power of the army, Argentine presidents were freer to concentrate power given the lack of a military threat.

It is important to note that, in the post-democratization period, the Chilean military was undoubtedly significantly stronger than the Argentine military. Whereas the Argentine military had been discredited in the early 1980s because of both economic mismanagement and the humiliation of Argentina's loss in the Falklands War, the Chilean military enjoyed substantially greater prestige. Unlike the Argentine military which lost power in a transition by collapse, the Chilean military gave up power in a pacted transition where it was able to gain numerous concessions. For example, the Chilean military emerged in the post-democratization period with a larger budget than its Argentine counterpart.

Despite the greater power of the Chilean military in the post-democratization period, the reason why I ultimately rejected this alternative explanation is that after 1990 there was never a serious threat in Chile that the military would seek to "knock over the board" and launch a coup. While Chilean presidents may have faced greater pressure from the military, it would be an exaggeration to argue that Chilean executives did not concentrate power out of fear of a backlash by the military. By the 1990s, the international environment had become significantly more hostile to authoritarian countries; also, a military coup would not have enjoyed legitimacy given that in the 1988 plebiscite, the population over-whelmingly voted by a margin of 56–44% against military rule.

The Approval Rating of Presidents

Another prominent alternative explanation for the degree of presiden-tial power in practice relates to the approval rating of the president. Based on this explanation, presidents that are highly popular should also have more de facto power. Popular presidents should have an eas-ier time getting the support of congress for their projects, and they would have more political capital to push through their reforms. How-ever, this alternative explanation is inconsistent with the cases of Ar-gentina and Chile. Using data from the Executive Approval database, I compared the approval rating for Argentine and Chilean presidents between 1990 and 2016. During this period, the average approval rat-ing for Chilean presidents was, in fact, *higher* than for Argentine pres-idents (while the average approval rating for Argentine presidents was 44.6%, for Chilean presidents, it was 49.0%). Nevertheless, the higher approval rating for Chilean presidents did not translate into more de facto presidential power. While this theory is certainly worth further research, in the cases of Argentina and Chile, the three independent variables I presented in this book provide a better explanation for presidential power.

Future Areas of Research Stemming from This Book

There are several future areas of research stemming from my book that would prove valuable for the political science literature. First, although I have identified three independent variables that together make it highly probable that a country will become hyperpresidential, more work is needed to determine how they interact.

Similarly, this book has highlighted the need for the development of a comprehensive index of presidential powers in practice. To date, there are no mainstream indexes that measure solely presidential power in practice outside of expert surveys, and the main indicators in existence include to varying extents the constitutional power of presidents. Although this book has pioneered the measurement of presidential power in practice through expert surveys of legislative and judicial constraints from Va-rieties of Democracy, ultimately, a broader and more systematic index of presidential power in practice is needed that moves beyond expert surveys.

Future research would also be particularly useful in expanding upon several alternative explanations. An explanation which I believe deserves particular attention is the role of crises that are not economic in nature. While in this book I have focused on economic crises as one of the critical factors resulting to hyperpresidentialism, virtually any crisis could have a similar effect. Future research could, for example, analyze how crises such as wars, terrorist threats, pandemics, or various forms of social upheaval affect the power of presidents. For example, further works could look at the effect of the COVID-19 pandemic on presidential power.

Another explanation which in my view warrants further study is the role of international factors. In this book, I have only focused on variables in the domestic realm, yet I acknowledge that presidential power in a country is also a function of foreign influences. For example, through mechanisms such as IMF conditionality, Western nations have been able to exert significant influence over less-developed states. Similarly, countries such as Russia and China have become increasingly assertive on the world stage. Western democracies would presumably frown upon attempts by presidents to concentrate power, whereas more autocratic superpowers might actively encourage the destruction of institutions of horizontal accountability.

More research would also be valuable in building on the survey that I performed in Argentina. As I mentioned in Chapter 5, whereas the survey was very informative in describing attitudes among citizens toward hyperpresdentialism, the study had two limitations. First, the survey results could have been skewed by the fact that the population had grown tired of unrestrained leaders after many years of hyperpresidentialism. Second, the survey was conducted during a year of economic growth, and it is possible that the results would be different if conducted during a year when a downturn is taking place. To build on these results, I would recommend asking these exact same questions to ascertain attitudes toward presidential power in Argentina at several points in time in future years. If people continue to have the same negative attitudes toward hyperpresidentialism even when an economic downturn hits the country, this would strengthen the finding in my book that presidents do not usurp power because the population desires it, but rather due to a high-level process involving only the top political actors.

Future works could expand the scope of this book beyond simply presidential systems to include parliamentary systems. Although I have not included parliamentary systems in this book, all three of the independent variables I presented that increase/decrease the power of presidents could also affect the power of prime ministers. For example, based on my findings, I would hypothesize that weak state institutions in a country, a large working majority in parliament, and a recent history of economic crises (especially those that take the form of a bust-boom cycle) could also help to strengthen the power of prime ministers and possibly lead to a situation of "hyper-prime ministers." Hungary under Viktor Orbán would be a particularly interesting case to study and seems to fit the patterns of my three independent variables. The country had weak institutions of horizontal accountability, Viktor Orbán was able to gain strong majorities in the legislature (large enough to modify the constitution), and the country faced a severe economic crisis in 2009.

More research is critical for strengthening the large-N analysis that I initiated in this book. I discovered a strong correlation between institutional strength and presidential power, and this relationship holds across various measurements of institutional strength (including the Corruption Perceptions Index and Quality of Government data). However, more work is needed to deepen this analysis. I also encourage quantitative analysis of my second and third independent variables.

Another avenue of research that would follow from this book would involve looking at *the nature of policies enacted under hyperpresidents.* How do laws crafted under conditions of hyperpresidentialism differ from laws that are the product of a representative system? I partially tackle this question in an article about policy stability,[14] where I suggest that hyperpresidents are able to pass their policies significantly more quickly than presidents who are more constrained, yet these policies are less likely to endure over time (since future presidents could change them with the same level of ease with which they were enacted). I also suggest that laws passed under conditions of hyperpresidentialism are of poorer quality than laws passed in a context of strong checks and balances. More research is however needed to analyze the effects of hyperpresidentialism on the quality and nature of laws passed, and there is significant potential for future work in this area.

Final Thoughts

The topic of this book is especially timely given the rising populism in many established Western democracies. In this context, my work adds to our understanding of the factors that allow some presidents to concentrate power as well as the factors that prevent other presidents from abusing their authority. In this book, I have attempted to not only explain the root causes behind presidential power in practice but have also offered easy-to-implement electoral changes that would help prevent hyperpresidentialism. I would also like to suggest that institutions such as the IMF and World Bank continue to strive to improve global financial stability, since as this book has argued, long-term economic stability not only improves the quality of life of the population but also ensures healthier democracies in which presidents are held accountable. This book also speaks to the importance of enacting reforms that strengthen state institutions and rule of law.

Understanding why presidents are able to concentrate power is a key first step in preventing future executive abuses. Identifying political systems that are at risk of hyperpresidentialism based on the three independent variables I have described in this book could help global policymakers focus their efforts on these countries. Established democracies could also use the framework that I described to identify warning signs and cracks within their own political systems. More broadly, I believe that my book, through its ability to identify countries vulnerable to hyperpresidentialism and through its recommendations for reducing the likelihood of hyperpresidentialism, represents a valuable and practical addition to the literature on democracy and regime politics.

Notes

1 Chaisty et al. 2018; p.1.
2 Chaisty et al. 2018; p.2.
3 Chaisty et al. 2018; p.2.
4 Chaisty et al. 2018; p.4.
5 Levitsky and Ziblatt 2018; p.187.
6 Levitsky and Ziblatt 2018; p.77.
7 Levitsky 2003; pp.144–145.
8 Author's interview with Luis Pastori (Federal Deputy (Misiones), UCR).
9 Author's interview with Mario Barletta (Federal Deputy (Santa Fe), ex-president of the UCR, 2011–2013).
10 Author's interview with Governor Ricardo Barrios Arrechea (Ex-Governor of the Province of Misiones, 1983–1987, and Federal Deputy during the 1990s).
11 Author's interview with Orlando Gallo (Ex. Federal Judge in Mercedes Province during the military period, ex-Federal Deputy 1991–1995).
12 Author's interview with Miguel Iturrieta (Ex-Deputy for Misiones 2005–2009, PJ-FPV bloc).
13 *Newsweek*, December 20, 2001.
14 Berbecel 2018.

Bibliography

Berbecel, Dan. "The Politics of Policy Stability: Explaining the Levels of Volatility in Economic Policymaking in Argentina and Brazil Between 1990 and 2010." *Canadian Journal of Latin American and Caribbean Studies/Revue canadienne des études latino- américaines et caraïbes.* Vol 43, Iss 1 (2018), pp. 18–46.

Chaisty, Paul, Nic Cheeseman, and Timothy Power. *Coalitional Presidentialism in Comparative Perspective.* Oxford: Oxford University Press, 2018.

Levitsky, Steven. *Transforming Labor-Based Parties in Latin America.* Cambridge: Cambridge University Press, 2003.

Levitsky, Steven, and Daniel Ziblatt. *How Democracies Die.* New York: Crown Publishing Group, 2018.

Appendix

Using Different Measurements Than the Corruption Perceptions Index to Illustrate the Correlation Between Institutional Strength and Presidential Power

In Chapter 3, I used the scores that a country received on the Corruption Perceptions Index as a proxy for institutional strength and rule of law. Recognizing that this is not a perfect indicator, in this appendix, I have also assessed institutional strength using several other measurements, namely indicators from the Quality of Government (QoG) Institute, an indicator from Freedom House, an indicator from the World Justice Project, and two indicators from the World Bank. My findings are very similar to those described in Chapter 3, and as scores improve on all of these indicators of rule of law, presidents become more constrained.

The first alternative measure of rule of law that I use is Freedom House's Functioning of Government Index (fh_fog). The definition of this variable is as follows:

> The variable examines in what extent the freely elected head of government and a national legislative representative determine the policies of the government; if the government is free from pervasive corruption; and if the government is accountable to the electorate between elections and operates with openness and transparency. Countries are graded between 0 (worst) and 12 (best).[1]

Figure A.1 illustrates the relationship between 2012 Functioning of Government (as a measure of institutional strength/rule of law) and 2012 Legislative Constraints on the Executive. Note that just like in the case of the Corruption Perceptions Index, as functioning of government increases, legislative constraints increase in a statistically significant manner.

Similarly, the World Bank uses an indicator called "Rule of Law" which includes many measurements of rule of law throughout the whole government bureaucracy. The value RL.EST is defined as follows:

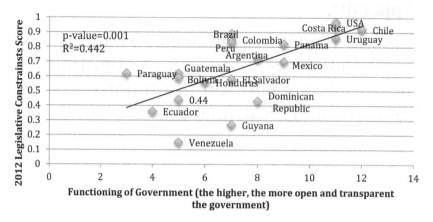

Figure A.1 Relationship between Functioning of Government (Freedom House measure) and Legislative Constraints on the Executive in the Western Hemisphere in 2012.

Rule of Law captures perceptions of the extent to which agents have confidence in and abide by the rules of society, and in particular the quality of contract enforcement, property rights, the police, and the courts, as well as the likelihood of crime and violence. Estimate gives the country's score on the aggregate indicator, in units of a standard normal distribution, i.e. ranging from approximately −2.5 to 2.5.[2]

The scatterplots in Figures A.2 and A.3 illustrate the strong correlation between the World Bank's Rule of Law indicator in 2012 and Legislative Constraints on the Executive in 2012 (higher values on this rule of law indicator reflect stronger state institutions).

An additional indicator from the World Bank that serves as a good proxy for institutional strength is "Control of Corruption." Figure A.4 compares the 2018 "Rule of Law" score with the 2018 score on the Legislative Constraints on the Executive index for the 20 democracies in the Western Hemisphere. As these scatterplots show, even when rule of law is measured using the alternative indicators supplied by the World Bank, the correlation between the strength of state institutions and Legislative Constraints on the Executive remains strong.

Another measurement of rule of law that will be used is the "Rule of Law Index" by the World Justice Project. The index is compiled "based on the experiences and perceptions of the general public and in-country experts worldwide."[3] For all democracies in the Western Hemisphere for which data was available, I studied the correlation between the 2017–2018 "Rule of Law" score and the 2018 "Legislative Constraints on the

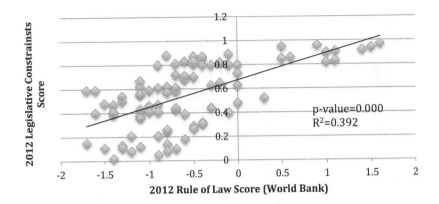

Figure A.2 Relationship between institutional strength (World Bank measure) and Legislative Constraints on the Executive in all presidential systems in the world in 2012.

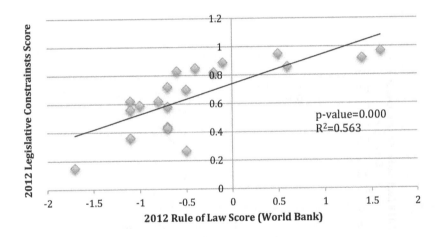

Figure A.3 Relationship between institutional strength (World Bank measure) and Legislative Constraints on the Executive in the 20 presidential democracies in the Western Hemisphere in 2012.

Executive" value. As the scatterplot in Figure A.5 demonstrates, this correlation is very strong and the greater the rule of law in a country, the greater the legislative constraints on the president.

Finally, the following four alternative measures of institutional strength in Figures A.6–A.9 are all based on data from the QoG Institute (using the sample of 20 presidential democracies in the Western Hemisphere).

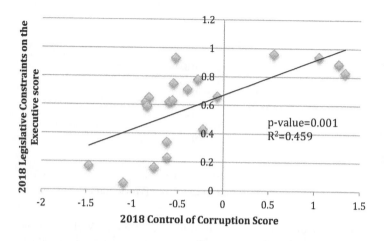

Figure A.4 Relationship between the 2018 Control of Corruption index (World Bank) and 2018 Legislative Constraints on the Executive in the dataset of 20 democracies in the Western Hemisphere.

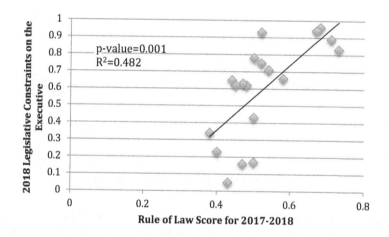

Figure A.5 Comparing the 2017–2018 Rule of Law Score (from the World Justice Project) and the 2018 Legislative Constraints on the Executive score for democracies in the Western Hemisphere.

As evidenced by the p-values and R-squared values, all of these measures of rule of law from the QoG dataset are highly correlated in a statistically significant way with legislative constraints on the executive in a manner similar to the Corruption Perceptions Index. Better scores on these

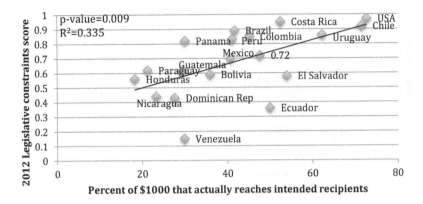

Figure A.6 Relationship between the perceived amount of money wasted or stolen in the bureaucracy and Legislative Constraints on the Executive in the Western Hemisphere in 2012.

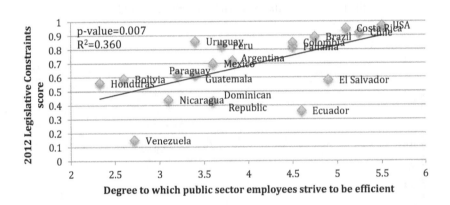

Figure A.7 Relationship between the degree to which public employees are perceived to strive to be efficient and Legislative Constraints on the Executive in the Western Hemisphere in 2012.

QoG indicators were correlated with higher legislative constraints on the executive.

The first measurement includes an expert survey where respondents were asked what percentage of $1,000 set aside for programs to reach the poor actually reached the poor after going through the government bureaucracy. Lower percentages would indicate more corruption/inefficiency and therefore less rule of law/institutional strength.

The second measurement drawn from the QoG dataset is an expert survey on the degree to which public employees are perceived to "strive

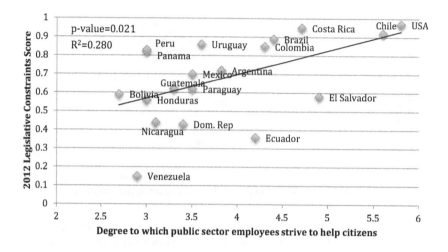

Figure A.8   Relationship between the degree to which public employees are perceived to strive to help other citizens and Legislative Constraints on the Executive in the Western Hemisphere in 2012.

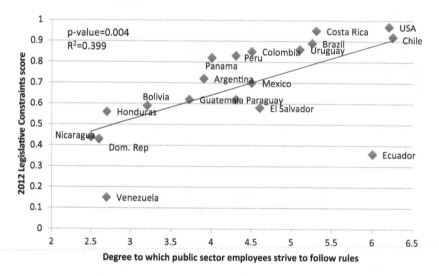

Figure A.9   Relationship between the degree to which public employees strive to follow rules and Legislative Constraints on the Executive in the Western Hemisphere in 2012.

to be efficient" (with a 1 indicating "not at all" and 7 "to a very large extent").

The third measurement drawn from the QoG dataset is an expert survey on the degree to which public employees are perceived to "strive to help other citizens" (with a 1 indicating "not at all" and 7 "to a very large extent").

The fourth measurement drawn from the QoG dataset is an expert survey on the degree to which public employees are perceived to "strive to follow rules" (with a 1 indicating "not at all" and 7 "to a very large extent").

Notes

1 QOG Standard Dataset December 20, 2013; p.81.
2 World Bank Data.
3 World Justice Project Rule of Law Index 2017–2018.

Interviews Cited

Note: The list below does not contain all of the interviews that I conducted in Argentina and Chile and includes only the individuals who were explicitly referenced in the book. Please note that the titles for these individuals were those *at the time of the interview* (on the date listed below).

Argentina

Juan Manuel Abal Medina—Senator and Former Chief of Cabinet of Ministers for President Cristina Kirchner
July 18, 2017

Raúl Allende—Head of the Press Department, *Auditoría General*
June 29, 2017

Ricardo Barrios Arrechea—Ex-Governor of the Province of Misiones, 1983–1987, and Federal Deputy during the 1990s
June 23, 2016

Mario Barletta—Federal Deputy (Santa Fe), ex-president of the UCR (2011–2013)
June 8, 2016

Ricardo Biazzi—Minister of Education of Argentina for 2 days in December 2001 under President Puerta (PJ), Professor of Constitutional Law
June 24, 2016

Germán Bordón—Lawyer and UCR Deputy in the Misiones Provincial Legislature, *Cámara de Representantes*
June 22, 2016

Julio Cobos—Ex-Vice President of Argentina, UCR senator from Mendoza
June 30, 2016

Javier David—Federal Deputy (Salta), Partido Justicialista
June 8, 2016

Gustavo Díaz—Employee at the *Defensor del Pueblo*
June 28, 2017

Luciana Díaz Frers—Employee of the *Auditoría General* (Senior Auditor)
June 1, 2017

Orlando Gallo—Ex. Federal Judge in Mercedes Province during the military period, ex-Federal Deputy 1991–1995 (Party: Movimiento para la Dignidad y la Independencia)
June 28, 2016

Germán Garavano—Justice Minister of Argentina
July 18, 2017

Patricia Giménez—Federal Deputy (UCR)
July 7, 2017

Matteo Goretti—Political scientist who coauthored a piece on decrees with Delia Ferreira Rubio
July 6, 2016

Miguel Iturrieta—Ex-Deputy for Misiones, 2005–2009 (PJ-FPV bloc)
June 24, 2016

Luis Jacobo—Former Minister of Education of the Province of Misiones (2011–2015) and the current representative of the province before the Federal Investment Council
June 23, 2016

Juan Pablo Jorge—Employee at the *Defensor del Pueblo*
June 28, 2017

Oscar Lamberto—Director of the Auditoría General
June 22, 2017

Esteban Lozina—Lawyer, ex-provincial deputy of the province of Misiones (FPV), former president of the Chamber of Deputies of Misiones
June 24, 2016

Raúl Madueño—Ex-Federal Judge
July 12, 2017

Martin Maquieyra—Federal Deputy (PRO)
June 28, 2017

Martín Medina—Political Scientist, Professor of Public Law at Universidad Cuenca del Plata
June 23, 2016

Néstor Migueliz—Director of *Asistencia de Apoyo Parlamentario*
June 27, 2016 and June 21, 2017

Ana María Mustapic—Professor who specializes in executive-legislative relations in Argentina
June 9, 2016

Juan Carlos Neves—A retired member of the navy and secretary-general of the political party, *Nueva Unión Ciudadana*
July 5, 2016

Luis Pastori—Federal Deputy (Misiones), UCR
June 8, 2016

Alfonso Prat Gay—Federal Deputy (City of Buenos Aires)
June 6, 2011

Ángel Rozas—Senator and ex-governor of Chaco, UCR
July 12, 2017

Delia Ferreira Rubio—Lawyer and scholar who specializes in Necessity and Urgency Decrees
July 1, 2016

Alicia Soraire—Federal Deputy (FPV)
July 6, 2017

Javier Zelaznik—Professor specializing in legislative politics
June 21, 2016

Chile

David Altman—Professor specializing in democratic institutions
August 12, 2016

Miguel Ángel Fernández—Professor and Director of the Public Law Department at the Pontificia Universidad Católica de Chile
July 21, 2016

Christian Anker—Employee at the *Consejo para la Transparencia*
August 17, 2017

Antonio Arancibia—Employee at the *Fiscalía Nacional* (Director of the Unit of International Cooperation)
August 14, 2017

Claudio Arriagada—National Deputy (Christian Democrat)
July 15, 2016

Jorge Bermúdez—Comptroller General of Chile (head of the *Contraloría*)
August 1, 2017

Carlos Carmona—Minister on the Constitutional Tribunal of Chile
July 24, 2017

José Luis Cea—Former Minister of the Constitutional Tribunal
August 2, 2016

Luis Cordero—Lawyer who specializes in public law and is an expert on the *Contraloría*
August 2, 2016

Alicia De La Cruz—Specialist on the Chilean *Contraloría*
August 2, 2016
July 27, 2017

Nicolás de la Cuesta—Manager of Human Resources, Central Bank of Chile
August 17, 2017

Rodrigo Egaña—National Director of the Civil Service
July 18, 2016

Claudio Fuentes—Professor specializing in Chilean politics
August 5, 2016

Juan José Guzmán—Minister on the Constitutional Tribunal
July 28, 2017

Claudia Heiss—Professor specializing in Constitutional Politics
July 27, 2016

Carlos Huneeus—Professor specializing in Chilean politics
August 4, 2016

Raúl Letelier—Professor specializing in Public Law
July 14, 2016

Francisca Moya—Employee in the Ministry General Secretariat of the Presidency (which is responsible for the relation between the executive and legislative branches)
August 1, 2016

Felipe de Mussy—National Deputy (UDI)
August 1, 2017

Ivan Obando—Professor specializing in Public Law and Political Science
July 25, 2016

Alejandro Olivares—Professor and Political Scientist
August 10, 2016

Valeria Palanza—Professor specializing in presidential decrees in Latin America
July 13, 2016

Guillermo Pattillo—Associate Director (*subdirector*) of DIPRES during the previous Piñera administration (DIPRES is the executive organ charged with drafting the budget)
August 8, 2016

Fernando Paulsen—Journalist and TV presenter
July 25, 2016

Gaspar Rivas—National Deputy (Independent)
July 12, 2016

Prof. Pablo Ruiz-Tagle—Specialist in Constitutional Law
August 3, 2016

Lucas Sierra—Vice president of the think tank, Centro de Estudios Publicos, CEP
August 16, 2017

Sebastián Soto—Head of the Juridical Legislative Division during the previous Piñera administration
July 29, 2016
July 26, 2017

Mario Venegas—National Deputy (Christian Democrat)
July 19, 2016

Patricio Walker—National Senator (ex-president of the Chamber of Deputies, and ex-president of the Senate), Christian Democrat
August 7, 2017

Newspapers, magazines, and other news sources:

Buenos Aires Herald

–January 25, 2014
–December 26, 2015
–May 30, 2015

Chequeado
–September 28, 2012

Clarín
–June 18, 2013
–May 9, 2016

CNN.com
–January 6, 2002

Diario Uchile
–April 18, 2015

Economist, The
–September 4, 2003
–August 10, 2006
–December 18, 2012

El Mostrador
–March 2, 2016

El Mercurio

La Arena
–April 26, 2013

La Nación
–November 22, 2007
–April 26, 2013

NACLA
–March 3, 2015

Newsweek
–December 20, 2001

New York Times, The
–May 16, 1989
–December 12, 2004
–August 8, 2013

Reuters
–February 23, 2013
–October 21, 2014
–March 11, 2016
–April 27, 2016
–August 10, 2016
–April 13, 2017

USA Today
–April 1, 2014

Voa News
–July 6, 2016

Wall Street Journal, The
–September 11, 2014
–March 15, 2015

Washington Post
–April 25, 2010
–August 20, 2015

Major Data Sources

Comparative Constitutions Project
        –Executive Power

Década Votada (congressional voting data organized by Andy Tow)

Elecciones Argentinas: Dirección Nacional Electoral

Freedom House
        –Freedom in the World
        –Functioning of Government Index (fh_fog)

Latinobarómetro
        –Confianza en Congreso
        –Confianza en Poder Judicial

Polity IV Project

Quality of Government Institute

Transparency International
        –Corruption Perceptions Index

Varieties of Democracy (V-Dem)
        –Legislative Constraints on the Executive
        –Judicial Constraints on the Executive
        –Legislative Party Cohesion
        –Codebook
        –Methodology book

World Bank
        –Indicators for GDP growth and inflation
        –Rule of Law
        –Control of Corruption

World Values Survey

Other Sources

Constitution of Argentina

Constitution of Chile

Supreme Court of the United States

Index

Note: **Bold** page numbers refer to tables; *italic* page numbers refer to figures and page numbers followed by "n" denote endnotes.